ABOUT THE AUTHOR:

Since 1935 Dr. Farrer has been Fellow and Chaplain of Trinity College, Oxford.

The first of his nine published works, *Finite and Infinite,* (1943, new edition 1959) recognized as a landmark in metaphysics, was followed by his Bampton Lectures, *The Glass of Vision,* which studied the working of the inspired mind and supernatural revelation as an extension of the natural powers of reasoning. Three works in biblical theology followed. In his latest book he is almost entirely concerned with a philosophical problem.

THE FREEDOM OF THE WILL

THE
FREEDOM OF THE WILL

BY

AUSTIN FARRER

DOCTOR OF DIVINITY AND FELLOW OF TRINITY COLLEGE
OXFORD

The Gifford Lectures
delivered in the
University of Edinburgh
1957

CHARLES SCRIBNER'S SONS
NEW YORK

To
THE KINDEST OF FRIENDS
AND BEST OF POETS
MARTYN SKINNER

FOREWORD

My friends said to me, 'How can you write a whole series of lectures on the Freedom of the Will?' I did not know; but in executing the task I have found the difficulty all the other way; all the most vital topics of philosophical concern come into the argument; and a series of lectures is little space enough. Looking at what I have done, I see that I have written a treatise on metaphysics; sadly superficial, no doubt. Yet I am still not convinced that, by narrowing the field, I could have cast more illumination on the freedom of the will. If in truth this question is inseparable from so many other questions, one would have done no good with it, by separating it.

After all, what can justify the composition of such a book as this is? A host of able men, their wits sharpened by logical training, have written ingenious papers lately in the philosophical journals, each discussing voluntary freedom within the area of a carefully limited question. I could not hope to vie with their detailed thoroughness, or formal elegance. If I was to contribute anything, it would have to be by aiming at greater completeness, and at a synthesis of topics. So that is what I have done, well or ill.

I have kept the contemporary debate in mind, but it seemed hopeless, where there were so many, to name or discuss contemporary philosophers. I have taken my start from three (somewhat popular) utterances; but after that, I have avoided the mention of other than classical names.

To keep myself and my readers awake, I have used the device of a running debate between the doctrines of freedom and of necessity. I hope that my readers will recognise this as what it is, a convenient method for discussing everything, first or last; and that they will not complain either because my determinist changes colour like a chameleon, or because, at any given point, he lacks the complexion of what they take to be the true doctrine. I can only beg them to read on (if they think it worth while) and see whether, at some point, I do not discuss the view they want to hear discussed.

My debts are great; first to the University of Edinburgh, for giving me the lectureship and even, in comfortable number, enduring the lectures; not to mention a hospitable kindness which I trust I shall never forget. And second, to Professor P. H. Nowell-Smith, for reading my original draft, and furnishing all those objections, the answering of which has given the book whatever life or relevance it can hope to possess. No one who has read his writings can be in any danger of saddling him with responsibility for my opinions.

OXFORD, *June* 1958

CONTENTS

CONTENTS

CONTENTS

THE FREEDOM OF THE WILL

CHAPTER I

BODY AND MIND

i. Introductory remarks

A GIFFORD Lecturer need not handle the substance of rational theology; he may discuss the preliminaries. There are two branches of these, logical and material. The logical branch examines the formal nature of theological statement, and the force of theological argument. The material branch traces in the world of our common experience those characteristics which lend support to theistic belief. We take the material branch. As to the logical or formal branch, the topics belonging to it have been much canvassed lately. We should ourselves have nothing to add to what such an author as Mr Ian Crombie has written about them, in a recently published book called *Faith and Logic*.[1]

The material branch certainly affords one plenty of scope. It is said in general, that the world is our evidence for the Power which has created it; and there is a fearful lot of the world. How are we to take hold of it? Traditional procedure begins an account of natural reality by scrutinising the experience of our senses. But it would be faintly ridiculous for a Gifford Lecturer to plunge into a discussion, say, of visual perception, even though the worthy Bishop of Cloyne walked straight through red and green patches into Supreme Spirit. But those were other days, and even Berkeley needed the analogy of active finite spirit, the human mind, to bear him out. Now-a-days it seems wiser to concentrate upon what Berkeley took too much for granted, and enquire how it is right to talk about the thing he called human spirit. Here at least is a purely philosophical enquiry, of which it can scarcely be

---

[1] A composite volume edited by Mr Basil Mitchell.

doubted that it has theological bearings. We should never so much as conceive a Supreme Mind, if we did not acknowledge mentality in ourselves, or in one another. Moreover it is plain that the way in which we find it proper to talk about the human being conditions, whether positively or negatively, our readiness to entertain belief in a Supreme Spirit.

Heaven knows the province of man has not been neglected in recent years, either by philosophical theologians, or by theologising philosophers. But they have often used a highly coloured language which baffles and scandalises the prevailing philosophy. 'I and Thou' seems to be one subject, 'You and Me' quite another. We will take the 'you and me' level, and make it our humble endeavour to keep our heels on the ground. We will maintain contact with the questions of current secular philosophy. If any of the insight of existentialists and metaphysicians trickles through the sieve of our common speech, so much the better; but if not, never mind. If we are trivial, at least let us be clear.

Of all that offers itself for discussion in the human person, it is on voluntary freedom that we will concentrate. We shall take 'freedom' in a psychological and moral, rather than in any social or political sense. Further than that we will not carry the definition of our subject beforehand. We wish to start from current questions, not from our own definitions.

ii. *The mind-body problem*

Over the whole debate about the voluntary freedom of man there hangs the shadow of physical determinism, a theory to which recent work on the brain has given a more definite outline. The functioning of the cerebral cortex is revealed as a system of electrical circuits; and apart from these (it is reasonable to suppose) no human thoughts are thought. Now the functioning of the circuits must presumably be understood physically or mechanically, that is to say, as exemplifying determined uniformities. How then —here is the difficulty—can it plausibly be maintained that an exercise of thought which has its being somehow in the functioning of a mechanical force, is really free? The thinking feels free, no doubt; but must not the feeling be delusive?

We may indeed still say if we like that every man is as free as he feels, much as we are accustomed to say that every man is as old, or as young, as he feels. But such a custom of speech is trivial; it is a mere determination to neglect all other aspects of youth or age, except the feeling of them. We know very well that a feeling of youth gives a man no mastery over the more compulsive aspects of age; it will not enable him to bring down the date of his birth or to put off the loss of teeth and hair. And similarly a man's feeling free will confer on him no absolute power ever to have acted otherwise than he did, or ever to have disappointed a perfectly informed prediction of his conduct, calculated on physical grounds. It may be, indeed, that in saying that a man is as young as he feels we are not being merely wilful, but suggesting that his youthful feeling is a symptom of his body's wearing well. By analogy, if a man feels free, the feeling may be an indication of good health and uninhibited performance on the part of his brain. But such a happy state of affairs may be no less the effect of determining physical causes, than a cramped or sluggish or diseased condition would be.

'But if the progress of brain-research has deterministic implications, are not they offset by the contemporary development of nuclear physics? Need we worry our heads about physical determinism, in an age which accepts the postulate of physical indeterminacy?' Ah, but the indeterminacy the physicist postulates, he places on the level of the most elementary and minute activities with which he has to reckon. All the stable and regular systems of nature belong to a higher level and have a larger scope. They preserve their stability in spite of the indeterminacy of their minute constituents. They profit (as it were) from a principle of statistical average, which makes the minute forces, though individually random, reliable in their mass effect. How, then, is such a physical hypothesis to affect our enquiry? We are dealing with a highly organised system, the working of human nerves; a system which has surely made its reckoning with elementary indeterminacy at a

B

3

lower level, so as to achieve a functioning which is stable and regular. What would interest us would be an indeterminacy on which conscious thought could (as it were) exercise a persuasive influence. But the idea of consciousness appealing over the head of a rigidly-organised system to its indeterminate and infinitely minute constituents, is grotesque. Let Western propaganda appeal over the head of a rigidly Marxist regime to its supposedly un-committed subjects, if it can; but consciousness is not going to by-pass neural pattern, and bear direct on underlying atomic elements.

No, it is with the nervous system as a system that consciousness must be correlated. And if the postulate of physical indeterminacy is to have any revelance, it must be through the way in which the system is organised. We shall have to suppose that it is unlike all other systems known to us. For, instead of counting out indeter-minacy by basing itself on statistical average, it somehow manages to take positive advantage of indeterminacy among its consti-tuents, so as to achieve a special sort of flexibility. Not, however, without keeping a firm hold on system at the same time; our flexible system must remain reliably systematic. We will not now pause even to consider whether such a hypothesis can be intelli-gibly stated, let alone made probable. We will content ourselves with pointing out that it is against the general analogy of nature; for natural system, as we know it, discounts the indeterminacy of the particles.

We turn back from so dizzy a contemplation to the established ground of a *de facto* mind-body parallel. Even here we must be on our guard against exaggerating our knowledge. However clearly the available evidence may point in general towards a close corre-lation between thought and motions in the brain, our ability to connect the detail of our thinking with detailed cerebral alter-ations is so far insignificant. For any practical consideration of mental questions, we are obliged to leave the brain out; to content ourselves with gyrating in a closed circle of perceptions, feelings, thoughts, decisions, acts; the circle, that is, of life as lived by him who lives it, and not as it may reveal itself to external investigation at the hands of surgeons or physiologists. Turning, then, in the closed world of personal experience, we may examine the question of free choice on a purely mental basis; we may ask about its freedom, not in respect of its physical organ, but in respect of its mental antecedents. Brain or no brain, did my previous sensations, or thoughts, or emotions lead me inevitably to the choice I made, or had I a sovereign liberty to have chosen otherwise? On such purely mental ground a libertarian or a determinist argument can still be advanced. But those who debate freedom on mental ground keep looking over their shoulders, like Tweedledum and Tweedledee under the approaching shadow of the monstrous crow. Is it not trifling to fight out the issue of an apparent liberty in the conscious exercise of choice, if physical determinism is about to be proved upon us?

The crow, in Carroll's fable, was equally hostile to both puny antagonists; the philosophical position is a little more complicated. For while it may be true that physical determinism makes nonsense of the whole mental debate, it is not indifferent as between the two sides. The physical determinist might go so far as to admit that on the merits of the mental debate the libertarian case was equally plausible, or even the more plausible of the two; but in saying so he would be passing an unfavourable judgement on the whole value of autonomous mental philosophy. Since mental philosophers are not likely to wish to pass such a condemnation on their own art, they will have a strong inclination, if they believe in the crow, to take the determinist side. They will tend to abandon the nice assessment of mental evidence on its own merits, and devote themselves to showing that the determinist case, even on mental grounds, is strong. For they will wish to have a mental doctrine and a physical doctrine capable of being brought into some tolerable parallel with one another; both being deterministic. And why not? Why should we even pretend to discuss the mental question in isolation? Why should not physical evidence tip the mental scales?

The moral of this state of affairs is obvious: settle with the crow first, and fight for the broken rattle afterwards, if it still seems worth while. What, then, is the crow? In the eyes of Tweedledum she may seem nothing but beak, for the beak is the business end of her, the threatening member; but the beak is merely the spear-head of body, wings and tail. We cannot isolate the offensive point, the threat against freedom which the correlation of thought and brain brings to bear. What we have to deal with is the whole relation of thought and brain. Only so can we see whether our opinion of being free is adversely affected, or not, by the physi-ologists' discoveries.

iii. Discussion of The Physical Basis of Mind

The problem of brain and thought was recently brought before the public in a series of broadcasts, afterwards published under the title, The Physical Basis of Mind. Seven scientists summarised in several aspects the present position of physiological knowledge. Three philosophers followed, and delivered their judgements. It will, perhaps, afford us as useful an entry to the subject as any other, if we give a brief account of the opinions of the three sages.

Viscount Samuel spoke first. In his opinion the general effect of physiological discovery has been to alter the boundary we are dis-posed to draw between the kingdom of vital consciousness and the kingdom of mechanical force. Uninstructed commonsense would suppose, and indeed used to suppose, that the boundary coincided with the surface of our bodies. Physical force played upon us from without; conscious vitality answered it from within. Heat, light, pressure, sound beat upon us in mechanical waves; sight, hearing, feeling, and all the actions consequent upon them were the work of living soul. Living soul had, of course, her organs, and one was free to doubt whether she was separable from them. But the prin-ciple of sentient reaction lay in the soul; the physical organs were no more than channels or passive instruments. But now (said Lord Samuel) the picture has been altered. We know that mechanical force does not finish its task when it reaches the sentient superficies of our body; it runs straight on and straight in; it con-tinues its operation through our nervous system, of which our

6

brain is but the headquarters. Mechanical force, producing movements of a certain kind in determinate regions of the brain, is the immediate and sufficient cause of all our sensory perceptions; other operations of the same mechanical force are the physical aspect and, as it were, embodiment of our deliberative thought; and yet further extensions of it are the sole motive power in the action of our limbs.

But (Lord Samuel continued) the all-pervasiveness of mechanism cannot banish consciousness, or make it other than we know it by direct experience to be. We still have mind on our hands, just as much as matter; neurological research has merely shifted the boundary between them. Consciousness is no longer to be set over against a mechanism outside us, but over against a total field of mechanism, outside us and within. The boundary between matter and mind is no longer to be seen as a demarcation of spatial areas, nor indeed as a boundary at all, except by metaphor. It is the point of linkage between two processes, the material and the mental.

So far Lord Samuel's argument (which we have taken the liberty to rearrange) scarcely offers a target to criticism. In saying this we do not, of course, mean to deny that philosophers can always torture the phrasing of any argument, and, by developing unthought-of implications, reveal preposterous consequences. Neither what Lord Samuel said, nor what we, far less competently, have made of his speech, will be immune from such unfavourable construction. But, treated with common benevolence, his account is, surely, a fair description of the state of things.

He was not, however, content to leave it at that. He made the additional point that the manner in which mind and matter are linked is a mystery to us in the present state of our knowledge. We can assert that the mental process and the material process are found *de facto* to accompany one another; but we can get no further than this sheer *de facto* concurrence. By what actual links they are attached to one another, or by what sort of interchange they affect one another, we have no notion; nor shall we have, until we have seen more deeply into the mental process, or the material process, or both.

7

Professor Ayer, the next speaker, fastened on the additional point of Lord Samuel's which we have just mentioned; and no wonder, for what a red rag is to a bull, a mystery is to Professor Ayer. He charges Lord Samuel with first creating a bogus problem, and then offering spurious hopes of its solution. If, says Professor Ayer, we know nothing of the link between matter and mind, it is because there is nothing to be known. Anyone who has reflected on what the expression of a mental state or act means, and on what a report about alterations in the brain means, will see that there can be no further link between them, than the link we have already acknowledged—that of a *de facto* concurrence. For what on earth could any further link be supposed to be? Not mental, presumably, and not physical. But surely there is no *tertium quid*. Or do we hope either to shade the mental off into the physical, or the physical into the mental? To find a phase of consciousness so crassified as to qualify for a place in the physical series, or a physical event so refined as to pass muster as an act of consciousness? To express such suggestions is merely to murder the language in which we try to frame them. For it is the business of consciousness-statements to express the consciousness-aspect of us and no other, just as it is the business of physiological statements to express the physiological aspect of us, and no other. If we can bring our descriptions of the two aspects into a *de facto* concurrence, we have done all there is to be done. How, then, can the advance of insight into either the material or the mental process ever do more than tighten the concurrence with which we are already acquainted? How can it reveal to us any link of a further kind, or make any difference of principle?

It is impossible to quarrel with the substance of Professor Ayer's contention. No bridge, we must agree, either mental or physical or neutral, is ever going to join the consciousness-story about us to the physiological story about us. If the two stories fit together—if there is an orderly concurrence between them—it is all we can ask for. Nevertheless Professor Ayer has been too severe upon Lord Samuel; Lord Samuel's words can be allowed to bear a perfectly creditable sense, if we interpret him instead of refuting him. We ought surely to suppose that Lord Samuel sees as well as we do that the brain-story and the thought-story cannot do more than concur; but surely the degree and even the type of concurrence can vary so greatly, that at one extreme it seems almost nothing, while at the other extreme it gives us all we are inclined to ask for.

The minimum concurrence would be a parallel between two staccato series of disconnected items, such that for every A on the one side there is an α on the other side; for every B a β, and so forth. The notation we have used is indeed, misleading, for A and α, β and B appear to have something to do with one another; and that is exactly what, in the case before us, we wish to deny. It would be better, perhaps, to pick our second set of symbols at random: what we observe, let us say, is that wherever A turns up on the one side μ turns up on the other; when B turns up, ζ comes opposite, and τ opposite to C. That would be a very weak type of concurrence, however repetitive it might be. What would be a strong type of concurrence? Suppose that the two series, mental and physiological, had each a sort of rhythm or pattern; and suppose that it were possible to talk of a formal similarity between the one rhythm and the other. A suggestion which is unquestionably false in fact may serve to illustrate such a correspondence. Let it be assumed that whenever I think of logical inclusion—that is, of the way in which a single genus embraces several species—I sketch to myself in imagination a large circle containing several smaller circles. And let it be further assumed that, whenever I think or imagine in this way, scientific detection, if brought to bear, is able to observe electric energy passing on a roughly circular path in my cerebral cortex, and then immediately proceeding to turn smaller circles within the area thus delineated. If these things were really so, might we not say that something in mind, and something in matter, had been discovered which really did appear to belong together, and not simply to happen together? And if we felt ourselves able to treat such a case as typical of the mind-brain relationship, should we feel it extravagant to claim that we could at last begin to understand what sort of relationship it was? And yet we should not have gone beyond concurrence;

9

we should not have disproved Professor Ayer, for we should have introduced no extraneous bridge, either mental or physical or neutral in kind, to join mind and body together.

The illustration we have used is purely mythical; it is, indeed, borrowed with a little adaptation from that storehouse of philosophical mythology, Plato's Timaeus. We are not accusing Lord Samuel of expecting that any progress either in neurological or in psychological research will prove such a fairy tale to be fact. He is doubtless too prudent to guess, in advance of discovery, what discovery will show. But, with all fair caution, he can surely be allowed to hope that the psychological story and the neurological story will come in time to reveal a formal similarity between them, quite beyond anything we have yet perceived. Now if some link of common form is what we hope for, and if hitherto we have found nothing we could call that, then it is no misuse of language to say, that we have not yet discovered the link, but that we hope we may, as research progresses.

The defence which we have ventured on behalf of Lord Samuel has been no sort of counter-attack on Professor Ayer's position. The effect of it has rather been to bring our two philosophers into essential harmony; and this seems a satisfying result. But the satisfaction threatens to be shortlived, for we turn the page and find Professor Ryle falling upon Professor Ayer and Lord Samuel, precisely in that point at which we have made them agree. Lord Samuel, he complains, spoke of two parallel systems or things, one mental, one material. And though Professor Ayer does not like to hear talk of parallel things or happenings, the only substitutes he has to offer are parallel tables of observations, these physical, those mental, with a one-for-one correspondence between certain recurrent items on either list. An irreducible duality remains. Either we shall talk about a man as a conscious subject, or we shall talk about him as a bodily being. The two ways of talking may fit, but they will never fuse. In speaking of any person, we must either ride our mental horse or our physical horse. The fact that the two horses keep in step with one another all along may make it comparatively easy to vault from the back of one to the back of the other, but our speech still cannot ride both at once; even less, by any logical magic, turn them into one horse, and ride that. Nonsense, says Professor Ryle. Our speech acknowledges no such impossibility. Common talk—the language of daily life—takes the sentient, intelligent, active, bodily man as its theme, and finds no difficulty in treating him as one.

It is easy to see what Professor Ryle means, but it is hard not to feel that he is aiming off the target. The discussion in which he has intervened is concerned with the special results of brain-research, and with the question how we are to fit them into our picture of human nature. And it seems a strange sort of answer, that if we avoid thinking about these special scientific results, and confine ourselves to hearty commonsense, we shall be free of the difficulties to which the special results give rise. What is this but Hume's prescription for philosophic headaches—carelessness and inattention, and a plunge into social life?

To whom, we may ask, is Professor Ryle's healing and reconciling gospel preached? Hardly to men wrestling with the relation between thinking and electric circuits in the brain. To whom, then? To a race of unreasonable pedants, who make the convention of talking in parallel columns, appropriate enough to one special issue, their model for all talk whatsoever about the human being; who pretend to think that 'He signed his name' is a slovenly shorthand, for which a correct speech would substitute something like the following: 'While he exercised the intention of signing his name, his hand carried his pen through the tracing of the characters.' And why is the longer form preferred? Merely out of false analogy with the genuinely correct form, 'While he exercised the mental activity of brooding on his opponent's argument, certain circulations of electricity took place in his cerebral cortex.' The distinction between brain event and thought is proper, the distinction between intentional act and bodily movement is improper. We ought to say 'He signed his name', but we ought not to say that, in his search for a weak spot in his opponent's argument, he circulated the electricity through his cerebral cortex. Wherein do the two cases differ? The use of the pen in signing his name is under the signatory's direct control, and is the very thing he means to do. The ponderer does not mean to circulate cerebral electricity, nor has he any direct control over the paths it takes. What he means to do is to find the weak spot in the opposing argument, and what he does is not to circulate electricity, but to make a review of the antagonist's points. But while he does so, some supersensitive detectors which have yet (I think) to be invented, reveal the paths of electric circulation in his brain to a scientific observer whom we will suppose to be present.

What is the conclusion? Mentality and corporeity coincide, when we use our hands to sign our names or our tongues to speak our thoughts. But they go apart into parallel columns when we use our brains to think; that is the trouble, a trouble which Professor Ryle (for anything I can see) does nothing to reduce or palliate. He tells us, if I understand him aright, that we mostly forget our brains and talk cheerfully enough about persons doing things. No doubt; but in a philosophic hour we sit down and reflect, and then it occurs to us that no human action is of any personal or social interest, unless it expresses some degree of intention or choice. It occurs to us besides that intentional choices only take place (if our scientists are to be believed) in connexion with electric circulations through the brain. Then we are bemused, or even distressed. For we cannot see how intention and choice can be what we have always taken them for, if they run in harness with processes supposedly mechanical. And in such a bemusement, we shall be little comforted by the exhortation to recall the way we think of persons when we are held in the vortex of common social life.

Lord Samuel, having spoken first, has no opportunity to criticise his fellow-speakers. It would be interesting to have his opinion on Professor Ryle's remarks. Might he not say, that the Professor has simply appealed to what Lord Samuel himself began by discarding, the pre-scientific picture of man? It may well be that such a picture continues to serve as our guide in daily life; but if so, what follows? Surely not, that we are let off considering that invasion or permeation of the human person by mechanical force, which science has now revealed to us. If Lord Samuel goes on from where Professor Ryle leaves off, the arguments of the three philosophers are left turning in a ring, like circus elephants, each twisting the tail of the one in front.

iv. *Reflections on* The Concept of Mind

But there is more in Professor Ryle's position than such an estimate allows. It is not his intention to dismiss the neurological account of man, but to uphold the commonsense description of him as the standard description, by which all other types of description must be judged, and to which they must somehow be accommodated. In his broadcast Professor Ryle finds no room to effect the accommodation—the accommodation, that is, of neuro-logical statements with ordinary personal statements. His full-scale study, *The Concept of Mind*, sheds more light. Not that *The Concept of Mind* deals explicitly with neurological statements; but it makes suggestions which, in my own fashion and at my own peril, I will develop.

Ryle begins *The Concept of Mind* with an onslaught on Des-cartes; I will not repeat what you have all read, but comment from a slightly more historical angle on Descartes's blunders. For it is surely an added support to Ryle's case, if it can be shewn that historical accident, rather than the claims either of science or of commonsense, led Descartes into the statement of that psycho-physical dualism which has become so inveterate and so baneful a mental habit with his successors.

What struck Descartes about himself was his thoroughness; what strikes us about him is his laziness, anyhow in metaphysics—his way of introducing into the traditional structure the minimum change necessary to accommodate new scientific ideas; his pulling of the time-worn elements round into a new arrangement, with-out apparently considering the resultant incongruities.

For the picture of body and mind which Descartes inherited we may turn to Aristotle *on the Soul*. In that treatise the philosopher had profited (we may now think) from the ambiguities of the Greek word, psyche, with its double sense of *life* and *consciousness*.

13

The body is alive, and therefore 'ensouled'; that is, it has the principles of action which are proper to animal life, whether conscious or otherwise. But some of its most important functions are, in fact, consciously exercised. In treating of sensation, imagination and instinctive behaviour, Aristotle is describing the functioning of a bodily system which enjoys consciousness in various degrees; for the action of soul on these levels is the action of living animal body. Since soul is defined as the active principle, sometimes sentient, of bodily function, the question which Ryle abominates, 'How do soul-action and body-action manage to concur?' simply does not arise; by definition, they cannot but concur, or rather, coincide.

But sensation, imagination, and bodily motion do not exhaust the powers of the soul; people also talk or think, moving with freedom in a world of general meanings. Thought, for various reasons, appeared to Aristotle to be an activity which had its cause in itself, directed indeed and occasioned by bodily circumstance and natural need, not however necessitated by either. The thinking soul transcended in a manner her bodily foundation; not that she could think without imaginative symbols of a bodily origin, but that the use she made of them was all her own. However little we may sympathise with Aristotle's apotheosis of pure thought, we must agree with him in marking the profound difference between sensation and discourse.

Descartes grew up in an Aristotelian world, but there was one feature of the Aristotelian picture that he could not stomach. The ruthless uniformity of his new physics demanded that the human body should be interpreted as physical clockwork; and to treat clockwork as the actual organ and sphere of conscious animal soul was a paradox before which Descartes recoiled. But animal soul had been for centuries defined as the active principle of living body; to separate it from body appeared a nonsensical operation, if you were going to have it at all. Animal soul, then, must be liquidated, and its functions distributed among its associates. The actual power of moving the bodily parts must be credited to bodily clockwork; all immediate feeling of bodily state and motion must be credited to the godlike thinking soul or mind, which is now left as the only soul there is.

Now of thinking soul or mind two things had been (as we have said) asserted. First, its characteristic action was to think, and the purer or more abstract the thought, the more characteristic of mind. And second, its action was self-caused or autonomous, however dependent upon *occasions* provided by the state of the living sensitive body, a sensitive body whose sentience carried overtones of imagination. Both doctrines remain in force with Descartes. As to the first—nothing but thought, *cogitatio,* reveals the nature of the mind; and since the mind is now burdened with sensitive and imaginative as well as ratiocinative functions, there is nothing for it, but to interpret sense and imagination as confused forms or modalities of thought. And as to the second doctrine: the whole action of the mind, as well in sense-awareness as in ratiocination, is still said to be autonomous, the mind itself being the sole agent-cause. All that the clockwork body does is to provide *occasions* upon which the mind acts, and apart from which it will not act.

It is surely plain that Descartes is murdering the language. If you extend *cogitare* to include sense-awareness, what meaning can *cogitare* any longer retain? To call sensation a confused mode of thought is about as useful as to call a frog a debased type of bull-calf. As with 'thought', so with 'occasion'. For thought to act of itself upon occasion of some fact, the fact must be already present to awareness, whether through sensation or through a previous piece of thinking. What can 'acting upon occasion' mean, when the thinking mind is said to act upon occasion of a state of affairs it does not see, so as to perform an act which constitutes its seeing of that state of affairs? And this is what happens, according to Descartes, when upon occasion of the piece of clockwork called my hand dropping from its position, my mind does that piece of confused thinking commonly called the sensation of my hand dropping. It is even worse when Descartes inverts the relation and makes the body act upon occasion of a mental decision. It may be paradoxical enough to say that a seeing agent takes action on occasion of visibilities which are, as it happens, to him invisible; it is even more paradoxical if we add that the agent is by nature blind, being, indeed, a piece of clockwork. Only a knowing agent can act on occasion of anything, a truth recognised by the Cartesian school in their scandalous recourse to theology. It must really be God who sees to it that my hand should act on occasion of my mental decision, and who directs or overrules the action of my mind when, on occasion of my hand slipping, my mind produces the sensation correctly corresponding. Once we have transferred the task of initiating actions upon occasion from God's creatures to God, the whole idea of occasional causality is exorcised from the field of natural observation. All that the natural scientist has before him is systems, bodily and mental, which *de facto* correspond, like two clocks keeping perfect time together. To inquire into the divine clockmaker or clock-setter is a task which may be left for the metaphysician.

It needs some apology, perhaps, to justify the repetition of textbook platitudes about the most overwritten episode of philosophical history; but it seems worth while to support Ryle's case by recalling how much of Descartes's formulation was the effect of historical accident, rather than any necessary impact of scientific advance. Descartes was not synthetising science and common experience; he was hashing Aristotle. It is, of course, absurd to treat the psychophysical dualism which has since prevailed as simply a Cartesian legacy, as though the eighteenth and nineteenth centuries were a second scholastic age, with Descartes in the position Aristotle had occupied throughout the first. Descartes was not so much authoritative, as typical; his contemporaries and successors had the same heavy metaphysical inheritance on their backs, and struggled with it in similar ways.

The Cartesian blunder against which Ryle protests may be stated in two theses: thought is the proper act of soul; and the proper form of statement about the human person is a statement in parallel columns, one about soul and the other about body. To make out a perfect opposition to Descartes, we might like to put exact antitheses into Ryle's mouth: the proper act of soul is heedful

bodily action in face of sense-perception; the proper form of statement about the human person is a single-column statement about
bodily experience or bodily behaviour. But these would not be
Rylean formulations. Of all the objections he would feel against
the suggested wording, the most relevant to our present purpose
would be his dislike of the phrase, 'Proper act of soul.' He would
not want to talk about 'soul', but simply 'person'; nor would he
even then wish to say that any form of activity was more *properly*
personal than another, so long as we were talking of activities
which current speech attributes without qualification to personal
subjects. But if for 'proper' we substitute 'basic', perhaps he might
agree that what we attribute to him is at least capable of decent
interpretation: 'the basic form of personal action is heedful bodily
behaviour in face of perceived facts; the basic form of statement
about the human person is a single-column statement about bodily
experience or bodily behaviour.'

The word 'basic' in these formulae must be understood in a
logical sense. What is meant by calling bodily perceptions and
bodily behaviour basic to the structure of human activities, is that
the types of human achievement which have traditionally been
thought most characteristic of mentality as such, presuppose
bodily action or perception, and concern themselves with it. To
deliberate, for example, may seem an admirable exercise, and one
that elevates us above the beasts. But about what do we deliberate? About doing this or that, about bodily action; an action
which must be not only bodily but heedful, or intentional, in
itself; for no one deliberates about reflex actions, about movements he can neither direct nor repress. It follows that deliberation
is not a form of activity on the same level with heedful doing, and
as it were alternative to it; it presupposes the idea of it, and is concerned about it. We can act intentionally without deliberating
previously, as when we make an immediate retort or an instan-
taneous counterstroke; but we cannot deliberate, except with a
view to intentional action.

As with deliberation, so it is with imagination and abstractive
thought. Imaginative experience, says Ryle, is not a field of enjoy-

ment in parallel with sense-perception, or with real bodily action; nor is it merely, as Hume taught, in causal dependence on the prior occurrence of physical experience. The dependence is logical. For what we imagine is the perceiving of things, or the things as we perceive them; or the doing, it may be, of this or that. Without bodily perception and bodily action, imagination would lack not so much a cause as a theme. The case of general or abstract thought is even more evident than that of imagination. Generalities and abstractions do not rest upon themselves. They refer to particular facts, of which apart from bodily experience we should have no notion.

Imagining, deliberating, theorising are activities of the person as real as any others, but not so primary, not so basic as doing and perceiving. They, no less than perceiving or doing, are somehow related to a physical instrument or vehicle, the nervous system; and to ask how they are related to it is a reasonable enough question. It is not, however, a question on which we can hope for any very direct light; for these forms of personal activity are not about themselves, let alone about their own bodily functioning; whereas what we have called the basic forms of personal activity are about themselves, about their own bodily selves. If I am in a hurry to cross a piece of rough ground, I push myself to run, and I place my steps with care. Here is conscious, bodily action concerned with its own bodily performance; here is the simple identity of body and mind, not as the sophisticated product of a philosophical reconciliation, but as the primary form of self-awareness; not the conclusion of speculation, but the beginning of experience.

To indulge, describe and isolate the active enjoyment of one's limbs may be the beginning of wisdom, but it is not the sum. We have to enlarge the picture of embodied consciousness, and work into it two sorts of facts undeniably relevant, though difficult to place: mental activities or states which ignore their own bodily performance; and events in the nervous system not directly represented in consciousness. We may not be able to see yet how either sort of fact is to be worked in; but we know, before we try, into what sort of unity we mean to work it: a unity of function directly enjoyed in primary or basic experience.

The importance which, in this enquiry, attaches to conscious bodily behaviour may be expressed by saying that it serves as a nucleus, a standard, and a clue. We treat it as a nucleus, when we regard it as affording a datum-area of psychophysical unity, an area we endeavour to extend by attaching to it further physical facts and further mental facts. It serves us as a standard, when we make it (as we must) our sample or defining instance of what we mean by unity between the mental and the bodily. When we are baffled about the relation of abstract thinking to motions in the cerebral cortex, what baffles us is nothing but the difficulty we experience of bringing such a case into line with our standard instance. We feel that act of thought and brain-event ought to be related as the mind to run is related to running, when we both have a mind to run, and run; and we want to be able to see the case of 'thinking with the brain' as at least an intelligible deviation from 'running with the feet'. But the experience which is our standard is equally our clue. If the direct experience of using our limbs is no clue at all to the unexperienced use we have of our brains when we think, then there is no clue to be had; of that we may as well be clear from the start.

We have drawn our own conclusions from Professor Ryle. He might disown them, but we will defend them. On the assumption that they are legitimate, let us turn back and apply to the debate of the three broadcasting philosophers what we have now deduced from *The Concept of Mind*.

In his broadcast, Ryle scarcely went beyond a single point. He said that it is absurd to raise a general problem about the unity of body and mind, since that unity is exercised in personal behaviour and expressed in common language. He appeared to be stone-walling on the wicket of commonsense and ignoring the special difficulties arising from cerebral discoveries. But having read *The Concept of Mind*—we hope not entirely between the lines—we judge that Ryle can perfectly well afford to take the scientific difficulty seriously. What he has shown is that the relation of brain-event to thought is not to be defined *in vacuo* with the help of whatever artificial terms may suggest themselves. No, it is to be worked into the picture of a given unity already expressed in natural language, that of the intelligent bodily person. We do not have to find out what psychophysical unity is, for we see it all the time. Our problem is, how to fit on to the unity we already see, certain facts which lie, as it were, outside the focus of vision in which we see it.

But in saying so much, are we not falling foul of Professor Ayer, and not only of him, but of our own previous agreement with what he said? 'No bridge' we agreed to think 'either mental, physical or neutral is ever going to join the consciousness story about us to the physiological story about us. If the two stories fit together—if there is an orderly concurrence between them—it is all we can ask for.' But are we not now suggesting some sort of a bridge, a bridge constituted by our direct experience of bodily behaviour? No, surely not; not in any sense which Ayer would need to deny. In spite of all that we have since said, the best that neurological statements and consciousness-statements can do, is to concur. The considerations we have been basing on *The Concept of Mind* do not turn the concurrence into anything other than concurrence; they teach us to reflect on the light in which such a concurrence is to be viewed. We are not—for example—to take the equation between thought and brain-event as the point in which the unity of our conscious bodily self is effectively revealed to us. We are, on the contrary, to regard it as an obscure or marginal case of such unity. Moreover, when we do contemplate thought and brain-event together, we must expect to find ourselves colouring our feeling of their mutual relation with a shade of negative analogy; it compares so unfavourably with cases which provide superior opportunities for observation. If I make a stroke with a tennis-racket, and you, observing it, describe it to me, 'Yes,' I say, 'that was what I did.' But if I do a piece of thinking, and you are able to observe and describe the electric circulations in my brain, all I can say is something like this: 'Well, I suppose that was what I did in thinking, but of course I had no idea of doing it.' And you may reply: 'No, in such cases one has no awareness of the physical motions one's performance involves.'

Let us wind up the three-cornered debate in a few words. There is no question of turning the relation between neurological statements and expressions of consciousness into anything but *de facto* concurrence: so much for Professor Ayer. Yet there is room for such a clarification of the concurrence, through increased exactitude both on the side of psychology and on that of neurology, that our knowledge of the relation might seem to be revolutionised: so much for Viscount Samuel. And the way we view, or as it were, value this concurrence, the place we assign it in our total thought about ourselves, may allow of careful reflection and delicate definition: so much for Professor Ryle, and so much, indeed, for us, since it is in such a field of reflection and definition that we propose to expatiate.

CHAPTER II

THE SEAT OF CONSCIOUSNESS

i. Where is consciousness seated?

WE concluded the previous chapter with a comparison between two relations. On the one side we put an act of thought as exercised by a thinker, with a corresponding cerebral event as observed by a physiologist. On the other side we put a bodily feat as performed by an athlete, with the visible phenomenon of it as watched by an onlooker. In the athlete's case, we said, there is a formal identity between what the doer does and what the observer observes, which is lacking in the case of the thinker. That was what we said; and if the comparison is allowed, the contrast must be admitted. But ought the comparison to be allowed? It may not be a crazy comparison, but it is at best a crooked one. It assumes that whereas the physical counterpart of athletic effort is visible behaviour, the physical counterpart of mental arithmetic is invisible nerve-activity. But is there no invisible nerve-activity, no microscopic redistribution of electric energy, in the case of the athletic feat? Of course there is. The carefully directed stroke at tennis is just as much dependent on minute happenings in the brain, as is the prodigy of mental arithmetic. Indeed (if I am rightly informed) the brain-events in the two cases are believed to be of much the same sort. Nor is this all. The sweep of the hand which holds the racket, at once so free and so beautifully controlled, is borne, as it were, on a stream of minute nervous and muscular action, all of it open to physiological investigation, and all of it ignored in common experience, as well by the player as by the onlooker.

How, then, ought we to express the contrast we are feeling

after, between the doing of mental arithmetic and the making of shots at tennis? Neither sort of action is unsupported by minute neural activity, with its controlling focus in the brain; but in the one case there is, and in the other case there is not, a large-scale sweep of motion in the limbs, spread, as it were, over part of the whole area of unperceived neural action, and constituting what the agent intends to do, as well as what the ordinary observer can see him to do.

The relation on which we are trying to cast some light is the relation of neural event to conscious performance in the mental arithmetician, and to make the comparison strict, we must compare it with the relation of neural event to conscious performance in the tennis-player. But can the tennis-player's case contribute any illumination? Is it not equally obscure? For he has no more direct concern with minute neural activity than the mental arithmetician has. No; but there is an intelligible relation between his conscious performance and his neural action which is lacking in the case of the mental arithmetician. Not, of course, in that part of neural action which takes place in the brain. In the brain they are equal. Each (we must believe) uses it, each is unaware of it, each employs it on, or about, something else, not itself. But in the region of the hand and arm the tennis-player intends and makes movements which, though they are not the minute neural activities observed by physiology, are nevertheless made up of those minute activities, in a sense of 'made up' which can be intelligibly defined. We will not strain for a definition here, but content ourselves with a parallel. If we press together the handles of a pair of self-extending tongs (lazy-tongs, some people call them) the several distinct movements of the criss-cross rods *make up* the total sweep of the elongation. In some such sense, what the nerve-threads in my arm do for me makes up what I both mean to do and feel myself to do; whereas what the nerve-clots in my brain do for me never makes up what I either mean to do or feel myself to do. The intelligible coincidence of mind and nerve is found not in the brain, but in the hand; not in abstract thought, but in bodily conduct.

23

But have we not reached a shocking conclusion and run into collision with physical evidence? Have not scientists, by experimenting with controlled interferences, proved that the brain is the seat of consciousness? Of course they have, in the sense which their experiments give to the phrase 'seat of consciousness'; a metaphor at the best, for consciousness cannot sit down, not having the wherewithal; and a metaphor which, like other metaphors, allows of various applications. If a physiologist speaks of the 'seat of consciousness', he will mean that part of the nervous system, upon the activation of which the occurrence of acts of consciousness is found to be (as it were causally) dependent. And he finds, for example, that although a certain sensation of touch has its normal remoter cause in the finger-tips, it is only when stimulation reaches a certain part of the brain, that tactual experience actually occurs. The finger-tip without the brain produces no tactual sensation; the brain, morbidly or artificially stimulated, will produce the sensation without the finger-tip. When the brain is said to be the seat of consciousness, it is this sort of evidence that is being summarised in the statement.

We get a different meaning for the phrase, if we start from the side of consciousness, and let her pick her own seat by sitting in it. Then we shall say that the sensation of touch is in the finger-tip, not in the brain at all. Even when tactual sensation is deranged, and the feeling produced by interference with the brain or with the intermediate nerves, and not by anything in the finger, it is still in the finger that it is felt. If the finger is amputated, it may continue to felt in a hallucinatory finger; and if, with the progress of time, we get rid of that hallucination, feeling will not in any case transfer itself to the brain, but, it may be, to the stump from which the finger has been cut. The brain is never the seat of consciousness, for consciousness never sits in it.

If we insist on mixing up the physiological and psychological senses attaching to 'seat of consciousness', we get a curious result. Consciousness sits in her chosen seat; and when that seat is pulled away from under her, she may continue to sit on what isn't there, like a country-house ghost in a modernised room. When, how-

ever, another chair well up the row from where she sits is pulled
away, she falls through the floor and disappears, however solid her
own chair may be. How, then, are we to find the seat of consciousness? By observing where she sits, or by pulling chairs out of
the row? The question is plainly absurd; it treats methods of looking for two different things as alternative ways to look for the
same thing. Yet the absurdity has an appeal, and it does not lie
merely in the ambiguity of a phrase. The two senses of 'seat of
consciousness' have something to do with one another, and ought
to be brought into a positive relation with one another. We will
endeavour, in the sequel, to do something about it.

Of the two methods we have mentioned, the method of physical interference is useless to our present enquiry. It is interesting
from many points of view to see what will happen to a complicated mechanism if you put sand in the fuel, cut this or that connexion, pull out a cog or two, or throw a spanner into the works.
By such experiments many useful lessons can be learnt, but one at
least will not be learnt, the normal capacity of the machine to
deliver the goods, or even (with certain types of machine) the sort
of goods it will deliver. So with the human system. To study its
performance when it is made to misperform is certainly to study
something, but it is no way of measuring its performance. To
show that it can be made to throw imperfect and hallucinatory
experiences, is like showing that a car engine can be made to purr
in the rhythm of 'Pop goes the weasel' when disconnected from
the wheels. Whereas if you want to judge the relation between
engine-rhythm and performance on the road, you must put the
car into gear and drive it out. Similarly if what you want to
investigate is the relation between neural activity and normal
consciousness, it is no use so monkeying with the neural activity
that you cut out the normal consciousness. And so, for the purposes of the enquiry we have in hand, we will disallow all inter-
ruptions of the form 'But if you were to disconnect the relevant
brain centres from the nerves of the arm . . .'. We are going
to talk about what happens when they are *not* disconnected;
about normal functioning, normal consciousness; about what

the human system is for—to risk a phrase now quite scandalous in philosophy.

When just now we were playing a childish game of musical chairs with the seat of consciousness, we found ourselves alternating between the placing of it in the tennis-player's hand, and the placing of it in his brain. But however it may be with the seat of consciousness, the area of physical or neural functioning to which the conscious act of making the tennis-stroke corresponds, is furnished neither by the brain as such, nor by the hand as such. When we are looking for the physical counterpart of a conscious act, we do ill to consider the human body in chunks, to take the arm as one, the spinal column as one, the brain as one, or even the regions of the brain severally—front cortex, back cortex, thalamus. The physical vehicle (as it were) of a conscious act is an immensely tenuous, elongated plant, rooted in several different regions of the brain, passing its stem through the spinal column, and flowering into performance in the hand. That to which the personal act directly corresponds is not, indeed, any system of stuff, however fine-drawn, but a sequence of activity. Yet we may think of this activity-sequence as picking out in red from the whole diagram of nervous tissue our body contains, the threads over which it runs. Then we shall find the path of the red to have the plantlike structure we have just described, rooted in the brain, flowering in the hand.

If we keep such a picture firmly in mind, the puzzle about 'the seat of consciousness' can be persuaded to disappear. The whole nerve-plant from brain to hand is the vehicle or instrument of the behaviour. And as for the consciousness—it is an obvious fact, apart from which our conscious life would be impossible, that consciousness broadens her effects; she does not represent separately the infinite detail of physical action, but employs a practical simplification. In the case before us, all the tennis-player intends to do, or is aware of doing, is to give a certain sweep with the arm, a certain turn of the wrist; he has no notion of the multiple energies in the minute parts which support the action he designs. As consciousness broadens, so she unifies; and since she is able to treat the whole action of the limb as a single business, it is no way incredible that she should treat the whole action from brain to finger-tip as a single business.

But if the broadening effect of consciousness is a commonplace, a certain narrowing effect is no less so. Consciousness concentrates upon, and high-lights the centre of interest, and throws the remaining area of action into the shade. The spot-light of consciousness falls on the tennis-player's wrist; if his control there is too good to need attention, the spot-light, with the aid of the eye, travels out to the tennis ball, and leaves the whole of the player's body in the dark. For the moment, however, we will think of a player whose mind is in his wrist. Such a concentration has in it something selective and, as it were, arbitrary. A large complex of controls and directions is necessary to achieve a successful hit; the feet must be planted right, the trunk correctly poised, and so on. If the ankle turned, no doubt the mind would fly down to it; but in the case we are considering, it leaves the rest of the system to look after itself, and concentrates in the wrist, for it is there that it is required.

We might make up a fable about a man who never had occasion to attend to the state or action of his feet, but only of his upper limbs and head; and who, in consequence, had no notion of such a thing as consciousness travelling down into his lower limbs. They would play their part, none the less, in his actual behaviour, and make their contribution to total performances which, like those of the tennis-player, spot-light the hands. But what is a fairy tale with regard to the feet is common experience with regard to the brain. We cannot conceive an occasion for spot-lighting what goes on there; the brain is not for dwelling on, because it is not for acting with; not, that is, in the common meaning of action, which concerns animal life, and the practical man. It is no cause for surprise that in the whole plant-like complex of activity which flowers through the hand, the spot-light of consciousness should never travel back to the root, and illuminate the brain. Always ignored, the brain is none the less vital to action. The tennis-player's ignoring of his feet does not mean that he could play the shot if they were suddenly amputated. There are other, less crude, ways of revealing the necessary function of the feet, than experimental amputation. In the case of the brain, we may be driven to crudities of this kind; though rats are a more favoured class of patients than men, for vivisectional experiment.

ii. A scale of mental actions

Our method in the present argument is to take a correlation which is not utterly obscure—that of bodily action as consciously exerted, and of the same action as externally observed—and to draw into analogy with it other and obscurer correlations, so that they may borrow a little light from it. The only other case we have so far mentioned is that of the mental arithmetician. But if we try to step in one stride from the tennis-player to the mental arithmetician, it is such a stretch, that the analogy breaks down between. What light can the identity of conscious act and physical event in the use of the hand throw on an act of thought which, so far as we have yet discovered, has no organ but the brain? For, properly speaking, the brain is no organ at all, but rather an instrument of organ-control.

We may hope to do better if we proceed in short steps, observing something nearer to the order of nature. The human animal took more than one step in advancing from the heedful management of his limbs to the doing of mental arithmetic; and the same remains true of the human infant, however civilised the nursery in which he is reared. The first step in being human was learning to talk. Now talking, shouting and singing are physical performances in the throat and mouth, and there is no reason to give a substantially different account of such performances, from the account we gave of shots at tennis. The spot-light of attention can be on the organs, if, for example, we are having a good shout, for shouting's sake, and are indifferent to the quality of the noise produced. But we early acquire a confidence (not always justified) in our control over the vocal organs, and so we take their manipulation for granted, and transfer our interest to the product. The singer's attention advances, as it were, just beyond his organs and

28

dwells on the series of sounds they produce; much as the mind of the tennis-player slips out beyond his hand, and dwells in what the middle of his racket is doing to the ball. Hearing assists the singer, as sight assists the tennis-player, to go beyond his skin. It is as though he lived, not in his throat, but in the sounds; as though the notes climbed up and down the scale in direct obedience to his will.

The unselfconscious talker goes a step further than the singer, and loses distinct awareness even of the sounds, in his concentration on the subject of his speech; he is not conscious of using such-and-such words, but of expressing such-and-such sentiments or ideas. It is unnecessary to ask how such a thing is possible, for we all do it. When we talk with complete freedom, we simply think aloud, or think communicatively; the meaning is in full control, many of the verbal expressions are taken for granted by the speaker, and he does not know whether he is using them or some others in their place. To be able to talk in such a manner is to have human mentality; and it is too late in the day to be surprised at being human, however odd it may be that we ever got that way. If we are out to do a bit of wondering, we may work up a fine astonishment at the tennis-player's shot; and so we do, if it is a good one. There are more sincere admirers at Wimbledon, than in the gallery of the House of Commons.

Suppose the orator to be engrossed in his matter, and the matter to be abstract—he is talking about moral principles, or laws of economic expediency, or, very likely, a fine hotch-potch of both. Where, then, does the spot-light of his attention rest? Not on his tongue, nor on the sounds his tongue is shaping; his tongue is in his mouth, the sounds spread forward from his face, but his mind is in neither. It is not anywhere, is not focused on any *thing*, if 'thing' be given its concrete sense. But there is no mystery here, additional to the fact that we can talk abstractions with undivided attention. To understand what it is like to do so, is to understand that the idea of a localised attention ceases to apply to the case. What is localised is not the meaning, to which we attend, but the management of the vocal sounds, from which we disattend. If we want to locate what is going on, all we have to do is to awake from our notional intoxication, and recall our attention to the wagging of our jaws.

I turn from the use of my hand to the use of my vocal parts, and again, from the conscious management of them to sheer thinking aloud. There is no reason to suppose that when I take either of these steps the part played by the brain changes radically. The action is still in the organ, not in the brain; the brain remains the control of action, not the organ of action. When we talk, there is no reason to think of the matter of our discourse as being pre-figured in the action of our brains. If a couple of gardeners are discussing tomatoes, it is their words which carry the precious truths they exchange about the culture of those useful plants, and it is their words that their brains direct. If anything were to be prefigured in their brains, it should be the pattern of the words, not the growth of the tomatoes. But why should the word-patterns themselves be prefigured in the brain? Does a control-mechanism need to prefigure what it controls? Surely not. It is not as though we had first to think with our brains, and afterwards transfer our thought to our tongues. We think aloud with brain and tongue, the control being in the brain, the action in the tongue. It is not the brain that thinks or talks, it is the man.

But surely, it will be said, to concentrate on the case of thinking aloud, is to evade the real difficulty about thinking in its relation to the brain. When we talk, we use our organs, who denies it? And so the whole performance remains in some sort of parallel with a bodily feat, where consciousness dwells in what we do. But does not the mystery of thought begin when we cease to use our organs—cease to talk, scribble, or gesture—and just think? The question asks for the answer Yes, and while we remain under the spell of the words, we are inclined to concede it. But if we break free, and make a few experiments, we shall begin to judge otherwise. Experience does not suggest that the boundary be-tween silent thought and thinking aloud is very marked, or that to cross it is to pass any very portentous metaphysical Rubicon. All too often, alas, I do not know whether I am thinking aloud, or not; and if I suddenly become aware that I am, and call myself to order, my impression is of trying to think more quietly—to do the same thing as before, only without waking the echoes. It seems quite immaterial, how far I permit the stirrings of action to come down into the vocal organs. I may move my lips and tongue, or only some obscure parts further back in my throat. Or I may seem to move none of these, but to be playing the parts behind them which, more vigorously exercised, would set them in motion.

It is no part of our purpose to suggest that all silent thought has the character of continuous formal speech, damped down, but otherwise unchanged. Silent thought is often happy to be delivered from the relentless march of words which utterance exacts. We go our own pace, we pay more attention to what we shall think, than to the formulated thinking of it; we run over and over a phrase, for the implications it may contain; we imagine a rudimentary diagram, for the suggestions we may find in it. Many flexibilities, many subtleties are the prerogatives of silent thought; and if we were aiming at completeness of treatment, or attempting a commentary on *The Concept of Mind*, we should have to detail their varieties. But however many they may be, interior speech plays a vital part in all of them, if they deserve the name of thought at all. If we could not speak, either inwardly or outwardly, we could not be said to think. It seems fair enough to take interior speech as typical of silent thought, and to use it as our example, in considering the physical basis of mind.

iii. Special problem of imagination

When we were describing the talker, or thinker aloud, we did not relate his meaning direct to his vocal action; we linked the two by means of the sounds which his vocal action was employed to produce. In the case of silent thought, does the link drop out? For in silent thought vocal action is reduced to the ghost of itself, and there are no sounds. Must we, then, attach the thinker's meaning direct to his ghostly vocal action, without any intermediate link? Not necessarily, for the ghost of action may be, and commonly is, accompanied by the ghost of sound: I imagine myself to hear the sounds which I play at producing, but do not produce; and the imagination of sound may be the vehicle of meaning. In so far as I concentrate on the meaning, I may forget, or be unaware, that I am imagining the vocal sounds which convey it. The thinker aloud may, for the same reason, be oblivious of the sounds he employs; but whereas he can be convicted by those who overhear him, the silent thinker's shadow-words are totally unobserved so long as he ignores them; they are the shyest of phenomena, but no less effective in playing their part, and sustaining the train of thought.

The ghost of vocal action, and the ghost of hearing, the two servants of interior speech, haunt, as ghosts should do, the scenes of their full-blooded life. The imagination of hearing haunts the hearing-nerves in and behind the ears, the imagination of speaking haunts the motor-nerves of tongue and throat; but neither of them haunts the brain.

The two ghosts we have mentioned are an odd pair of companions, and it may not be easy to see how they manage to join hands. That actual speech should arouse actual hearing in the speaker's ears, is no mystery; he hears the physical noise he makes. But how does the ghost of speech (which, by hypothesis, is voiceless) arouse the ghost of sound? The two ghostly experiences belong to totally different systems; what is the bridge between them? To play at talking, even without talking, has the nature of action and employs executive nerves. But to imagine oneself hearing is to call into play a system not active, but receptive or sensory. Though there would, indeed, be no hearing but for the responsive action of the sensory nerves, the response is dictated from without. We cannot hear what we choose, but only what is sounded, and the more completely our hearing is dictated by exterior forces, the more it deserves the name of hearing. Grammar confuses difference under common form, when it makes 'to hear' and 'to speak' equally active verbs; they are no more truly active in the same sense, than are 'to fall' and 'to run'. Nature is more discriminating than grammar, for she has ordered the sensory nerves and the executive in distinct systems, like the water and the electricity in our streets; only that (unlike water and electricity) they come together at headquarters, and are correlated in the brain.

Our puzzle is, how the ghost of hearing can be aroused by the ghost of talking; but the problem is, in fact, a general one: how can the ghost of hearing, or of any other receptive, sensory experience, ever be set going at all? There is no corresponding mystery about raising the ghost of speech; for speaking is active behaviour; if I want to speak silently, all I have to do is to talk, but not quite. Whereas to imagine sights is not a matter of seeing, but not quite; it is not done by looking at a real object, and failing to see it properly; there is no object. But if there is no object, how is a sensory, receptive faculty to be set going at all? It can, of course, be set going by morbid causes, or by interference, as when the nerves between the organ and the brain are tampered with; but the effect of that is not imagination, it is hallucination. Speech has its natural cause in ourselves, and so we can 'ghost' speech. But hearing has not its natural cause in ourselves; so how can we 'ghost' hearing? And if we do not 'ghost' it, how does it ever get 'ghosted'?

It seems that sensory imagination cannot really be the ghost of simple sensation, as imagined action is the ghost of action; and such is the moral of a famous discussion of the imagination in *The Concept of Mind*. Professor Ryle exposes the dangers of any direct comparison between the exercise of visual imagination, and the enjoyment of normal sight. The most misleading point in such a comparison is the suggestion that the interior view, like the exterior, provides a datum for study. 'Look out of window, and see what you can see' is a sensible request; but 'Look into your imagination, and see what you can see' is nonsense; or, if it does preserve a sense, it does so by altering the meaning of the words. I cannot look into my imagination, as I might look into the garden, because what I shall see in imagination is not what awaits my contemplation; it is whatever I may imagine, when I imagine. And so 'Look into your imagination, and see what you can see' will have to mean something different, if it is to be possible we should act on the advice. It may mean 'Use your imagination, and see what you can evoke' by way of an image (let us say) of the Eiffel Tower. Or it may mean 'Turn your imagination loose, and see what images it raises'—a request not very easy to follow. Or, in a third and quite different application, it may mean 'Turn your attention on an imaginative content already in your mind, from which you have been dis-attending'. If, for example, I have been doing mental arithmetic, I may have so concentrated on the logical operation, as to be unaware whether I was supporting it with visual images of arabic numerals, or auditory imaginings of their names. Exhorted by you, I attend to the imaginative embodiment of my thought, and decide that it is visual. But to do this is not like looking into the garden, and discovering what is there; it is like realising that I have been seeing the garden trees for the past minute or two, without taking them in. It is not like the exercise of a virgin act of apprehension, it is like reflection upon an old one.

There is, indeed, the exceptional case, when imagination is not what we construct but what presents itself; in dreaming, most markedly; in visionary experiences which lack the full-blooded character of sensory hallucinations; to some extent in daydreaming and in what is called creation, or happy invention. I say 'To some extent', for which of us does not cook the dénouement of his day-dream, and how many of our happy inventions fall out of a blue sky, without any setting of the mind in the required direction? But even when imagination is most wilful and least welcome, it is superstition to look for its usual cause outside the mind, or in anything but a dissociated action of the mind itself. It is a tale we are telling ourselves, without knowing that we are telling it, or why. Yet by subsequent reflection, and sometimes with psychiatric aid, we need not despair of getting round on to our own track, and finding out what we were up to; and, like the clever kitten, catching the tail which danced so provokingly always just out of the focus of sight.

It is plain, then, that imagination is not in any of its forms the ghost of sight, or of any other simple sensation. If we look for its prototypes in full-blooded life, we must seek them in experiences compounded of active and receptive elements; as when I follow with my eye what I write with my hand, or hear what I say; or, a closer correlation still, when I both move my limbs and feel the movement. Then what the executive nerves do in working the muscles, is what the sensory nerves in the same bodily parts immediately report; so that I have some difficulty in distinguishing the working of my limbs, and the feeling I have of doing it. Berkeleian idealism exploits the confusion, in support of the preposterous doctrine that bodily actions consist in certain series of feelings; such feelings being immediately subject to our voluntary direction, and in this way differing from the sensations of touch, hearing and sight, which we cannot directly occasion, but merely lay ourselves open to receive, from the impress of some exterior power. We must insist, on the contrary, that no sensations, whether of movement or anything else, are directly produced. They are produced indirectly by executive action making changes in the body, and it is these changes that are reported by sensation. Nevertheless, our power to give ourselves sensations within certain ranges often appears for all practical purposes absolute; and so provides a full-blooded analogy to the ghostly experience of imagination, where also, within limits, we can imagine what we will.

We are tempted to call 'analogy' too weak a word here, and to claim that such compound experiences of full-blooded life are the actual prototypes, or parents, of imagination; that all we need to do is to reduce such experiences to the shadow of themselves by faint performance, and we have imagination without more ado. But such a suggestion merely brings us back to the difficulty from which we started, and which we were considering in the special case of the step from thinking aloud to silent thought. He who thinks aloud produces in his throat the sounds he hears, and hears them in his ears, through the bones of his head. But it is not to be supposed that the ghost of talking, in its faint agitation of the vocal parts, produces ghostly sounds which actually vibrate in the ear, and produce the ghostly image of hearing. If anything of the sort happens, the thought is not, after all, silent, and the sounds are not imagined, but heard. No; the connexion of ghostly speech and ghostly hearing is not in the ears and throat, but in the brain; not at the exterior termini of the two nervous systems involved, but at their interior.

Now it would indeed be difficult to make the step from thinking aloud to silent thought, if in the one activity the attachment of the executive and receptive systems were at their exterior termini only, and in the other at their interior termini only. How should we suddenly abandon the only link we have, and begin to use one of a completely different sort? Fortunately for us, no such revolutionary step is demanded of us. When we think aloud, the line of vocal activity and the line of auditory sensation are already attached at both ends. When we learn to think silently, what we learn is to dispense with the exterior link, and make do with the other. Let us consider a little further how this happens.

Our receptive organs themselves, such as the ears and eyes, are not unprovided with executive controls. We do not commonly hear without listening, or see without looking: activities which involve a setting of the organs, as well as an attention of the mind —if, indeed, the two are separable; and the setting of the organs is the work of executive nerves, not receptive. Now listening and looking can be, and usually are, particular, not general. We do not commonly listen, or look, for noises or sights without specifying which, but for special sights or noises. When we ourselves produce the sounds we are to hear, as in the case of our thinking aloud, we are not likely to give ourselves many surprises, or often to listen for the wrong thing. In such a case, the anticipatory adaptation of our receptive organ for what it is to receive may be reckoned to be perfect. We may think of what happens as the bifurcation of a single executive action; the intention is to have certain sounds, and energy proceeds from the brain down two associated channels, one leading to the throat, for the production of the sounds, and one to the ears, to dispose them for receiving the same sounds.

Now it is a familiar experience that what we expect to hear or to see, we often imagine, and in this way sometimes deceive ourselves. Physiologically this should mean that the disposal of the organ to receive a certain sensation can suffice for stimulating the receptive nerves to make a ghostly report of the expected sensation, even though no full-blooded report falls into step with it, in response to any exterior stimulation. All, then, that silent thought needs to do is to dispense with the exterior stimulation and the full-blooded report. The silent thinker plays at speaking, he does not speak; but the play in the throat is enough to set going the anticipatory adaptation of the ears; and that is enough to produce phantasms of the sounds.

The variety of imaginative experience is great, but for our present purposes the example we have taken may suffice. We put forward the generalisation that, whereas the cause of sight is what we see, the cause of visual imagination is how we look; and so with hearing and the other senses which have counterparts in the imagination. There is a passive or receptive element in genuine imagination, the enjoyment of the phantasms; and this, like the enjoyment of full-blooded sensation, is in the receptive nerves. But the determining cause why we imagine one thing rather than another, must be sought in the adaptation of our organs for imaginary experiences; and this adaptation is the work of the executive nervous system, not the receptive.

The old-fashioned philosophical psychology treated words as the conventional substitutes for images, and images as the pale doubles of sights and sounds; and since we are passive, or receptive, in hearing and seeing, it was concluded that we are equally passive in imagining. Imagination being taken as the substance of thought, thought was easily regarded as a dream which dreamt itself, and into which the subjective laws of the mind introduced whatever discipline of logical order it exhibited. Professor Ryle appears to believe that in *The Concept of Mind* he has pickled a rod for the back of Descartes; but it is Hume who takes the beating. Descartes used a crude mythology of description which is certainly misleading, but the sheer empirical errors which Ryle exposes are the property of Hume. After all, Descartes did know that thinking is something we do, and that imagining is a sort of thinking.

For us (though not, of course, for Descartes) to ask whether we ever think with our brains alone, may come down to the same thing as asking whether we ever think without doing anything, even of the ghostliest kind; for if we *do* anything, our brain will presumably be setting in motion, or at least endeavouring to set in motion, some part of the executive system. Surely the burden of proof lies on the man who says that there is ever thought without so much as the ghost of motion; and it will be hard for him to prove the negative part of his case. 'Not even the ghost. . . .' How could he be sure of that?

But perhaps he feels that he is under no necessity to prove an entire negative. He may say: 'I am willing to grant that when I perform a sheer act of unsupported thought, there may be some frisking and whisking of the nerves, experienced by me, perhaps, as the flick of the shadow of a gesture. What I deny is that anything of this kind can act as the vehicle for the important transition of thought, which contemporaneously occurs.' Well, but why should it not? What have we here but a striking case of a very general fact about the mind: that the significance of what is consciously done, said or felt largely depends on what is not consciously done, said or felt, but lies somehow in the margin of the mind, out of the mind's reach? The meaning adhering to any single word I use in common speech, lies in the confused feeling of a whole complex of references to possible thoughts or buried memories; references which I could pause to take up, but which I do not in fact take up, being unwilling to break the thread of my discourse. What is in consciousness somehow focuses what is *not*: an apparent paradox, but, no doubt, apparent only. For in so far as what is not itself the focus of consciousness is focused there, it becomes present in consciousness in the degree in which it is so focused; we have no need to say it is both really absent and effectively present at the same time. But we can afford to leave verbal niceties for another occasion, since none of us will presumably deny that any phrase or other mental symbol draws its

38

meaning from a wide penumbra of references or connexions, which make themselves felt for the moment in that phrase or symbol, and not in anything else. The symbol may be attenuated to the merest flick of the shadow of an action, and still provide a pin-point on which a crowd of angels—or rather, a complex of references—can stand.

What, then, is our conclusion? That thinking is a sort of shadowy doing, having a symbolical or representational, anyhow not a directly practical, value, and concerned always with something else, and not with itself. Thinking points away from itself, from its own embodiment; and this is awkward for us, since in the present enquiry our curiosity points at it. After all that either physiology or introspection can do for us, we are bound to interpret the cognitive shadow by the executive substance, to regard it simply as the shadow of that substance. The shadow of doing, which is thought, must be interpreted by full-blooded doing, a doing concerned with itself, and pointing to its own bodily enactment. Indeed, we make the interpretation instinctively. When we say that thought is something we *do*, we use the analogy of bodily behaviour; and we are wise.

CHAPTER III

THE INSTRUMENT OF PERSONAL ACTION

i. *Physical locus of decision between acts*

ALL that we accomplished in the last chapter was to bring every sort of doing, mental and bodily, under a single formula. In every action, from pitch-and-toss to mental arithmetic, we found ourselves putting some organ to a use. The use, physiologically speaking, was a pattern of minute events, or rather, a series of such patterns; each pattern being a self-discharging system of which the mechanism can be studied by neurologists. The gun discharges itself—if the trigger is pulled; but what about the pulling of the trigger? We have cast no light at all on the question of free-will, when we have said that it takes effect in, or concerns itself with, the triggering-off of self-discharging mechanisms. For freedom lies, if anywhere, in the ability to trigger off whatever action we choose, in preference to several alternatives; as though we were in Robinson Crusoe's stockade, with the loaded pieces in position at the several gun-holes, free to let off which we liked. What concerns us is not the act of execution, but the act of choice.

We ought not, indeed, to speak as though there were two actions: an act of deciding on action, and an act of acting. The two may be distinct in special circumstances, as when we decide to act on some future occasion, and then do act when the occasion arrives. But the typical case is that in which we decide to act, by acting. When, for example, decision is the decision to make a bodily movement, it is commonly made, or anyhow made decisive, by our moving, and by nothing else. We need not distinguish between two actions, the act of moving and the act of deciding; we can draw the distinction within one and the same voluntary movement, by considering first its movingness, then its decisiveness. The movingness lies in the execution of the act, the decisiveness in the preference of it to any other; the movingness is in relation to the effect produced, the decisiveness is in relation to rival projects. The action both discards its rivals and enacts its effect, and we may be conscious of both these things. But while the enactment is experienced as physical, the discarding is experienced as mental, or logical only: as the doing of this, *not* that or the other.

Not belongs to logic, there is no *not* in nature, no physical act (for example) which consists in negating. Sea-anemones, in a manner of speaking, say *No* to sand and *Yes* to seaweed, but they say their *No* by regurgitation, an act just as positive as ingestion is. And if there is a physical performance involved in our negative choices, it must consist in some positive business, some disengagement from, or suppression of, or draining away, by diversion of energy. Yet we are not aware of starving the acts we do not perform, as we are aware of moving our limbs; all we are aware of is negating alternatives, a mental business. The corresponding physical business goes through in the brain, without there being any direct consciousness of it.

Rejection is only the negative aspect of selection. It is the function of our brain to supply us with alternatives from which to select; and this we suppose it to do through tracings left behind by previous actions, and leading towards a repetition of the same actions; tracings into which a mechanism of association directs the brain-energy again, on occasion of our responses to the present situation. Our whole capacity to profit from past experience depends on the recording power of the brain. Much physiological speculation, and even some physiological discovery, has accumulated on the subject of the memory-record; and it is a fair field for physical explanation. There may be mental reasons why some things are initially recorded while others are not, or again, why some registrations attract our subsequent attention, others not. But how things are registered, what the register substantially is, and how it comes into play again, there must be questions for physiology alone. They are not, in any case, our questions. We will take it for granted that many suggestions are present in consciousness because associative machinery has operated; just as hearings of sound, and seeings of colour are present in consciousness because sensory mechanism has operated, and for no other reason. Accepting, therefore, the suggestions from our brain, we will watch ourselves choosing between them.

For the sake of simplicity we take an elementary case, into which language does not enter. We will not have a man discussing alternative suggestions with himself, or developing them for himself. We will have a car-driver confronted with an immediate choice. The lorry he is following slows down and he itches to pass it. But a blind view in front pushes his foot towards the brake. He brakes. The suggestion of overtaking lies in the imagined feel of doing it; and so with the suggestion of braking. Now physiologically viewed, these imagined feels of action should arise from a faint play in the same nerves as would execute the action itself. When, therefore, the brain supplies the alternative suggestions, what happens physically is not confined to the brain. In a former chapter we drew the physical diagram of action: a tenuous plant, rooted in the cortex, running a stem through the spinal column, and finally branching in the hand. The physical diagram of *imagined* action, where the imagination is muscular rather than (say) visual, will be identical. We must suppose, then, that by the mere working of associative machinery, two momentary action-plants flourish side by side in a ghostly form, awaking the consciousness proper to each. In the case we have taken, the consciousness of the acceleration-project is no sooner complete, than the driver decides against it. And how? By treading on the brake; that is, by enacting the alternative. There is no more to be said. Intentional action is an ultimate. We know that we can act; this means that we can operate the action-pattern, can put life into the nerve-plant. The action-pattern does the rest; it sets minute mechanism to the draining of force from the ghostly alternative, and the direction of force into the operative nerves. The brain-circuits connected with the discarded project cease to function, while those leading to the adopted project function with effect.

The purpose of the example we have taken is merely to explode a spurious problem. How can it be, we are inclined to ask, that in making decisions we use our brains without knowing it? The moral of our example is that we do not, in the relevant sense, use our brains at all. We enact the chosen project, that is what we do. The disengagement from, and drying up of the alternative project happens in the brain (and outwards from it); we do not personally do it, the system does it for us. Mr John Betjeman has an anecdote about a Victorian architect. When his pupils pointed out to him that his neo-Jacobean designing had balanced a pillar over the edge of a sheet of glass, or involved some minor structural inconvenience of the kind, he replied: 'The man will see to it.' He was an architect, not an artisan. It was for the master to draw elevations, for the man to make them stand up. The man would see to it; the man was competent with iron rods and rules-of-thumb. It became a saying in the office, and we might adapt it for the lecture-room: The system will see to it. The actions we intend are architecturally, not mechanically, defined. We enact the chosen alternative; as to the elimination of the other, the system will see to it, as it will to the pulling of the muscles.

The car-driver has supplied us with an example in which we suppose alternatives to be presented by the brain, so that mental direction is limited to the act of deciding. But mental direction has a wider scope than this. When I talk to myself or to others, aloud or silently, the function of consciousness is not to opt between words, phrases or even sentences put up ready-made by the brain. On occasion, no doubt, it may be so. I have two ready-made anecdotes, stereotyped to the last syllable, one about Pat, the other about Mike. The topic 'Irish humour' brings both into my head, and I despair of being allowed to give both recitations; I must choose between Mike and Pat. But on other occasions, as when I was composing these lectures, I make it up as I go along. In a sense, the brain's associative mechanism supplies my talking self with ready grown nerve-plants (as we have called them), the action-patterns involved in saying, or imaging, the words; and not content with that, groups them for me in many convenient bunches. But the language-system is *embarras de richesse* to the speaker. It is ridiculous to say that, as I compose a sentence, all possibly relevant words, phrases and syntactical forms line up before my attention; so that the adoption of a word is like the picking of a suspect out of an identification-parade. Mental spontaneity in the management of words does not take the form of mere decision, but of inventive construction. We do not choose between materials that come to hand; we know how to put our hand on the materials we require, as a mason might know his way blindfold about a builder's yard. There is no *embarras de richesse*, once we know our way round the storeroom.

We may know how to produce the word we want; but how do we decide what word we want? There is no general answer to this question, only particular answers, such as 'Well, you are talking about so-and-so' or 'Well, such-and-such an alternative word wouldn't do, would it?' Constructive spontaneity is an ultimate fact about us men; we exercise it, and we can recognise it. If anyone pretends not to know it, we can only cite examples; inventive talking is one, inventive dancing is another. Within the rhythm of a given dance the imaginative dancer may extemporise variations. We may compare the set rhythm of the dance to the language-system, the dancer's extemporisation to the sentence freely thought. The extemporisation is not a single movement, but a series of movements so related to one another that it is possible to pass rhythmically from one into the next. It would suit our prejudice in favour of diagrammatic tidiness if we could say either that we made it up one movement at a time, or that we first imagined the whole series as a group, and then proceeded to execute it *seriatim*. But neither alternative is (or anyhow need be) true. We can make up the whole thing as we go along. We might say that it dawns on us as we go on with it. But the suggestion of passivity in 'dawns on us' is false. I do not open the gradual eye of dawn; dawn opens it on me. Whereas what I invent, I invent.

As with extemporised dancing, so with the use of language. No one speaking easily, inventively and continuously says a word except with a view to the sentence, or a sentence (it may be) except with a view to the argument. And yet he who says the word has not prefabricated the sentence. Still less has he who says the sentence prefabricated the argument. We might say that our meaning outran our words, only in a molten state, and that it was cast into form as the words were supplied. But do not such metaphors mystify more than they enlighten? After all, we know what it is to invent an argument, or a description, in speaking it; what is the use of multiplying words on such a subject?

Perhaps a different sort of comparison may be more illuminating. In physical nature we accept the sway of whole fixed patterns or rhythms. Free energy proceeds in whole waves, tied energy in whole gyrations; animal life in pulsations and circulations of various sorts. Each of these motion-units escapes from the mathematical moment and embraces a tract of time. At any indivisible instant it is in process of taking place. Why, then, should it surprise us, if conscious spontaneity has its action-units, more extensive than the present moment or the indivisible act? They are not, of course, fixed and given before the event, like those of physical nature, or where would be the spontaneity? We throw them as we proceed. Invention makes its own periodisations; its own sentences and arguments in discourse, its own figures in dancing.

We are digressing. It is not our concern to be picturesque about invention, or witty about wit, but to relate such forms of mental action to nervous structure. He who invents his discourse passes, with meaning as the sole consideration, from the utterance of one word to the utterance of another. Physically speaking, each word is an action-pattern, a nerve-plant: really, no doubt, a bunch of nerve-plants, but for simplicity we will use the singular. The passage of our conscious action from word to word, then, has its physical counterpart in a passage of energy from one nerve-plant to another. We know how to go from word to word; we are not conscious of any steps between one word and the next. But the physical transition from one nerve plant to another goes by way of the roots, so intricately interwoven in the cortex. We must suppose that our intentional operating of action-patterns in continuous series forces a way through the cortical maze, guided by existing paths, yet ignoring all but helpful turnings, and (to change the figure) constantly tipping the balance of minute energies in the direction of the required channel. What we can do in the way of invention is conditioned by all this, and yet *we* do none of it, the system does it. We are the master architects of our discourse; we leave mechanics to the man.

To summarise: intentional action is not concerned with the brain, but with acts carried by action-patterns rooted in the brain. In the simplest cases of practical decision the brain may be credited with supplying alternative projects; if they are before the mind, it is because brain-mechanism has set two or more action-patterns tingling in a ghostly way. Our decision is just the intentional and full-blooded enactment of one alternative. Invention is another thing, concerned with a transition, but not the transition between project and execution. Invention is indifferent to the very distinction between shadow-action and action proper; whether we utter our words, or merely imagine them, makes no odds; we may be equally inventive in either case. Invention has her physical existence in the passage from action-pattern to action-pattern. She applies her vigour to the picking of sequences, not the actualisation of projects. Without the machinery of the brain, she could not step from one pattern of action to another; yet the step she takes is from one use of the organs to another such; she never (as it were) sets foot on anything in the brain.

ii. *What is the instrument of free action?*

We have endeavoured some sort of description, at once personal and physical, of typical human activities. We have made no pretence to be exhaustive; we have said nothing, for example, about constructive picturing or wilful day-dreaming. But we hope it will be evident that the formula we have used is adaptable to any variety of human action. We will, therefore, let ourselves off making further applications, and turn to consider a criticism against the formula itself.

Our friends, reflecting on what we have said, may offer some such comment as this. 'You seem to be telling us that we draw on the activity of our brains as a milkmaid draws on the udder of a cow, not by handling the main body, but by pulling at the teats which hang out from it. For it is by working the nerve-systems dependent from the brain that we set the brain's associative mechanism working, or afterwards profit from the work it has done. Such is your story, and we have no quarrel with it as an interpretation of personal experience, for consciousness identifies itself with the organs, not with the brain. Our difficulty is over the squaring of your story with physical theory. For of the action-systems proceeding from the brain, a virtually watertight physical account surely should be, and to a large extent already is, forthcoming. It is only in the cortex that it would be tolerable to suppose a certain play of the mechanism, allowing of intentional control; and the language you use appears to admit this. According to your physical theory, then, there is nothing for intention to get a grip on, outside the brain. According to your psychophysical story, intention never does take hold within the brain. Is not this a manifest contradiction? Some while ago, you yourself brought before us the paradox about the seat of consciousness, physically in the brain, experientially in the limb or organ. You agreed that the paradox could be exploded as verbal; but you were not content with a verbal solution. The two seats of consciousness, though "seats" in different senses, ought (you said) to be coordinated in a single story. Such a story (we presume) you now claim to have given us. But what has the story done? It has hardened a verbal paradox into a physical contradiction.'

In answer to this objection we have two points to develop, one about the seat, or physical counterpart, of consciousness; the other about the sense in which bodily functions can be called mechanical. We will take them in order.

The detailed working out, or self-discharge of the action-pattern we have called mechanical; but we never correlated the operation of intention with the self-discharge of the action-pattern, but with its occurrence. The physical effect of intention is that a certain action-pattern should occur. It occurs, no doubt, only in discharging itself, and so intention bears upon a patterned discharge. But it bears upon it under the aspect of its pattern, not under the aspect of its discharging mechanism; for with this it is evident that intention has nothing directly to do.

We may call the occurrence of the pattern the physical counterpart of intention, always provided that 'intention' is taken in the sense of 'that which is intended', not in the sense of 'our intending' whatever we do intend. The two senses are, of course, inextricably connected: there cannot be any intending, where nothing is intended; nor can there be anything intended, where there is no intending. There is however, a difference of time between the two. The intending is ahead of the intended, though it be but a hairsbreadth. We may intend the further steps of what is already initiated, or the continuance of what is already in operation; but it is the continuance, and the further steps, that we intend, not anything that already is. If, then, the physical counterpart of the intended lies in the occurrence of the action-pattern, the physical counterpart of the intending should lie in what leads to the occurrence of the intended action-pattern, rather than of any other; and so, presumably, in the brain-events decisive for its enactment. Intending, then, has its seat in the brain and outwards; the act intended has its seat in the limb. But since intending is a consciousness not of itself, but of what it intends, the perceptible coincidence of the physical and intentional systems is in the limb, not in the brain. In the analogy drawn by the objectors to our story, the milkmaid works the udder by pulling on the teats. But the milkmaid is seated on the milking stool, whereas intentional activity is seated in the brain; as though the udder set itself to work, by a spasmodic action of its teats.

But if we seat intending in the brain (and outwards), how shall we justify the formula, previously insisted on, that we do not use our brains in intentional activity, but rather the part of the action-pattern which has its life in our hand, or throat, or tongue? The question whether we *use* our brains or not is a verbal question, and therefore, no doubt, a philosophical question. What is the proper application of the verb 'to use', and how far are we prepared to stretch it? We are first said to use instruments, not parts of ourselves. When I use a pen, I do not use my hand; my hand is part of the me who does the using, and not merely a part, but the operative part, in which I come to bear upon the pen. But because the hand can sometimes do the job for which an instrument is designed, we say, when offered an instrument and told to 'use this', 'No thank you; I prefer to use my hand.' The first speaker to make the answer was probably thought to be a wit, like the man who first had the idea of trotting home on Shanks's mare. Reflection takes hold of the joke and develops the parallel. When I use a pen to write, my purpose is to make it do this or that, and my attention dwells on the tip of it; and the same things may be said of my finger, when I model with it. And if my modelling finger, why not my babbling tongue? Here indeed the element of local attention commonly fails, for I take my tongue's performance for granted, unless I get tongue-tied. But what of that? The practised and absorbed writer may take his pen's performance for granted, but he uses it, none the less for that.

Once the gallop of analogy starts, it is not soon halted. If I use my vocal organs to speak aloud, do not I make a shadowy use of them in discoursing silently with myself, and similarly a phantom-use of my limbs in imagined gestures? But now, I reflect, imagined gestures are physically an actual play of some kind in the nerves controlling my limbs. So shall not I say that in the imaginary gestures I really use not my limbs, but my nerves? And from here it is a short step to the position, that I do not really, or physically, use my executive nerves in independence of their roots in the brain; what I use is the whole action-plant from root to tip. And surely this is an under-statement, for it is the brain part of the system in which intention takes hold of mechanism, and where the using really happens; so let us say that really it is my brain I use.

But when I reach this point, I begin to feel a certain uneasiness. Surely I have overdone it somehow; for by the same reasoning, the part of my pen I really use will be the handle, not the tip of the nib. And that is contrary to the proper mode of speech. For if we are prepared to discriminate at all, and not merely to say that we use the whole pen, we shall discriminate in favour of the operative point. Apply this rule to our verbal house-of-cards, and down it comes with a run. What we most properly use will always be the limb. As for the brain, we never use it at all; for we can only pretend to use what we can pretend to exteriorise. We do not need to exteriorise the pen, it is external anyhow. But as I write, I may in a manner exteriorise my hand, by attending to the motions through which I put it, in guiding the pen; in using the pen, I am using it. So with my arm; so, even, with phantom-gestures and mental picturings. But I cannot exteriorise my brain, or seem to wield that.

It is not for a philosopher to prohibit verbal usages, but to point out their dangers. If what I mean by 'I use my brain' is that it comes into play when I use other things, there is no harm done; but will it not be at once safer and more illuminating, to say that our using of whatever we do use has its physical seat in the brain and outwards? The using, not the use; for 'use' in English does not easily mean the act of using, but the employment to which the thing used is put; and we never put our brain to any use, but only our limbs or our organs. Consciousness, indeed, is more closely identified with uses than with organs used; but that does nothing towards identifying it with anything in the brain. The only place where anything of which consciousness is conscious and anything which physiology describes can be said to coincide, is where a certain system of physiological events make up an action we design to execute, or a use to which we put our limbs.

So ends the first part of our reply to the objection. Before we proceed to the second part we will revive the still outstanding half of the objection itself, or rather, we will let the objector have a second innings. 'It is all very well,' he says 'for you to put *using* in the brain and treat the hand as something we use, or put to a use, so long as your object is to correct our language about the brain. It will not do, if the object is to define the action of the hand. It cannot be said absolutely that my hand is an instrument I use, for, as you yourself began by admitting, in the properest mode of speech, my hand is part of me, the user, and what I do with it belongs at least as properly to my act of using, as it does to any instrumental use. The act of using continues into, and is alive in, the hand, when, for example, I model clay with my fingers. Moreover it is in the hand, as you yourself say, that consciousness experiences itself as identified with physical event. Now according to you (says the objector) this experience of psychophysical identity is to be accepted as veridical, and taken as the clue to the whole relation of the personal with the bodily. But how can this be so? For what physical process is there in the limb, with which consciousness could veraciously identify itself? There is nothing there but an action of the executive nerves, which you yourself confess to be inexorably mechanical. You are up against the same difficulty as Descartes, and you haven't the grace to own it. Descartes, seeing the nervous system to be a causal mechanism, abandoned the attempt to correlate consciousness directly with it. He looked for some interior point at the heart of the web, where he could postulate a sensitive spot, responsive to the mind. Now you, says the objector, following your physiological masters, spread out Descartes's sensitive spot into a sensitive complex, a tissue of cortical circuits. But instead of simply adapting Descartes's scheme to the revised physiological theory, and confining the seat of consciousness to the sensitive area, you extend it over the mechanical outworks. Indeed it is here, you say, that the flowering of consciousness is found; it is only the roots you locate in the brain.'

We will answer the objection by putting yet another word through the hoops. This time 'mechanical' is the victim. Of Cartesian neurology it can be used literally; not of ours. Mechanism properly so-called finds its type in clockwork. It is a system capable of being put in motion, composed of solid, inert and separate parts, so set that when the movement is started up, they move one another in a determined order. Descartes did not think that the neural system was clockwork, but he did think that it was made up of inert stuff in small solid blocks, displacing one another. For he thought that all physical systems whatsoever were composed in this way. It is well known that nobody today thinks anything like this either about physical nature in general or about the nervous system in particular. Energy, rather than stuff, is our ultimate. When we say that a mechanical account can or should be given of neural activity, we mean no more than this: it can be practically described as a series of minute energisings following one another with quantitative uniformity, according to rules which can be stated. When we accept a mechanical account of the process, we accept nothing which excludes our regarding it as a manifestation of physical life. A physical system does not need to die, or even to petrify in parts, in order to reap the advantages of regular action in those of its functions which demand regularity. The minute elements function regularly, and yet allow themselves to be overruled by the requirements of their action-pattern. The action-pattern functions normally, and yet allows itself to be initiated by voluntary choice. The whole system is alive and conscious with a total consciousness, a consciousness at any moment dormant or virtual only in most of its parts, and yet effectively focused somehow or concentrated in lively patches, such as those concerned with intentional action. We have been examining such patches of consciousness and finding them to be correlated with patterns of physical functioning, each pattern made up in part of events which can be interpreted 'mechanically', and in part of events which require further principles to explain them. If it is the 'mechanical' part that carries the accent of consciousness, it is not because it is mechanical, but because it is executive, thus coinciding with the deed intended and performed.

CHAPTER IV

THE ACTION-PATTERN, AND ALTERNATIVE THEORIES

i. *The action-pattern*

WHAT would Professor Ayer say? Would he pass the general drift of our last chapter, or would he complain that we were introducing that impermissible bridge, that nonsensical *tertium quid* between consciousness reports and physiological assertions, which, at an earlier point, he persuaded us to banish? It is uncertain what he would say: an uncertainty which merely illustrates the limited usefulness of principles laid down in advance of discussion. They may look clear, they may carry conviction; so that we proceed to discuss, with the comfortable assurance of possessing a touchstone for sound and rotten hypothesis. A hypothesis comes up, and we put the touchstone to it, only to find that we cannot read the result of the test. In our previous chapter we certainly introduced a *tertium quid*, neither the subject of consciousness-reports nor the subject of neurophysical statements; but whether this *tertium quid* has the damnable characteristics banned by the Professor's logical exorcism, is not immediately clear.

Our *tertium quid* is the unit of bodily functioning involved in, or corresponding to, a conscious act. A player makes the careful shot at tennis, about which we have talked already. A whole of activity extending from brain to hand functions as the unit of his act—the unit of his act, not the subject of his consciousness. Consciousness we saw to be a sort of spot-light, lighting up a part of the process, and shifting at will. Now it is in the elbow and wrist, now in the fingers. But its range is limited; there are parts of the process, for example in the brain, on which neither intention nor sensation ever dwells at all. These parts of the process are not shown to belong to the functioning of consciousness by any direct report on the part of consciousness; what shows their indispensability is the experimental observation that consciousness fails or is disordered, if they are physically tampered with. Our *tertium quid* is a unit of which the extent and the coherence is revealed neither by consciousness alone nor by neurology alone; it is, as we have called it, a third thing on which they both cast light. But not only are they both required, to delimit it physically; they are both required to define it logically. What are we talking about? Not a stretch of consciousness as such, but an area of that functioning which neurophysiology investigates. But what area? An area picked out by the action of consciousness, not by neural action as such. For neural activity, we take it, is always going on in the human body; a minute excitation, constantly wearing its natural channels, and weaving its patterns: patterns which have only a relative distinctness one from another, and only a relative unity each in itself. Seen from the level of neurophysical functioning, none of these patterns is a single whole. Neurophysiology uses a microscopic scale; its unit of time is a moment which allows room for no more than the excitation of this part of this nerve, or that part of that. The whole system of movement is pulled together into one, in being wielded by a single act of consciousness.

Let us hope that our *tertium quid* will escape Professor Ayer's condemnation of intermediaries. For though it is not a pattern belonging to pure neurophysical science, it is still a physical pattern, a moving physical mosaic made up of neural movements. It is not a bridge between the mental and the physical, but firmly on the physical bank; it is that physical to which the mental corresponds. Ought we to add: 'And to which the *behavioural* corresponds'? Those who study the behaviour of animals abstract from the question how far the behaviour is conscious, let alone chosen; they concentrate on what the animals do, and on the predictable sequences which are to be found in their doings. Such a study is bound to work with units of action, with jumping up, chasing, attacking, eating—sorts of unit which might be the subjects of conscious intention, if the animal could be credited with anything of the kind. The study of behaviour no more takes us into the brain, than the personal interpretation of human conduct does. To consider how an animal behaves is to consider how it behaves; you need not go inside its skin for that. But then, of course, you may; for you may wish to take into account facts which you accept, even though they are formally extraneous to the matter of your study. You cannot but believe that the action exhibited in the behaviour works out from the brain through the nerves; and if you trace it back to its roots, you draw yourself the same diagram of the attenuated nerve-plant, you work with the same unit of neurophysical action as the philosopher does when he studies the place of consciousness in bodily conduct.

From certain points of view it may seem that behaviour is a more useful category than conscious action. It is both wider and more stable. The fitful light of consciousness moves hither and thither, it waxes and wanes, in the area of a behaviour which goes steadily on. Why not discount the consciousness as much as possible? For many purposes it is convenient to do so, but not, of course, if what we want to know is how consciousness operates. And in any case the study of mere behaviour, even in animals, is a painful abstraction. It is a moral certainty with all of us that consciousness plays a part in making them tick, anyhow so far as the higher animals are concerned. We abstract from the consciousness, because we can get no nearer to it than fancy takes us. The trouble is, as schoolgirls like to remark, that our animals cannot talk to us, poor things; and what is even more impoverishing for them, they are unprovided with anything to say. Meanwhile we can scarcely separate the idea of animal behaviour from a sneaking attribution of intention. In the case of mankind there is no need to attempt the separation, for men can talk; and how they talk!

Conscious intention may provide a more full-blooded approach to our *tertium quid*, but, we have claimed, mere behaviour affords a wider approach to it. The claim may be allowed to stand, so long as we limit our view to the field of overt bodily action. Here the range of behaviour is wider than the range of intention. But intention beckons us into a field of her own, to which behaviour has no access; a realm of thought not directly expressed in overt action; of shadow-acts, which, however shadowy, are not performed without employing our *tertium quid*.

The status of the *tertium quid*, or—to give it back the name we have already coined for it—of the action-pattern, may be clarified by asking, what work is required of it. We do not need it to double the work of intention, where intention is present. Intention is the direction of an act personally exercised; and we do not want any physical principle to explain over again the action's taking the intended direction. What we require of our physical pattern is that it should fill the gap between what we intend and what happens. We intend a macroscopic effect, but it cannot come about except through many microscopic events. It is nonsensical to claim that intention bears directly on the microscopic. Intention, by definition, bears on what it intends; we cannot intend that of which we have neither sense nor notion. No doubt the grand sweep of action, which we now direct by a single intention, is made up of many small actions, once learnt by us with labour and pain. I do not now agonise to put one foot before another without falling over, but once I did. Yet if we resolve action into the least elements our infancy studied to manage, we come no nearer the microscopic level. What we once studied to manage was always the control of our limbs, never the speeding of energy through our nerves. There must always (it would seem) have been a physical or natural, not a conscious or intentional, action-pattern, to bring the microscopic components of our action into line.

Deny this, and what results? Everything that happens, including the formation of the pattern, must be explicable without invoking the formative influence of the pattern itself: explicable, that is, from the minute neural activities themselves, interacting by their own principles of action. I dare say this is very improper language. Examples may show better what is meant. The tides along our coasts are an impressive phenomenon. They ebb and they flow in a balanced rhythm; the variations of height from day to day are not haphazard but fulfil a cycle of changes. We may speak of the cycle *governing* the tides, but we do not take such language seriously. We know that the cyclic rhythm is a mere resultant, a mass effect of the behaviour of water-molecules under the influence of gravitation. 'The tide' is not a pulsating agency, it's a composite effect. The total rhythm does no work; it is the large-scale result of working forces.

There are plenty more examples of what we are after. To find examples on the opposite side is not so easy; not, anyhow, examples which are undisputed. For whatever organic whole we may cite, there will always be intransigent atomists ready to deny any working principles of wholeness in it; or that anything happens in the organism, which is not the simple result of action exerted by the constituent elements. Out-and-out atomism is a paradoxical opinion, nevertheless; and those scientists seem wise who admit that in cellular organisation the molecular constituents are caught, and as it were bewitched, by larger patterns of action; and that the cells in their turn are similarly caught in the pattern of the animal body. Even where the real efficacy of higher organising principles is denied by scientists, it is not necessary for the philosopher to take the denial at what is to him its face value. When the scientist rejects a principle of explanation, he does not mean that it is unnecessary from a speculative point of view, let alone that it is refutable. He means either that he is in no position to put it to the experimental test, or that he fears its acceptance will be a psychological discouragement to hopeful enquiries. Where scientists grudge to admit real efficacy on the part of principles of higher organisation, both considerations may operate. They do not see what experiments would prove it; and they fear *ignava ratio*. For will not students be apt to think that if a principle of higher-level organisation is involved, it must be a waste of time to look for any mechanism of the elements organised, through which the organisation works? Rather than risk the numbing effects of *ignava ratio* it is better to ignore the force of organising principles, and to aim at explaining everything by autonomous combinations of the elements. For you never know how much, or exactly what, you will be able to explain from below. Yet the real power of the higher forms of organisation to bewitch the lower forms, and lead them a new dance, seems undeniable, when we stand back from the business of our research, and survey the field. If no new principles of action come into play at successive levels of organisation, the electrons composing the atoms have it in them to be you and me, precisely as the water-molecules have it in them to be the tide; and that is a tall story.

So far we have discussed the real efficacy of organising patterns, as though the difficulties to which it gave rise were purely scientific. But there may be difficulties of a more philosophical sort; that is to say, difficulties about the question to be asked, rather than about the answer to be given. We have put the question thus: Do higher forms of organisation really affect (or, overrule) the operations of lower forms? To phrase the question in this way is to assume that the units and patterns of the lower organisation are what the higher organisation organises; just as human individuals are what political society organises. But the relation may not be so straight as such a comparison suggests. A more fitting parable might be found in the statement that games-players are what political society organises. It is, indeed, probably true that all the citizens of a civilised state divert themselves in one way or another. A study of their games-playing habits, skills and preferences might be full of interest, and well worth the award of a junior research degree. But a thesis on games-playing would not directly set out those passions, concerns and activities of the citizen, which enter into the pattern of the body politic. The question, whether games-players ever act as they would not otherwise act, in consequence of their inclusion in a political state, is a confusing one. If we undertook to answer it, we should want to introduce a distinction. The persons who are games-players (we should say) act otherwise through being citizens than they would act if they were not; but they do not play their games otherwise.

In the good old days physicists were convinced that the subject of their study was *the* constitution, the operative principle of the ultimate elements in nature. On such a view, there was nothing for any higher principles to organise, but that which the theorems of physics had defined. Science enjoys no such confidence now. No more would now be claimed for physical theory, than that it systematises the answers given by nature to questions we have thought of asking, or her reactions to tests we have been able to devise. If we map two levels of organisation by applying different arts of enquiry, there may be a certain irrelevance between the two sets of results we obtain. The higher organisation which we have managed to diagrammatise may draw upon, or employ, active properties of minute Nature which have escaped the net of our atomic studies; may (to return to the political parable) organise householders, where we have been studying games-players.

The parable in this form manifestly exaggerates. Statistical observation would prove, anyhow in large measure, the irrelevance of games-playing to political conduct, whereas experimental enquiry shows the relevance of much minute physical organisation to the working of higher patterns. If there is a logical hiatus, it must be more like that which is involved in basing politics on economic man, than in basing them on games-playing man. The action of political states varies in direct proportion to the citizen body's economic interest and behaviour; and yet to understand economics is not to understand politics; politics can touch many other springs in the human heart.

I would undertake for a bet, though not for a small bet, to write a piece of space-fiction about a planetary people whose political system was affected by their economic behaviour, while their economic behaviour remained unaffected by their political system. About such a people three things might be true: their political organisation does real work, in making them act as they would not otherwise have acted; it responds to their economic behaviour; their economic behaviour is not reciprocally affected by it. If, now, we called upon the economists of our planetary utopia to make room for the bending of economic generalisation before political pressures, they would rightly refuse. And such, for all I know, may be the correct attitude for physicists to adopt, when called upon by biologists to allow for the overruling of physical uniformities by biological organisation. But the intransigence of the physicists, however well justified, need not contradict the claims of the biologists to be studying a pattern of action which does real work at its own level, and leads the minute parts of Nature a dance they would not otherwise tread.

We have no present concern with boundary disputes between the positive sciences. All we are interested to show is the meaningfulness of the suggestion that a high-level pattern of action may do some real work, and not be reducible to the mass-effect of low-level action on the part of minute constituents. And we are happy if we can show at the same time how the claims to exactitude advanced by minute physics need not stand in the way of our entertaining such a suggestion.

ii. Philosophical objections considered

To return from the general to the particular, we will ask whether that action-pattern in the human body which is correlative with consciousness acts upon, overrules, the minute patterns of action which neurophysiologists study; and we will claim for our form of enquiry the merit, that it escapes the criticism levelled by Professor Ryle and his friends against any question of interaction between mind and body. The very idea is denounced as involving a Category-Mistake. If mind and body are to interact (or for that matter, to fail of interaction), two suppositions are required: first, that mind and body are in the same category; second, that they are numerically distinct. But (say our philosophers) the combination of these two suppositions is linguistically intolerable. If mind is distinguished from body, it is not as a rival substance, but as a special class of capacities possessed by a bodily person. Whereas if mind, or soul, is understood substantially, it denotes the bodily person in his exercise of these capacities. In illustration of their contention, our philosophers point with complacency to the different usages of old regional English. If you were born in one county you were a nice body to your neighbours, if born in another, you were a good soul. In either case the same thing was meant. The 'body' was understood to be ensouled, and no one imagined the 'soul' to be disembodied.

When our philosophers talk in this way it is reasonable to suspect them of a side-thrust against the hope of everlasting life. We take note and pass on. Perhaps we will make a remark about it later. For the present we are content to say that we should not dream of basing the hope of man's perpetuity hereafter on the incompleteness of his embodiment now. The soul is perfectly embodied, and does nothing here without the body. We should need first to disembody the soul, before we could speak of interaction, cooperation, or conflict between naked soul and physical body. But if we had disembodied the soul, could we talk of her interaction with body, even then? If there are to be any acts or motions of the soul with which body could interact, they must be cast in a bodily shape, they must be the acts of an embodied soul. The conclusion is evident: the only interaction we can even consider is one that lies between different patterns of bodily action; but of these some may be actions of the embodied soul in a way that others are not. For there are, it must surely be admitted, distinct trains of events going on in one living body. The body is no single fixed system of motions; it is not at all like a simple piece of clockwork, in which all the moveable parts are so geared together, that no one of them can move without all moving, in a manner determined by the motion of that one. Not only are there distinct trains of motion in the body; there are several levels of motion, traced by different sorts of evidence. There are macroscopic patterns, such as I personally execute, and you see me perform; and microscopic patterns, detected by the interference of special instruments. Yet both come down to a common denominator, in so far as they are motions in the body; and there can surely be no Category-Mistake or other logical impropriety involved in our considering their mutual relation.

Even supposing that our doctrine escapes the charge of involving a Category-Mistake, it will still have further accusations to face. It will be said to be an empirical hypothesis, and therefore no proper piece of philosophy. Not that our philosophers have any objection to empirical hypotheses—far from it; they regard them as the very stuff of science, and, indeed, of common knowledge. But, they hold, it is not the business of a philosopher either to frame empirical hypotheses, or to favour one against another. It is his business to examine the logical form of such hypotheses, and their logical relation to other statements or types of statement.

Our immediate reaction to this line of criticism may well be a gesture of impatience. Who cares whether what we are doing is philosophy, or not? We want to understand the body-mind relationship. It seems likely enough that in such an enquiry we shall wish to consider empirical hypotheses, not only in point of form, but in point of factual content. After all, the body-mind question, as we now know it, has been created by the acceptance of empirical hypotheses about the nervous system. These hypotheses have to be related to direct descriptions of subjective experience; for what the hypotheses themselves describe is supposed to be, in some manner, the vehicle of such experience. But, taken as they stand, do our neural hypotheses allow of being brought into immediate relation with subjective descriptions? Or do they need first, perhaps, to be rounded off, or completed, on a side which positive science has so far neglected? Surely it cannot be denied, *a priori*, that the rounding-off needs to be done. It is no use saying either that there can be no gap between one set of facts and another, or that if there is a gap, science must have mapped it already. A knows all about guns and B is a veterinary surgeon. A understands the firing of the rifle and B the death of the deer, and the two events are certainly connected. Yet neither A nor B, it may chance, can give you a scientific account of the trajectory of the bullet in its relation to gravitation and atmosphere. And it is perfectly possible to imagine a time at which no one was able to supply this account, even though the mechanics of the rifle, and the physiology of animal death, were well understood.

The filling of the gap between the gun-story and the death-story will, of course, touch no distinctively philosophical issues;

it belongs first to last within the area of science and commonsense. The case we are considering does involve philosophy; indeed, it begins from philosophy. We find ourselves engaged on a philosophical attempt—to define the different ways in which consciousness-descriptions and neurological descriptions refer to the same events. To adapt Professor Ayer's phraseology, we are trying to span a logical river with a logical bridge. But when we come to make the attempt, we find a factual gap on the neurological side. The neurological mapping is all concerned (as it were) with fields and hedgerows back inside the country; it does not define the shore which our bridge is to connect with the shore of consciousness. The gap is a gap in empirical mapping, but the filling of it has a philosophical importance; for until it is filled, we do not know what to join with the opposite bank by means of our logical bridge.

That philosophers should refrain as far as possible from sketching in hypotheses about matters of fact, is a sound maxim; above all, that they should not pit their speculative constructions against hypotheses empirically verified. If philosophers do make such sketches, they should always, perhaps, regard them as guesses in anticipation of scientific exploration. But where there is a burning philosophical interest in the relating of A to C, and where A can be related to C only by being rounded out into AB, philosophers will make the conjectures necessary to the rounding-out. They would certainly not show themselves any more philosophical, if they preferred to construct spurious logical bridges direct from A to C.

iii. *Parallel descriptions not to be accepted without justification*

Whether, in fact, our action-pattern is a pure speculation of the philosophical mind, or is a conception with some scientific employment on the borderland of neurology and animal psychology, is a question we leave for those competent to discuss it. Meanwhile, here comes the next wave of the philosophical attack. 'If only' our friends say to us, 'you would take to heart the lessons of linguistic philosophy, you would stop thinking that there is any gap to fill. Do not we keep describing different aspects of things under different linguistic conventions? Isn't that how language works? And what is there to worry us, if we find ourselves talking both personal-life language and neurophysical language about the human body? The physical language is to tell us how it works and what it will do; the personal-life language expresses how it feels itself from inside.'

What could sound more unexceptionable? That is how language works: it expresses different aspects of things under different conventions of speech; or, to put it more philosophically, we find that by using different conventions of speech we can arrive at descriptions which are useful in different ways. Certainly. But do we make it a linguistic rule, never to attempt the relating to one another of our different descriptions—or shall we say, of the aspects of things captured by our different descriptions? Surely that way schizophrenia lies. We do, we must, relate them. What, then, is meant when the purely general fact of multiple description is invoked to palliate a mere parallelism between personal talk and physical talk? Did anyone ever doubt that these two lines of talk employed different types of description? But it remains to ask, how the matters they describe go together in one world. The general analogy of multiple description will cast no light on so particular a question.

Everything turns on the tone of voice, the emphasis. If it is said that personal-life language and neurophysical language give us aspects of the same man, described in strikingly different conventions, a problem is apparently being raised: 'How can they be mutually related?' But if it is said that the two types of language give us aspects of the same man, merely described under different conventions, a problem is apparently being exploded; it is suggested to us that we know what a relation of differently described aspects is like.

Well, perhaps we do; as we might be said to know, in general, what a fourfooted beast is like. But if anybody said to us that, knowing what a fourfooted beast is like, we need feel no qualms about admitting the biological possibility of mantichores, we might fairly reply that 'fourfooted beast' is too general a notion to support the conclusion. To show the possibility of a species it is not enough to invoke the genus; we must work from the analogy offered by some admitted species. Similarly, it is useless to invoke anything so general as the frequent acceptability of parallel descriptions, to palliate the oddity of relation between personal-life language and neurophysiology. Nothing could palliate the oddity, or cast any light on it, unless it were some other particular pair of parallel descriptions; a pair both acceptable in itself, and significantly analogous to the pair which concerns us.

Is any such analogous example brought forward? Yes, and more than one. Happily there are few that are of weight; we will confine ourselves to the examination of two: sense-experience language in its relation to physical-object language, and sensible-quality language in its relation to physical-force language. There is a sort of inevitability about the choice of these examples. If we are puzzled by a double way of talking about what we call ourselves, to what can we turn for comparison, but to double ways of talking about our environment? And of double ways for talking about our environment there turn out to be two which, as we shall see, have an obvious relevance to our enquiry. First, then, we take sense-experience language in its relation to physical-object language.

In certain cases, which Bishop Berkeley made much of, we find ourselves to hesitate between taking a sensation as the quality of a physical object, and taking it as a feeling in ourselves. Is it heat in the fire-bar which I touch, or is it pain in me who touch it? Beginning from such cases of natural ambiguity, we may build a system of universal double interpretation. We may construe all that we see or hear *either* as selections from the sensible aspects of a physical world, *or* as transitory phenomena having their place in the stream of our experience. So we have on the one hand a body of physical-object statements, on the other of sense-phenomenon statements; and the difference between the two arises simply from a difference of interpretation; as is, indeed, immediately obvious when we reflect that the sense-phenomenon world belongs neither to science nor to commonsense, but is the wilful creation of an artificial philosophy. Since nothing is employed for its creation but a sophisticated descriptive convention, what else but a convention of description can distinguish it from its rival?

Since it is the fit, or unity, between personal-life statements and neurological statements that we are trying to illuminate, it is on this point in the analogy we have quoted, that it concerns us to concentrate. What is it, then, that bridges the duality between our two types of statement, the physical-object type and the sense-phenomenon type? The answer is clear. The bridge between them is the identity of the data for both. The physical objects are 'constructed' from the same data, possible or actual, as the sense-phenomena; and any difference of detail in the one system involves a corresponding difference of detail in the other.

Well, and can we say the same of the body and the mind? Are they alternative constructions out of identical data? The answer will depend on what we mean by 'the body'. If we take 'body' in one sense, then, Yes; if in another sense, then No. Yes, if the body we speak of is the body as the man whose body it is, experiences it. No, if the body is taken as what the neurophysiologist observes and theorises about.

To take the negative first: it hardly needs pointing out that the data for neurological statements and for the corresponding consciousness-statements are totally different; that is, they differ both in number and in kind. The consciousness-datum may be a visual image, where the neural datum is an electric registration. The image is obtained by one experient, the registration by another. Even if, by a system of wonderful contrivances, we made every man his own phrenologist, and turned his neurological research upon his own brain, the registrations he read in our supposed instrument of self-observation would be a quite separate set of phenomena from the thoughts or mental images he concurrently enjoyed.

Perhaps the point we are making may be most strikingly exhibited by a comparison of the fields for empirical discovery offered by the two cases. In the parallel of physical objects and sense-phenomena, it would be a mere joke to claim new empirical findings about the detailed correspondence of the one system with the other. We cannot seriously exclaim 'Goodness me! Who'd have thought it! Where, in the one story, I speak of a red ball in front of my eyes, here is the other story mentioning a circular red patch shaded away round the edges!' If there is any discovery at all here, it is not a discovery of detailed correspondence, but of interpretative convention. For the physical-object interpretation at least is natural, not wilful; we do not do it by the book, we do it without intention, and only catch ourselves doing it when we philosophise. So it may not have occurred to us until the present moment that 'shaded round the edges' is often our warrant for 'convex'; and to discover this is to discover something, i.e. how we are wont to interpret. There is, of course, a genuinely empirical fact connected with the interpretative rule. If circular visual patches shaded away round the edges were not normal signs of the availability of further data, especially tactual, we should not make it a rule to interpret as spherical the shaded visual round. The connexion between shaded visual rounds and corresponding tactual data is a matter of empirical observation; but not of an observation which connects anything proper to the physical-object world with anything proper to the sense-phenomenon world. Both tactual data and visual belong to either world indifferently; so does the *de facto* connexion between them. Only, this connexion is differently interpreted in our sense-phenomenon language and our physical-object language respectively.

How different it is with the parallel between neurophysical statements and consciousness-statements! Here empirical discovery of correspondences between the two series is not merely a logical possibility, but a scientific pursuit. We endeavour to find out what, by way of stimulation in determinate areas, is happening to the brain, when such-and-such a sensation, mental image or the like is present to the man whose brain it is; and the stimulation is betrayed to us by phenomena totally different from those which either constitute, or reveal, the subjective experience.

We have said enough to show that the bridge between sense-phenomenon language and physical-object language offers no analogy which can help us over the gulf between consciousness-language and neurophysical language; or, as we put it less exactly, the gulf between body and mind, where 'body' is understood in neurophysical terms. But, we said, if 'body' is understood in other terms—as what the man whose body it is feels it to be—then the analogy fairly applies. That this is so, is evident. All we need do is go back to our starting-point, and rejoin Bishop Berkeley in his consideration of the ambiguous sensation. Is it heat in the fire-bar, or is it my pain? We take the liberty of pointing out to the Bishop an equally common case; the ambiguity not between a quality imputed to a physical object, and a pain of mine, but between pains of mine and events perceived in my arm. I begin by feeling my arm displaced and forced back. What I seem to perceive so far is, so to speak, the contemporary physical history of my arm. But the further twist it proceeds to undergo ceases to be perceived as physical history—it becomes a flame of agony: not what is happening to my arm, but what poor I am suffering.

The ambiguity is simpler and more general in those experiences of voluntary movement which we have discussed at large. My action of throwing the ball is a history also of my shoulder, arm and hand; my speech against governmental iniquity is a history also of my tongue and throat; and even (a fact we seldom notice) my silent philosophical rumination is a history of motor nerves in the vocal region.

If we feel any hesitation in speaking of the consciousness-statement, body-statement relation as receiving illumination from the sense-phenomenon, physical-object analogy, it is not that the analogy fails, but that the illumination flows the opposite way. For, as we said, the general re-interpretation of the physical-object world in sense-phenomenon language is a philosophical artificiality, whereas the simultaneous interpretation of what happens in our bodies as being what we also do or suffer, is natural and indeed inevitable. Is the double interpretation of the external world anything but an unnatural extension, beyond the confines of our bodies, of a double interpretation which within these confines is axiomatic? What happens in my arm is alternatively a phase of my action; what passes in the scene before me, I cannot seriously take to be a phase of my sight.

You will think that we are proposing a short way with phenomenalism, and that a famous philosophical question cannot be as simple as that. But phenomenalism is not our present business. We are concerned to point out no more than this: the sense-phenomenon, physical-object duality deals in two ways with things as they appear, and leaves untouched the relation of such appearances to scientific doctrines about underlying atomic structure; and in just the same way the consciousness-statement, body-statement duality deals in two ways with the self as it is felt, leaving untouched the relation of such feelings to underlying neural structure. There is just the same gap between the limb as felt and its minute constituent parts, as there is between the action exerted and its minute component events; and it is this gap that our talk about action-patterns is intended to reduce.

But our present business is with the suggestion, that any talk about action-patterns is perfectly superfluous, because language about systems of minute neural events, and language about actions exerted or felt, are harmlessly parallel descriptions of the same things. We are still searching for an analogy to help us see that the parallel really is harmless. If there is such an analogy to be had, it is surely plain enough by now what analogy it will have to be. The phenomena presented to our senses, whether interpreted as elements in our experience or as characters inherent in objects, are habitually related by us to the mysterious states of affairs which we understand physicists to describe. And in like manner what we are aware of in ourselves, whether interpreted as personal experience or as bodily fact, is somehow related by us to what neurophysiologists, we take it, are describing.

The distinction between the object of physical science and the object of direct experience has a long philosophical history. Something very near to it meets us in our old philosophers, under the name of a difference between the primary and the secondary qualities of things. The so-called secondary qualities have an indisputable phenomenal reality, being immediate objects of our awareness—colours, sounds, scents, tastes, temperatures, and varieties of surface-quality under our organs of touch. These are real 'distinct natures'; and yet they correspond in a determinate order to something quite different, once called the primary quality of things, but now seen to be their active force; a force explored by us through interfering with it, discovering how it interferes with us, and setting one item of it to interfere with another. The active forces of things can be known in the gross by direct experience, just as much as their secondary qualities; try walking against the wind, or even better, try walking through a brick wall, and you will see.

Here, then, are two classes of characteristics, both directly known, both somehow belonging to the same things, quite disparate in kind, and in external correspondence with one another. And since the relation of secondary quality to active force is spread over the whole face of our daily experience, no one can complain that the notion of the parallel it exhibits is an out-of-the-way notion, or profess surprise if consciousness and neural activity, in their mutual relation, afford another instance of the same kind.

However long we continued our search, we should not find an example anything like as apposite as this. When, being confronted with parallel descriptions of the human person, first in mental, then in neurophysical terms, people appeal to the general acceptability of parallel descriptions, they cannot do better than appeal to the analogy supplied by secondary quality and active force. The appeal may seem persuasive; for we accept the quality-force parallel, right enough. But as what do we accept it? Not as a parallel between rival accounts of the way things work. Force is effective by definition. Secondary quality does no work at all. To know force is to know what things do; to know secondary quality is to know how they look, sound, smell or feel, but never how they act. Nothing is more difficult to wade through for being blue, or lighter to lift because it is silky. It is not the tones of sound, but the waves of force, which break our ear-drums.

Force is omnicompetent, and it takes secondary quality into its province. The way things look, sound or otherwise appear, arises out of what they do. That is what we all believe. If, then, we are being asked to accept the mental and the neurophysical side by side, as we accept secondary quality and active force side by side, we may reply that we do not accept the latter of these pairs as simply side by side, nor have we ever been willing to do so. Whatever complacency we feel about the odd parallel in which we are obliged to place them, depends on our being able to view secondary quality as dependent on active force.

It follows that a doctrine about mind and body which is built on the analogy we have been considering is not what used to be called psychophysical parallelism, but what used to be called epiphenomenalism: that is, it makes of consciousness an epiphenomenon, a mere experiencedness of the bodily process in subjective colours, founded in the physical events of that process, and without reciprocal effect upon them.

The conclusion will probably be resisted. It will be objected, first, that the appeal was not to the analogy of secondary quality and active force, but to the general acceptability of parallel description. Even granting that the instance named is the strongest, it is only as an example of side-by-sideness that it is invoked. Everything else that may be true of it is abstracted from. We reply, that the appeal is to the *acceptability* of parallel description, and therefore it is inadmissible to abstract from what makes it acceptable. Or, if you do, what you know from the analogy can only be that parallel description may be acceptable, where sufficient special grounds are present to make it so; but that these grounds may be various in different cases. It is then incumbent upon you to reveal what are the special grounds, the special modalities of relation, which make it acceptable in the case of body and mind. But that is merely to formulate the enquiry upon which we are ourselves engaged.

A second line of defence may be tried. It may be agreed that the appeal really is to the analogy of secondary quality and active force, and to whatever makes parallel descriptions acceptable in that instance. But it may be held that it is more natural, or even more proper, to take the relation of quality and force, or should we say of secondary quality and primary quality, at a prescientific level. For our immediate understanding of everyday experience remains at that level, however much science we have read. Is not science a special language for out-of-the-way occasions only? And according to commonsense, secondary qualities are not secondary at all; they are on all fours with primary qualities. The (secondary) qualities of things tell us of what nature they are; their active properties tell us what they are apt to do.

The trouble about this defence is, that in saving the equality of the two terms, it loses the analogical relevance of the relation between them. In the commonsense view of the world, the primary and secondary characteristics of things fit together in the things, as the six sides of a box fit together in the box. It is a neat job, certainly; but it is so neat, that no question of parallel description arises. It is only in the sophisticated view of science, that we find ourselves puzzling over the relation between a story about a refraction of light-waves, and a report of a red expanse seen. What the defence we are rebutting really does is to employ the analogy on the scientific level, and interpret it from the prescientific level. It may be well that we should reason with the learned and feel with the vulgar, but not that we should run with the hare and hunt with the hounds.

We shall insist, then, upon our contention. An appeal to the general acceptability of parallel description is an appeal to analogy. The only analogy which will give us any support is the case of secondary quality. And to rest on this analogy is epiphenomenalism. Indeed, the proposition can be converted: epiphenomenalism consists in nothing but the pressing of this analogy.

iv. Epiphenomenalism

The relevance of epiphenomenalism to our main line of argument will, then, be this. The epiphenomenalist is the only man who has anything plausible to say in palliation of a direct parallel between neurology and personal statement; the only man, therefore, in a position to dispense with any real work on the part of our action-pattern, or *tertium quid*. As the multitude of water-molecules, drawn by gravitation, appear as the tide, but the tide as such does no work; so the multitude of minute forces appear as an expanse of green, but the green does no work; and so, in the third place, says epiphenomenalism, the multitude of minute neural energies appear as such-and-such a phenomenon of consciousness, without the consciousness doing any work, or commanding an action-pattern through which to do any.

But such a formulation awakens misgivings in a fresh direction. Secondary qualities do no work. Yet to say of anything *in rerum natura* that it exerts no effect on anything, seems excessively odd. Even if there is no philosophical reason against attributing such dead-end characteristics to the world, we are nevertheless not going to believe in them. In our ordinary view of things, we do not have to; for we suppose that secondary qualities, though not active in the manner of physical force, have their effect on the course of events through informing the mind; since the mind, or rather the man, acts on information thus received; as when the light turns from green to amber and the driver puts his foot down on the brake. Admittedly there is a certain prodigality of nature here—not every flash of sensible quality is taken into active reckoning. But that does not puzzle us, for it seems to enhance the efficacy of our mental powers that they are played upon by a range of phenomena greater than they directly respond to, and within which they are bound to exercise a selective choice.

Secondary qualities indeed (to take the example of colour) are the way things look, not the way we see. Yet nothing, surely, looks thus or thus, where no one sees;[1] the qualities, though they are not in the percipient, lie on the approaches to the gates of perception. They are not so independent of the mind, that their occurrence can be used to cast light on the absolute existence of anything, and in the present case, of consciousness. And this seems so fatal to the whole epiphenomenalist analogy, that we might be tempted to

[1] Any more than anything acts where nothing is affected. Secondary qualities are no more 'relative' than active forces, but their correlatives are fewer and more specialised.

73

drop the discussion at this point, as though epiphenomenalism were exploded.

But there is no satisfaction in exploding anything. When we have exploded epiphenomenalism, we still want to know what people are doing when they think of consciousness as an epiphenomenon or (to dispense with jargon) as a felt aspect of neurophysical being. We might offer some such account as follows.

Although nothing looks thus or thus where no one sees, yet he who sees counts himself out, or takes his seeing for granted. The concern of seeing is not with itself, but with the way things look. And so it is very natural to think of a realm of secondary quality as having an absolute existence, yet an existence grounded (as scientific enquiry teaches us) in the active forces of things. It is this incomplete, but natural, view which gives us the notion of the sheer epiphenomenon, doing no work itself, but grounded in what works. And surely to prescind the world from the onlooker is no very violent proceeding; we do it for the most of our waking lives. If it is such a view that gives us the epiphenomenon, the epiphenomenon may be thought solid enough to act as a parable of mind.

Let us proceed, then, to apply the parable. A convenient way of doing it is by means of a simple manoeuvre. We keep the abstracted view of secondary quality before us just long enough to get it fixed in our heads that there is such a thing as the mere epiphenomenon. But once the idea is fixed, we give way and admit the inadequacy of a view of secondary quality which leaves the onlooker out. No (we now say) sheer epiphenomenality needs to be moved a stage further on; the dead end is not secondary quality but that consciousness to which secondary quality appeals. Mind really is the dead-end; not (as Aristotle vainly supposed) the prime mover, itself unmoved by anything; but the ultimate moveable, itself moving nothing. Aristotle is only the tallest of many ninepins to go down before the epiphenomenalist ball. The man in the street shares the fate of the philosopher. For commonsense admits no dead-end in the mind. It supposes that, just as things, through the way they look, are reflected in our seeing of them, so our seeing of them is reflected in our taking action about them. And since our taking of action introduces real physical changes into the world, it sets ripples spreading over the physical pond which will reach no dead end, perhaps, until all active force in the universe is balanced out and cancelled.

So commonsense may hold; but, epiphenomenalism will say, so much the worse for commonsense. Our consciousness of seeing things is veridical, our sense of doing things on the basis of what we see is delusive. Perception is a priceless, and intention a worthless, clue to the functions of the mind. In spite of appearances, our mind does nothing but perceive. In perception commonly so-called, we are aware of things with which our nervous system is engaged. In thought we are aware of the tentative re-actions of our bodily system to what has been perceived on a more immediate level. In decision and in action it is the effective reaction of the organism which makes itself felt. At every stage consciousness reflects with broad, simplified and conventionalised effects a highly complicated physical reaction-system in play. If thought and decision do not seem like perception, it is because we are self-identified with our nerves and with what we do, in a way in which we cannot be self-identified with the exterior objects of our sensation. But in spite of all differences of feel, there is essen-tially one function, awareness. That which consciousness repre-sents, or identifies itself with, does the whole work of man; the conscious representation does no work. It is a causal dead-end all the time, a strengthless shadow cast by real act.

Where the neural reaction is taking place on a certain level, it just is a law of nature that consciousness should accompany it; and so we are not to be surprised (the epiphenomenalist will say) if there are certain self-adjustments to circumstance which we find ourselves unable to make, without consciousness going along with the mechanism as it taps out its answers. In the same way we just cannot bang a gong without some rather noisy epiphenomena supervening; so nature has decreed. Apart from our own case, we can scarcely guess where such natural laws will, or will not, take effect. What are we to say of the ingenious devices somewhat portentously called mechanical brains? How much cleverer shall we need to make them, before they begin being conscious in their higher moments? When will they qualify for the supreme hand-out covenanted to its progressive elements by the Welfare-State of Nature—a mind?

Surely the conception of Natural Law which allows such questions to be entertained is utterly mythical. Are we to suppose that something called the nature of things (nature of *what* things?) keeps laws laid up in pickle for future contingencies nowhere yet exemplified, laws which spring into operation, when the instances arise against which they were provided? So that (for example) there were special laws regulating the behaviour of living tissue, before there was any life? Let us hope that the Law of Nature has provided for *all* possible future contingencies; and if it has, what an interesting body of legislation it must be!

Such ideas have been entertained by great men, and retailed by Gifford Lecturers, but that does not make it any more possible for us to take them seriously. We must regard the Laws of Nature as generalisations about the working uniformity of existing things. If so the laws (or at least the by-laws) can be no static *corpus juris*; they must receive additions, in proportion as new types of things and new rhythms of performance develop. We can never invoke pre-existent law to explain any step of innovation in existing Nature. For the purpose of understanding what followed, we must always make do with what already was; we must try to see how natural agencies, complicating and developing their operations, established new levels of existence and revealed fresh qualities. We may not think it good sense to believe that they did it un-aided; not, anyhow, if we are theists. But we shall interpret the aided process as the process it was, and the aid given by the process aided; we shall not invoke *ex machina* any *lex divina*.

We have, then, to understand the development of conscious-ness in the world as a natural fact. We must not say (so to speak) that when the silent film of physical nature advances into techni-color it bursts into song, the song of consciousness. If there is any song it is because there is a sound-track, and how did the sound-track come to be there? Even if it were tolerable to suppose that consciousness flickered up somewhere by a happy accident, how did it establish itself, make good its place in Nature and elaborate its forms at leisure? Let the Darwinians, let the materialists reply. On the supposition that consciousness does no physical work, they will not be ready with an answer. On the supposition that many reactions of conscious animals work through their being conscious and not otherwise, they will be supplied with as convincing an answer as they could wish. They may, indeed, feel that Nature could have managed better. When our inventors have devised a few thousand machines which, between them, do everything one human brain can do, they may then turn to commiserate Nature. Poor blind, blundering Cause, she never achieved the supreme economy of doing all things without a mind; even simple arithmetic, by her contrivance, works through an agony of thought. Had she been as clever as we are, there need never have been a trace of sentience. But since she was so stupid, and made the act of sentience the point of control in all her higher mechanisms, it is not to be wondered at that conscious mentality has received the prodigious development we observe; for nothing succeeds like success, and nothing has been so successful as intelligence.

A philosophical Darwinian, let us hope, would smile at the crudity of our tirade. He would say that to commiserate Nature and to congratulate her was equally impertinent. And as for our demand for a survival-value account of the rise of consciousness, he might say that it had nothing to do with him. The Darwinian theories are concerned with working physical forms. Consciousness is another affair entirely, and belongs to a different province of study.

Nature ought neither to be congratulated nor commiserated, for there is not such a person. But crude teleology, renounced by our lips, and expelled from the field of our professional study, continues to hold sway over the unexamined corners of our minds. Who can say how much the epiphenomenalist case is bolstered up by the unconscious persuasion that *consciousness is a treat*, and so great a treat, that there is no need to justify its appearance in the world by survival-value or anything else? It has its own value, or rather, in it and for it alone do any values arise. A philosopher will lay his finger at once on the equivocation over the words 'value' and 'justification' here. A Darwinian justification is not a proof that anything is worth while, but only that it has survival-value; and survival-value is not a value properly so-called, but a tendency to keep going. Survival-values flourish in an impersonal world; but we must personify Nature with a vengeance, before we can begin to think that anything is more likely to happen, because it is a treat.

However it may really be with the cosmic assumptions which epiphenomenalists consciously or unconsciously entertain, the treat-attitude squares happily with the epiphenomenalist doctrine. Treats are ends in themselves; and if consciousness is to him a dead-end, the epiphenomenalist has no need to worry; for what is a dead-end causally is an end in itself teleologically. One might explore the affinity of such an attitude with intellectualism, aestheticism, hedonism and other forms of moral frivolity; but this is hardly the time.

Whatever attractiveness attaches to the picture of consciousness as a rainbow on the scene of Nature, is likely to depend on our not looking at it too closely. It may do well, so long as we can think in a broad way of consciousness as embracing our whole awareness of our state, and the whole business of our reflection upon it. When Aristotle extolled the delights of philosophical contemplation, was he not vaunting the highest charms of consciousness? And what am I doing, in pursuing these present lines of reflection, but tasting in my humbler way the universal treat? At the same time, it must be admitted, I am wagging my tongue, and there's the trouble. For apart from gestures of the sort, whether movements of my tongue or mere flicks of my nerves, it does not seem that I can think. Now according to the theory these gestures, being physical, ought to be moves in a practical game of physical response to physical environment. And yet they seem to be moves of which the whole function is to serve as symbols for contemplative reflections. They have, it would appear, been bewitched by consciousness and brought to play the consciousness game. But admit this, and the whole theory crumbles; for if consciousness can have the physical motions playing her game in moments of pure speculation, why not on other occasions also? Why should not she guide their practical performances, as commonsense supposes her to do?

To admit that Aristotle's meaning has captured the direction of his nerves must be fatal to the theory; yet how are we to help admitting it? Shall we, perhaps, try to say that the nervous system has a spare-time activity, and that this activity consists in tapping out all sorts of possible correlations in the calculative machinery it has built up? That there is no need for such an activity to have a directly practical bearing; it is enough that it should be practical indirectly, by building up combinations which may one day find an application? This, then, is what the brain of Aristotle was doing when he thought out the *Metaphysics*. Or was it? Well, it does not look as if it were. And anyone who holds that when we think or talk the meaning is a by-product, is maintaining a paradox.

We may summarise the case against epiphenomenalism under three heads. (1) It does not deal equitably with the balance of mental life; for it declares perception to be the whole nature of the mind, and mental action to be illusory. (2) It takes mind clean out of the system of nature, by denying it any physical effect, or natural utility. (3) It counters the whole assumption of logical study, by denying that meaning governs the formation of discourse.

To belabour epiphenomenalism may be to flog a dead horse. But however many times defunct it always revives, and appears in new disguises. Linguistic philosophy is the professed enemy of mystification, but misemployed, can become its ally; as happens when talk about the acceptability of parallel description is used to block enquiry into a natural relation. Metaphysical argument may be the grand cause of logical mirage; but linguistic conjuring is unrivalled for vanishing-tricks, and can make the most urgent question seem to disappear. The linguistic method, however, is the cure for its own diseases. If an appeal to logical considerations explodes a genuine question, it is because the logic has not been tailored to fit the case. The remedy is not less logic, but more.

By whatever philosophy the attempt is made to place physiological and personal language in simple parallel, epiphenomenalism is the result. For a mere parallelism will never content us, we shall always want to put in a natural relation, and that relation will be one-sided. For consciousness seems conceivable as the mass-effect of minute physiological events, whereas they do not even seem conceivable as effects of conscious intention; not, that is, without the admission of a *tertium quid*, a large-scale pattern of physical action directly correlative with consciousness at certain points, and productive of real physical effects. And the postulation of such a principle is no mere evasion of an unwelcome or even of an untenable alternative. It is the giving of full value to the only clue we have for the relation between mental activity and bodily performance—the case where what I mentally enact I physically perform.

NOTE ON PSYCHOPHYSICAL PARALLELISM

In the preceding chapter we have reduced psychophysical parallelism to epiphenomenalism in so summary a fashion as to suggest the puzzle, how parallelism can ever have maintained itself? For even as a working hypothesis it is quite inapplicable. What is the use of recommending us to explain our sensations from our past personal life, never from the physical facts to which they call our attention? To explain a sudden toothache in a new place from previous jaw-experience or thought-experience or any other experience, rather than from the state of the stuff in our jaw?

We may give two reasons for the appeal of the theory: philosophical confusion and the exigences of debate. If we are debating in defence of anyhow some independent action on the part of our mental life—if we are vindicating the mental aspect of ourselves from the suspicion of being merely consequential on the physiological aspect—it may seem a strong position, to deny that the antecedents which directly explain an occurrence in consciousness are *ever* to be found in physiological facts. But how can we uphold this universal negative? Only by the aid of a philosophical confusion.

The confusion may be conveniently exhibited as an equivocation on the phrase 'mental story'. We say that we are discussing the relation between the 'mental story' about life as experienced or exercised, and the 'physical story' about life as somehow constituted by the facts physiology investigates. But are not all stories mental, in so far as they are stories, even if they talk physiology? For all stories are talkings, and all talking is mental. I cannot seek the explanation of the toothache sensation in the sheer facts which constitute the state of my jaw, but only in a story representing to me those facts; and the story is just as mental as the toothache. And if you press me to go behind the story to its justification, I still find something mental, sensations of the scientific observer. I do not deny that there are physical facts; I merely claim that there is a complete mental counterpart covering them, so far as they are anything to us. All explanation of the toothache will be a cross-referring within the mental realm: a realm which we (admittedly) believe to have a physical double.

The confused nature of such reasoning is obvious. It substitutes the distinction between thought and whatever it can think about, for a distinction between two different things about which thought can think: personal life as lived, and physiological states of affairs as experimentally established. Either we can think about physiological states of affairs, or we cannot. If we can, then we can also compare them (as we are able to think of them) with our personal life (as we are able to think of that); and it is irrelevant to point out that thinking, even about physiological states of affairs, is itself part of our personal life. It is, indeed; and if we were thinking about *thinking about* physiological states of affairs, we should be thinking about a piece of our personal life. But this is not what we are doing; we are just thinking about physiological states of affairs, and it is these, not our thoughts about them, that we compare with our personal life. All stories are mental in so far as they are stories; but when we constrast a mental story with a physiological story we are considering differences of subject-matter, not identities of medium.

81

CHAPTER V

MECHANISM OVERRULED BY MENTALITY

i. *The mechanism of choice*

THE object of this chapter will be to examine a point of detail. The previous chapter laid down a principle: it had to be allowed that the pattern of action directly operated by intentional behaviour exercised a real directive sway over the minute physical energies in our bodies, causing them to do what, left to themselves, they would not do. Such was the principle. We propose now to apply it at a particular point: the relation between personal intention, involving choice, and the minute mechanism of the cerebral cortex.

In taking up such a topic, we are moved to observe the present state of physiological knowledge. It is characteristic of working scientists to be modest in the statement of their results. The neurophysiologists make clear to us the great inequality, in degree of closeness or exactitude, exhibited by their present acquaintance with different parts of the physical mechanism underlying our personal life. An inequality of progress on different lines of research may be due to quite accidental causes; the availability of instruments, or the hobbies of investigators. But it may just as well be due to the greater intractability of some matters as compared with others; and in the field we are speaking of, appearances suggest something of the kind. The most complete story available about the physical counterpart to any whole act of consciousness deals with sensation. The physiologists can tell us under what conditions of stimulation the sensory organ excites the nerve, what sort of wave the nerve transmits, by which line it passes through the brain, and (finally) what area of the cortex must be stimu-

lated, to produce any one of the special sorts of quality-conscious-
ness; this and much more they can tell us, contributory to the same
result. Thus to the question, 'What happens to my body and in
my body, when I see patches of colour?' a remarkably complete
answer can be given.

The executive part of our nervous system is equally well
known. Supposing that I decide to move any one of my limbs, the
transmissions of energy can be mapped from brain to muscle.
Though we cannot speak here, as we could with colour-vision, of
a complete physical story covering a whole act of consciousness.
For the clear part of the physical story leaves out the decision,
through which *this* movement rather than any other is performed;
and the decision is part and parcel of the personal act. My consciousness is of doing *this* (rather than that); not of finding myself
engaged upon *this*. But the part of the process which can be
physiologically mapped is the execution of the movement. As to
the steps by which I engage in it, physiology can speak in generalities only—they will consist of some combination of electric circuits, passing through some part or other of a considerable area in
the cortex. And so it is with the physiology of thinking; the same
kind of vague generality must content us.

We threw out a hint, to the effect that the inequality of present
knowledge might prove to be of some philosophical interest; and
even the few examples we have mentioned suffice to show that it
is so. Can it be fortuitous, that a clear mechanical account is available for precisely those parts of conscious life which an anti-
mechanist would expect to find mechanised? However spiritual-
minded we are, it will give us no comfort to believe that sight or
hearing is spontaneous. How we choose to look or listen may, no
doubt, determine antecedently the state of the receptive organ.
But once granted that the organ is in a given receptive state, we
all devoutly hope that it will register mechanically the external
stimuli affecting it. Heaven forbid that the spontaneous initiatives
of the mind should be able further to intervene, until the stage of
interpretation is reached. Our feeling about the executive apparatus is the same. However fondly we cherish the faith that we do

THE FREEDOM OF THE WILL

what we choose to do, none of us regrets the mechanical obedience of his limbs in the detailed execution of his voluntary acts.
The alternative is pins-and-needles, paralysis or ataxia; and if
anything of the sort happens to us, we lament a mechanical
breakdown, not a spiritual disorder; that is just where good sense,
however spiritual-minded, parts company with Mary Baker Eddy.

Where, on the other hand, the theorist who gives full credit to
the apparent spontaneity of mental action expects to find a hiatus
in mechanical explanation, there is a hiatus in our present knowledge. Thought, practical decision, the directing of voluntary
movement, these activities cannot be physically mapped at present,
except in the vaguest way. We say 'At present', for we are not
conducting an obscurantist apologetic. We do not say that a
proper physical account of characteristically spontaneous action
should be despaired of. We say that in such areas physical investigation and physical description might be expected to be difficult,
and this for two reasons. First, the mechanisms which are sensitive to
intentional direction must surely be of the highest complexity or
subtlety. And secondly, it cannot be easy to sort out the working
of a system, when one of its determining principles is imperceptible on the level of investigation we are employing; as the
action of intention presumably must be on the level of neurophysiology.

Since the spiritualising philosopher is commonly suspected of
scientific obscurantism, it may be of interest to consider what sort
of physical evidence would do his case most good. A blank inability of science to map the physiology of thought and decision
would provide no positive evidence for the real efficacy of mental
action. It would still be open for a physical determinist to say that
a description, could it be arrived at, would prove causally watertight, and leave to consciousness no function but that of being
conscious. But suppose it were possible to describe exactly the
pattern of physical forces coincident with the act of decision in
any case; and suppose it were found that the whole structure of the
pattern tended towards the production of a delicate balance, with
many open possibilities this way and that, according as the balance

might incline; but that the inclination of the scale, if it had to be accounted for mechanically, would have to be put down to an operation of forces which, relatively to the bodily system, would be accidental or fortuitous; as the way the dice fall is fortuitous relatively to the system employed for throwing them. If such were the physical evidence, the spiritualising—or, shall we say, mentalist—philosopher would have a strong case. For, he would say, it is evident that actions taken upon what is subjectively experienced as decision are not the effects of accident. They might, for the sake of argument, be attributed to the mechanical working of a supersubtle electronic calculator. But, he would say, our evidence is that the calculating mechanism (if we may so call it) of the brain builds up to an indeterminate balance at the crucial point. We can but conclude that the overruling power of some consciously-operated pattern draws the minute forces and tips the scale.

Since we are launched upon the enjoyable course of making up the facts to fit our theory, let us see if we cannot make them better still. Let us suppose that the balance of minute forces at the crucial point is such, that the law of averages makes it unlikely to tip one way or the other. For, we will suppose, it rests upon a little chaos of motions whose average tendency is to cancel one another out and hold the balance stable. Yet in fact the balance inclines decisively, as often as we act definitely or think purposefully. How can such a thing happen, apart from the one-way pull of some overruling power—presumably that of some pattern consciously operated?

Our new supposition sounds well in the abstract, but not so well in the context of physical theory. For, according to a view widely held, the average stability of minute chaos is the basis of all physical necessity, and the bed-rock of natural law. So that if our hypothetical brain-system builds up to a balance resting on such a foundation, then on physical evidence it builds up to a jam, and leaves no play at all; and the actual moving of the balance is a downright miracle. If we want to quote physical evidence for a mechanism tending to a sensitive balance at the crucial point, the balance will have to be genuinely precarious, and allow of decisive swings this way or that on mere physical average. There will then be no physical mystery about the inclinations of the scale, so long as we keep to the microscopic level. But when we shift to the macroscopic, we see so many chances falling out exactly à propos for human or animal purposes, as to explode the hypothesis of accident. Somewhat as though we had a gaming-top with twenty-six divisions for the letters of the alphabet, and found that by writing down in sequence the letters it gave us, we were composing good consecutive prose. There would be no physical mystery about the top's stopping at any single letter, and yet the linguistic value of the series would call for further explanation.[1]

It sounds scandalous, certainly, to lay down in advance 'of research the sort of thing we would like the physiologists to discover. But we are not inviting *bien pensant* investigators to prove a pious fraud for the mere confirmation of faith. We look to see the facts, when they are arrived at, disconcert whatever detailed expectations we may form beforehand. All we have wished to do is to show that the mentalist case does not depend on the obscurity of physical fact. For the purpose of such a demonstration it was sufficient to give an imaginary forecast of detailed discovery which would not merely allow, but commend the mentalist doctrine. That the neurological facts, if ever they are firmly established, will prove compatible with the mentalist case, we are confident on quite other grounds, as we explained in the preceding chapter.

ii. *Theory of Professor Eccles considered*

Before we pass on, it seems right to mention the much-discussed speculation of Professor Eccles.[2] The Professor begins, as we do, from the assumption that in an act of consciousness it must be possible for meaning or intention to be decisive. He differs from us by knowing what he is talking about on the side of the brain.

---

[1] The spelling-top would give itself away by defying mere average; there would not be enough Z's and X's. There is no reason why this feature should be reproduced in the brain-structure hypothesis.
[2] J. C. Eccles: *The Neurophysiological Basis of Mind.*

And so he is able to say, as we are not, that there are known facts about the brain, as well as highly general facts about physical structure, which make very tenable a hypothesis of delicate balance in that cortical region where thought and decision have their physical seat. He encourages us to think of systems in the cortex highly responsive to the least pressures: reactors, as it were, of the greatest liveliness and sensitivity. To what, then, do the reactors react? To motions of the soul, says Professor Eccles. He makes it plain that he accepts the Cartesian metaphysics. By 'soul' he means a separate substance, acting upon body, and conditioned by it. His difference from Descartes is in physiology. Descartes, with his simple clockwork mechanism, was not able to make it intelligible that the brain should lie open to spiritual direction. Professor Eccles feels that he has the advantage here.

It is of interest to us to observe that the physical part of the Professor's speculation is perfectly separable from his Cartesian pneumatology. Any of his readers who hold that cortical mechanism must be open to direction on the part of meaning may be grateful for his physical hypothesis, whatever their attitude to Cartesianism may be. We for our part would not attempt to defend his metaphysics against Professor Ryle or, for that matter, against St Thomas Aquinas. We will have nothing to do with the fantastic suggestion, that what the supersensitive 'reactors' in the cortex react to, is the initiative of a virtually disembodied soul. To what, then, are we to say that they do react? What else, than to the motions of the *embodied* soul, that is to say, other motions in the same nervous system? The thesis which the mentalist philosopher needs to maintain is that there are motions in the brain capable of reacting to meaning, not mechanism. He has no need to maintain that the meaning to which they react is disembodied. The response of one cerebral motion to another can in this respect be usefully compared with the reception of a signal by one person from another. The receiver reacts to the meaning of the emitter; yet the emission of the signal is as physical a business as any other.

Let us suppose three signallers, Tom, Dick and Harry. Tom is semaphoring to Dick by the use of flags. Dick transmits the message to Harry by telephone. Both Tom and Dick are going through physical motions; Tom waving flags, Dick making vocal noises. There is nothing in the least mysterious about either system of motions, physically considered. Each has its physical effects: Tom's flag-waving not only agitates the air, it disturbs the distribution of light, thereby affecting Dick's visual nerves; Dick's talking into the telephone similarly disturbs the current carried by the wire, thereby producing noises in Harry's instrument. So far the parallel holds. But the tale uttered by Dick into the telephone, and the tale uttered by the telephone into Harry's ear, respond in different ways to the actions respectively of Tom and of Dick. Dick's tale responds to the meaning, not the force, of Tom's semaphoring. The telephone's tale responds to the force, not the meaning, of Dick's voice.

In drawing the distinction we are not denying that Dick's talking has physical causes. We could trace the energy expended in his vocal effort and find its sources in his body, and ultimately, it may be, in sunlight, diet, and other more remote origins. But we do deny that the physical causes of Dick's talking prescribe the speech-pattern adopted by Dick, as the physical causes of the telephone's talking prescribe the speech-pattern reproduced by the telephone. For in his talking Dick steers himself by what Tom's semaphoring *means*.

Let us drop the parable. What we are saying is that all mental events are also physical events, deriving from physical causes and carrying physical effects; that in some of them (as in the telephone-noises) physical causes simply determine that sequence of pattern which is mentally significant; but that with others of them it is not so—the significant sequence is determined in response to the meaning carried by previous mental events. Now in so far as physicomental events take shape in response to meaning, they are not determined by physical causes.

'Drop the parable.' But when we turn from Tom, Dick and Harry to relations within the brain, are we discarding a parable, or simply giving the inner side of our story? We say that Dick responds to Tom's signalling. But he would not respond to it if he were blind, nor if his eyes, however sharp, were untrained in semaphore. What is this but to say that the signalling which determines Dick's response extends through his eyes and visual nerves, and on into his brain, there to set a very delicate receiving-mechanism in agitation? We may say if we like that Dick responds to the whole signalling process, from flag-waving at one end, to cerebral agitations at the other. Yet the business-end of the process is the terminal event; it is here that Dick's reaction to it picks it up, and responds to it. Responds to it, we say, by telephoning to Harry. Yet (once again) the business-end of the responsive process is in Dick's brain; for here it is initiated, and here it is in contact with that to which it responds. And so we justify the contention that the tale of Tom, Dick and Harry is not a parable about the mutual relation of events in our brains, but a story of the mutual relation of events in Dick's brain, only told from the outside.

What shall we say to this contention? There is no denying that the brain of a signaller busied with the transmission of messages provides an actual example of inter-cerebral relations; nor that our story of the signallers was introduced to illustrate just such relations. But something more ambiguous is affirmed, when it is said that the response of one cerebral motion to another simply is the second signaller's response to the first. The ambiguity lies in the word 'response'. Literally, no doubt, to respond is to answer; it implies that the person responding has been addressed in audible speech, and that his answer is directed back to the speaker. When we have Dick responding to Tom's signal by telephoning to Harry, the sense of 'responding' has already been stretched in two directions. That to which Dick responds is no longer audible speech, but significant gesture; and his response is directed not back to Tom, but on to Harry. Yet this at least of the original meaning remains: he who is said to respond *perceives* that to which he responds; and on the basis of his perception, he *intends* what he does by way of response to it. Whereas when we say that a second cerebral motion responds to the first, all this part of the meaning has evaporated. The first motion is not perceived, nor is the second intended. With a similar impoverishment of the word, we might say that a willow responded to the neighbourhood of water, by pushing its roots that way. All we mean is that the second fact was occasioned by the first, and that it has a teleological look.

We are in a dilemma. We are trying to say that cerebral motions are often responsive to meanings; and therefore we cannot be content with the weak sense of 'respond', typified in the willow tree; for the willow tree does not respond to the meaning of anything, but at the most looks somewhat as though it did. On the other hand, for reasons already given, we cannot affirm the strong sense, typified in the story of our friend Dick. We had better abandon this line of approach, and take a fresh look at the facts.

Whether we are talking about Dick the man, or Dick the brain, as the subject of a response to meaning, the meaning responded to will be the same. It lies in the signals Tom is perceived or understood to give; it lies (for Dick) in Tom himself, gesturing away over there with his flags. Dick is probably quite unconscious of his own visual organs, let alone the nerves behind them. The meaning he appreciates is incarnate in what Tom visibly does. Even if Dick reflects that the visibility of Tom depends on the openness, direction, and soundness of his eyes, he regards these facts as constituting the mere absence of obstacles to sight, or at the most as *conditiones sine quibus non* for its enjoyment. And when a neurologist gives a more elaborate account of the visual organ, backing it with nerves and rooting it in the cortex, the relation between the organ and what Dick perceives through the organ is unaffected by the elaboration. The meaning is still expressed in the flag-waving, not in any wriggling of Dick's cortical nerves.

If Dick is a thoughtful man, he may say to himself something like this. 'Organs are odd things, and one can't see how they act as channels for our perceptions. Still, we must swallow it—they do; and it seems only reasonable that, if they are to do their job, they should run all the way in.' All the way in—to where? To where Dick is? But isn't Dick all over himself? Yes, but he is in different parts of himself for different purposes. So let us say, 'Right in to where Dick is, for the purpose of initiating the sort of action he might want to take in response to what he sees with his eyes.' The roots of the organ, then, should twine with the roots of action.

Having got so far, Dick may start at the other end, and consider his responsive act. This is not in his brain, either, but in his vocal parts. Still, it seems equally reasonable that the roots of the action system should run all the way back. Back to where? To the place into which the roots of the visual organ run right back. Then the seeing and the response to the seeing will be in direct touch. Such is Dick's reasoning, and so far as it goes, it locates the point where the organ is rooted by the point where the action is rooted, and vice versa; much as though one should say that the South Pole is where Amundsen planted his flag, and that if you want to know where he planted his flag, it was at the South Pole. To be any better informed about the absolute position of the spot he is talking about, Dick must put himself into the hands of anatomists.

There is only one response of Dick's to what he sees, and that is his talking. But this response has a complex instrument, and the root of the instrument is in the cerebral cortex. The responsive action may be said to consist in the voluntary discharge of ready-made mechanisms. But if this is to be done, there must be something not prefabricated, to set off one mechanism rather than another. What must not be prefabricated, is the selection of the train of action. What can well be prefabricated, and, so far as we can judge, must be, is the selective apparatus: prefabricated as a system which allows of switching this way and that, through a wide variety of alternatives.

And what does the switching? It switches itself, being the instrument of life, or rather, the appropriate organ of a living person. Yet for this very reason it does not switch itself, not it, that is, taken in isolation. For the person is whole, and life, consciousness, action are whole. They concentrate themselves, indeed, on single acts through single systems of organs; but the system operated has always a considerable sweep of extent, and is never in the brain alone. Dick talks with his vocal parts, a system of which the initiating or controlling switch is in the brain.

We are now, perhaps, in a position usefully to reconsider Professor Eccles. He wanted to think of the subtle reactors in the brain as having so delicate or precarious a balance, as to allow of their reacting to the virtually discarnate soul. Our first move was to say, No; they react to the 'soul' incarnate in previous meaningful actions, or reactions, of the bodily man. But now we have worked round to the making of a second move. We say that the reactions of the reactors are, in cases of free will, themselves the work of soul, or personal life, incarnate in, and active through, these very reactors. It is of this that their delicate balance, or mechanical flexibility, allows.

iii. Mixed descriptions and mixed explanations

There is an objection which we have several times touched, but neither stated nor answered; and it seems high time we gave it proper consideration. The objection may be put like this: 'You tell us', say our friends 'that our soul is incarnate, or, in less picturesque language, that all mental events are also physical events. But to physical events, surely, none but physical explanations apply. If there is a gap in the physical explanation of physical events, then there is a gap in the explanation of those events, which nothing else can fill. But you (our friends say) introduce such a gap. For you say that there are events which, while being mental, are also physical; and which, nevertheless, take on a shape of decisive significance for our personal life, not in response to physical action but in response to a meaning. So there you are, holding open a gap in physical explanation, to allow room for a different sort of explanation. But no other sort of explanation for physical events (and these are physical events) is allowable. You do not merely say that in such cases you cannot find the physical explanation—that would be laudable modesty. You say there is no physical explanation to find—and this is damnable obscurantism. We observe, of course, that you try to cover yourself. You say that events determined in response to meaning are not without physical causes. The soldier who translates the semaphore *viva voce* into the telephone speaks out of the vigour native to his body, and the past history of the elements of energy active in his speaking could (theoretically at least) be traced. So you say, but the evasion will not serve. All you have said is that the event is not wholly without physical causes or conditions. One would hope not, indeed. But you deny that the shape taken by the event is sufficiently explained in such factors; indeed you assert that there is an aspect of it which is not, in these terms, explicable at all. And what is this, but to assert a gap in physical explanation of the physical?'

Such is the objection. And here is the reply. We concede that physical events have none but physical causes, and none but physical effects—if we are to speak of immediate effects. But we do not concede that the events under discussion are mere physical events. We do not, indeed, know for certain that the world contains any mere physical events, if that means events which are nothing but exemplifications of principles handled by the physical sciences. The most we can say is that there are events of which every aspect but the physical can usefully be neglected. We can say the same of events in the human body, but only at a certain level, and only for certain purposes. When we are talking about physical events which, in another aspect, are also mental events, we are not free to neglect the mental aspect. We are talking about a single history—the history of a man's nervous system or rather of some small parts in it. And this history is a physicomental history—that is, it is partly determined by physical factors, partly by mental. It is really useless to protest against such a mixed history, as being a monstrosity of description; it is the typical sort of history, we know of no other. We scarcely have a history of angels, history is of men. And how does the historian view his characters—how, for that matter, do we view one another in common life—if not as agents both physical and thoughtful, whose actions are not understood if either aspect of our nature is neglected? I say, '*Are* not understood.' No doubt some men hold, as a speculative hypothesis, that it ought to be possible to give a full explanation of human conduct in purely physical terms. We have argued, and are arguing, that the hypothesis is false. But whether it is false or not, it remains that for all practical purposes mixed explanations of human action are always given and always accepted. 'He panted his way up the hill, *because* he was a seventeen-stone man' (physical), 'and *because* he was resolved to keep the appointment on time' (mental). This being our most common and indeed instinctive form of thought, it is useless to call a history which employs mixed explanations a monstrosity of description. We ought to distinguish the aspects, but we ought to unify the event; and we ought not to pretend, as Spinoza did, that a complete explanation of the event can always be given under either aspect in abstraction from the other.

If we accept mixed explanations of behaviour in the total bulk of a man's person, why boggle at accepting them for the most lively and, as it were, mental parts of his person, the elements of his nervous system? Not, evidently, because they are these parts rather than some other parts of the man, but because they are parts. Mixed explanation belongs to history, and history is of persons; it is only by an extension of the natural usage, and almost by metaphor, that we bring ourselves to speak of a nerve as having a history. And if we feel a sense of strain, or mental disquiet in so using the word 'history', we are reacting very properly. For a given part of the nervous system only has a history through being part of the man; its history is part of his history. In an idiom now virtually obsolete one said 'The Chancellor's hand was active in the business' or 'The King's heart went out to his son'. But no one supposed that the Chancellor's hand, or the King's heart, had a biography of its own, or that the biographies of the men were made up out of the biographies of their several organs. The motive of the old epical particularisation was obvious enough: it reminded us that, for the purpose of action, a man is in his hand, and for purposes of emotion, in the region of his heart. Our present motive for particularising is different; a purely philosophical enquiry has fixed our attention on small physical elements which, from the physical point of view, interplay on a minute scale. But since their physical action is not self-contained, but serves on occasion as the instrument of personal history, we break off from the history of the person those fragments of it which take effect through the minute parts or systems we are examining; and we call each fragment of the man's history the history of the part to which it is referred.

Now the fragmentation of a man's history—or, shall we say, of his personal activity—and the distribution of it among his organs, is in a manner natural, and in a manner forced. It is natural, because human activity distributes itself in a multitude of separate acts, and so may be said to subdivide itself. What is more, the subdivisions of our activity may be said to localise themselves. For we do not employ our whole body equally in every action, but bring all our other processes to support a single action-pattern, or rather, as we have said, a single sequence of such patterns. And so it may seem that a man's active history can fairly be divided into subsidiary histories, of which the subjects are several systems in his body carrying the several trains of his action.

Nevertheless, such a use of the word 'history' is forced. The organ does not have a history, for its history is not its own, but a fragment of the man's. By making the organ the subject of a history which concerns it, we attribute a personal agency to it, and such an attribution is mythical. Human agency issues from the total balance of particular or localised systems within the man; only the man acts, none of the systems act. And that which does not 'act' in the personal sense of 'act' has no history.

The purpose of our discussion has been neither to recommend nor to prohibit talk about the histories of, let us say, circuits in the cerebral cortex. We hope we have made it clear how such language can illuminate, and how it can mislead. Our present business with it is not to guard against its erroneous implications, but to draw from it what light we can. So we have said that by viewing the activities of certain bodily elements as pieces of history, we shall assist our imaginations to accept mixed explanations for them, part physical and part mental; such an acceptance being the only true wisdom in this regard.

iv. Physical shocks to mental complacency

The explanations we accept, and should accept for conduct are part physical, part mental; and the balance of the two factors is a matter for empirical observation. To reject physical determinism is not to claim that all acts are free from virtual determination by physiological causes, but only that some are. We are not even saying that all acts which seem to determine themselves in response to meaning, really do so. Nor are we saying that certain areas of activity in which mental determination commonly prevails are guaranteed against irruptions of overpowering physical determination, either open or disguised.

A sudden breaking-in of physical determination where we do not expect it, gives a painful shock to mental habit, and is capable of undermining our confidence in our liberty, to a degree which seems irrational and disproportionate. Is it not surprising to hear a competent philosopher confess in private conversation, that he would feel the force of the libertarian case, were it not for lobotomy? Is not this on a level with the readiness of an adolescent to believe a beneficent Providence, were it not for spiders and wasps? Are spiders and wasps uniquely dysteleological? And what is there so startling about the effects of lobotomy? Mental patients, a prey to crippling anxiety, can sometimes be relieved by the disjoining of certain connexions in the forepart of their cerebral cortex. But the relief is purchased at a price. The whole range and depth of their response to the world is reduced. They are different men, and, by comparison with their former selves, shallow or insensitive. No doubt it is disconcerting to their friends, but what is there in it to surprise philosophers? Who ever doubted that physical causes could affect the whole character of a man? Many illnesses do so, and many drugs, with sudden and dramatic effect.

The soul is not a goddess enjoying Olympian detachment. Her actions have their roots in the body, however freely she may act in the development of those actions; and the bodily roots of action being altered or affected, there will be a corresponding alteration in the resultant conduct. The most freedom we can have, is to make the best of ourselves, and the self of which we hope to make the best is in large measure physically defined; it is not the same self when we are well or ill, famished or replete, drunk or sober, young or old—so why not add, unlobotomised or lobotomised?

The alteration of our physical condition may shift the basis of our conduct without reducing our freedom; or, again, it may virtually remove it. Hunger affects our conduct powerfully, but it does not remove free choice; a hungry man cannot fail to be interested in food, but he may still be free not to monopolise a tempting dish. But famine, long tantalised on the brink of death, will reduce men to the condition of wolves; they are scarcely to be held responsible, though they eat one another. Perhaps lobotomy falls somewhere between common hunger and bestial famine. It neither removes freedom nor merely changes the subjects of its concern; it curtails it.

There are many ways of affecting a man's conduct by variously tampering with his body. But so there are of affecting violin-music by tampering with the instrument. The music, like the conduct, we take to be freely and personally produced. But it cannot in any case exceed the capacities of the violin, and however competent the performer, his music will not remain unaffected if we loosen the strings equally—he will lose pitch—or unequally—he will go out of tune—or if we knock holes in the soundbox—he will lose resonance. At some point a degree of interference will have been reached, such that he can produce no semblance of music. Just as some men go mad, and all of us die; though it be, that God will raise us up, and put the instruments of a new music into our hands.

Since no one presumably disputes the drift of what we have been saying, how can the consideration of any single new fact like lobotomy incline men to talk physical determinism? Is it perhaps that in practice libertarianism and determinism are not so much alternative beliefs as rival emphases? No one in practice thinks as though his thought were the mere self-recording of a physical process, and no one acts on the assumption that his conduct is wholly unconditioned by his bodily state or constitution. May not the cash-value of physical determinism amount to such assertions as that we are in no action free from physical determination of some kind, that we are physically determined in more ways and on more occasions than we are aware, and that we habitually exaggerate the scope of choice? And may not the cash-value of the opposite doctrine reduce to the proclamation of a corresponding set of contrary slogans? If the battle is a competition between compensatory emphases, no wonder a new and striking fact, revealing a physical check on mental liberty, should make people shout determinism for a day or two.

v. Conclusion on body and mind

In taking up the question of physical determinism, we declared it to be nothing but a special deduction from assumptions held about the general relation of the bodily to the mental. We had no complaint to make about the logic of the deduction, supposing the assumptions. And so we examined the mind-body relationship, not any short proofs or refutations of physical determinism. No formal refutation would, in any case, be likely to give us solid satisfaction. We might wonder whether, after all, it did not contain a trick, which cleverer heads might presently expose; or whether the definition of physical determinism demolished in the refutation was the only definition, or even the best, that could be offered.

It seemed a better initial move to correct our speech about bodily facts, mental facts and the relation between them. Having made it as correct as we could, we would see whether physical determinism did or did not appear to result. We might then hope to form an opinion which nothing was likely to overthrow, except a better appreciation of the facts themselves. He who sees all he can see, and then judges, is not immune from correction by new facts, or by a better view of the old. But he who puts his confidence in a single and supposedly cogent argument is liable to have ambushes sprung on him by what he knows already, and has failed to draw into consideration.

We have now made our attempt to talk straight about the body and the mind; though, no doubt, there is a deal more to be said, we shall not say it. And now that we come to draw our conclusions, we see that whatever argument we have to offer against physical determinism is already contained in what we have said.

Classical determinism drew its strength from the conviction that our intentional actions were, on their physical side, reducible to events exemplifying perfect uniformities; uniformities which could be given the exactitude of mathematical expression, and which would yield strict quantitative predictions. But in the bodies of animals exactitude of this kind is obtainable at a microscopic level only, and only in so far as the physical elements are viewed as interacting by merely physical rules. Even then, there are such astronomical numbers of minute elements in any biologically significant part of an animal body, that our practical concern will always be with mass effects. The operation of mere physical rules does not give a sufficient account of animal action; and as soon as we allow for the operation of what we have called action-patterns, we introduce a factor which cannot be reduced to physical arithmetic.

But though the bewitching (as we have called it) of our minute physical energies by organising patterns may remove their operations from the sway of physical exactitude, it does not break at one stroke the shackles of physiological determinism. For even when our energies are seduced from strict physicality into the service of action-patterns, they continue to work with a regularity on which (whether mathematically perfect or not) we confidently rely. If I set myself to walk over level ground, the action-patterns I put to work command the services of their physical constituents in such a manner, that they discharge their tasks with a quasi-mechanical reliability. It would be disastrous for me if it were otherwise. No one in fact supposes that our freedom is to be found in the manner in which action-patterns control (as it were) their minute constituents. No one says that a walker is *free* to engage the several minute parts of his legs and feet in the action of his walking. He is free in the initiation or direction of the action itself: in the actualisation of one action-pattern, rather than of any alternative—if we are to employ our own jargon.

When we have insisted on the requirement that consciousness should do some real work, and not exhaust her efficacy in the mere business of being conscious, the work we have spoken of lies in making the transition from one quasiautomatic action-system to another. Our claim has been that the actualisation of an action-pattern may be consequent upon previous action-patterns, or previous perceptual reactions, not in virtue of their physical efficacy, but in virtue of what they mean. It has simply to be accepted that the cortical mechanism allows of being governed by a response to meaning. The response inheres in the action of the cortex itself, as constituting the intention of that action; but not of that action in isolation. The action which has intention is the action not of the cortex, but of the man, concentrating upon certain of his organs. The cortical mechanisms are the sensitive roots of intentional action-systems, through which they feel one another, as it were, and respond to one another; feel also, of course, and respond to external sensations. How in detail this mutual feeling and responding function, should become clearer with the progress of cortical research. The mechanics of it, that is, should become clearer; the linguistics will remain as awkward as before. We shall never be able to talk about this 'feeling' or 'responding' without the use of these, or other, analogical terms, all equally derived from the experiences of the whole man. Let us hope we have said enough to justify and to illustrate the way such analogies are used.

NOTE ON THE SEPARABILITY OF THE SOUL

We have done an injustice to Professor Eccles in suggesting that his theory of mind and brain is motived by a conviction about the efficacy of mental initiatives alone. If it were so, he might not judge as he does. In fact he is at least equally concerned to make sense of revealed truth—a creditable desire on the part of any believer.[1] His Cartesianism, being a thoroughgoing separation of soul and body, is likely to attract a believer in immortality who is neither theologian nor philosopher. Unless we can show the soul to be a 'separate substance', how shall we understand her to be naturally immortal?

[1] This aspect of his thought appeared in a discourse given in Oxford to the Newman Society. I have ventured to depend on my recollection of it.

Professor Eccles is too philosophical, all the same, not to feel the difficulties of the theory. He may separate the soul, but he cannot deny that the body is her instrument for contact with the world, and for the recording of that contact. He cannot but think that the soul's acts of reminiscence resemble the behaviour of a man with no memory for tune, who revives the experience of the concert by playing himself a record. If the soul could recover the past without the physical gramophone, it would be an absurd dispensation which provided her in this life with so elaborate an instrument, and made her powers of recall vary with its physical state. If, on the other hand, memory is stored in the brain, what sort of identity remains between the soul liberated from the bodily instrument, and her former embodied self? It may be too much to say that I am my memory, but it is a truism that I have no self apart from it.

Faced by these difficulties, Professor Eccles adopts heroic remedies. He reduces the memory of the separated soul to a general disposition, the spiritual fruit of particular experience; a disposition which, even in this life, the Cartesian must presumably attribute to the soul, if the soul is to be the moral subject. He opines that such a general and virtual memory will allow the soul, in a purgatorial state, to repent her sin against her Creator and his creatures. Nothing more is required of her own recollective powers. Her final beatitude will consist in a new and present contact with God and the Blessed; and, according to the orthodox belief, she will then be equipped with a 'spiritual' reconstitution of her bodily being.

We will agree with Professor Eccles that active disposition is something real in the highest process of our personal being, something out of which, or in which, we act. It is no mere construction built by observers out of our previous conduct, and used by guessers to forecast our coming behaviour. Neither is it a mere mechanism of physical habit limiting the action of the person. It is a direction of personal action itself. But its 'reality' does not imply its independence of instruments. A personal skill in the painter is still a skill in using brushes, and an ability to find one's way about a library is not a recipe for being happy without books. To cut the soul's mnemic dispositions loose from her mnemic materials is a desperate enterprise. The soul's dispositions, about which she can hereafter repent, must include dispositions toward fellow-creatures. How can such dispositions be merely general? How can they be anything at all, apart from habits and policies of speech, action and sentiment, responsive to recurrent types of personal situations, and directed upon individual friends or enemies?

Professor Eccles might reasonably complain that our criticisms are unfair. He speaks as a believer, and we judge him as a rationalist. No Christian supposes that the soul comes out of the body like a cork out of a bottle, without any transformation. Does not the soul's Creator adapt her to her new existence? And may not the adaptation include such a development of her acquired dispositions as to compensate the loss of her physical records; so that her sentiments (let us say) about particular persons carry with them some representation of those persons?

Here is a line of defence perfectly reasonable in itself; but it admits a principle which endangers the Cartesian approach. Once we allow a divine transformation or supplementation of the disembodied soul, we confront a fundamental question about the philosophical expectations our faith will lead us to entertain. Shall we expect the analysis of our personal being to isolate a spirit capable of continuing its proper existence without the body? Or shall we merely expect our personal being to deserve such a description, as makes its continuation by God credible in a transformed state? I should judge that the first of these expectations is doomed to disappointment, and not merely because Professor Eccles's attempt disappoints it. If, on the other hand, we adopt the second expectation, does not the two-substance hypothesis lose its initial attractiveness?

We may put the same issue in another way by considering the 'natural' immortality of the soul. History shows us Christian belief turning, after some initial hesitations, against the equation of immortality with salvation; salvation is what God does with the immortality of the redeemed; it is not their immortality itself.

Immortality is not a gift of grace; the soul is naturally immortal. But what does 'naturally immortal' mean? No Christian takes it to mean 'immortal independently of God'. We do not deify the soul. When we have set aside such an impiety, we have still two interpretations of natural immortality to consider. 'Soul is naturally immortal' might be analogous to 'Granite is naturally durable'. In the system of created nature in which we have our present being, the destruction of granite can be seen to be difficult, and the perishing of the soul (we should be taken to hold) impossible. Such an interpretation takes 'naturally' to mean 'in accordance with the laws of nature', i.e. of this created universe. But it is not necessary to take 'naturally' thus. We might find the naturalness of the soul's immortality to lie in her relation with her Creator, not in her relation with the rest of the created world. Because other created things lack certain characteristics, it is natural they should be allowed to perish; because the human soul, or person, has these characteristics, it is natural God should conserve us always.

We cannot pretend to hesitate between these two interpretations. If the soul were immortal by the laws of the natural world, we should have no reason to hope for her survival except as a part of that world. But our faith not merely is that she will ultimately survive the world, but that her immediate survival of death coincides with her being taken out of the world. The naturalness of her immortality, then, must lie in a relation between her nature and the Divine Nature.

In view of the distinction we have made, what are we to say of the Cartesian argument for separability? Does it profess to show a natural fitness in the soul for survival in a created order open to our inspection—an ability to do without her bodily envelope, as a hermit-crab can do without his shell? Or does it detach the soul from the body merely to prove her spirituality, and to suggest her permanent place in the creative counsels of God? We should like to adopt the second interpretation; but it is difficult to believe that anyone who thought singlemindedly along such a line would strike into the Cartesian road. If the soul is neither intrinsically immortal (like the divine nature) nor immortal relatively to the order in which she now finds herself, her immortality must depend upon an act of God, placing her in another order, an order in which that immortality will have its context. And if this be so, is not the act of God the sole and sufficient cause of her survival? What interest, on this supposition, can belong to a Cartesian insistence on her substantial detachment from conditions contextually indispensable to her present phase? Such a detachment will not enable her to give herself a new and different phase of being; nor, surely, will it afford a reason why God should give her one. If there is a reason, it must lie in her capacities to love, to know and to devise; not in the special type of relation these capacities are deemed to bear to their bodily 'instruments'.

The Cartesian thinker has still a rejoinder to make. 'It may be' he says 'that the natural evidence for the soul's immortality lies in her godlike endowments. But there remains a philosophical question which has nothing to do with the evidence for anything. If we say, for whatever reason, that the human person is continued in another form of being after the death of the body, it is incumbent upon us to indicate what is continued, for the body (evidently) is not. To speak of immortality is to make a distinction between something which undergoes a transformation, and circumstances in the alteration of which that transformation consists. A complete account should specify (a) what abides, (b) what circumstances are removed, (c) what circumstances take their place. It has to be conceded that we cannot give a proper account of (c) this side of the grave. But unless we can distinguish (a) from (b) we cannot talk about immortality. How, then, are we to draw the distinction? Where death draws it. We know what perishes. If any soul remains, it must be as the subject of acts which we can be understood to perform bodiless.'

We agree with the first part of the foregoing speech. It is incumbent on the believer to distinguish what survives from what it survives. But we disagree with the proposed way of drawing the distinction. We cannot distinguish acts possible without the bodily instrument from acts requiring its use. We can distinguish acts simply directive of the bodily system from acts which use it freely for other ends—we can distinguish the putting of food into one's mouth from the use of one's tongue to work through a philosophical discussion. But nowhere are there bodiless acts.

How, then, distinguish what survives from what it survives? First, distinguish form from matter. The form, pattern or rhythm of our lives operates a matter of minute physical energies, but is not (as we have argued) reducible to them. We may suppose it translated to operate in another medium. But how are we in any way to conceive that medium, or rather, how to avoid conceiving it as identical with the matter we know? By attending to purposes. The soul in this life is not the simple mistress of her matter, but enslaved by her dependence on it. That is to say, many of her acts have a material purpose; they are directed to maintain the position, and the favourable position, of the soul in the material field. By death she loses, or is relieved of, that position. Her new existence will not fight for it again, but pursue purposes which emerged in the course of the fight. Whatever the medium of her existence will be, it will allow such a simplification of purpose. We will not here speak of the state of the damned. Our faith makes the high purposes of the redeemed soul a content for immortal existence. Flat humanism, of course, does not. But that is another argument.

CHAPTER VI

FREEWILL DEFINED

i. 'Free' as a value-word

THE relation of the mental and the physical in our being is a subject in itself so intriguing, that once taken up, it is not easily set aside. But we must be strong-minded if we are ever to write this book; we must have done with a theme which we introduced simply as an obstacle to be removed, before we could fairly enter on our chosen path. Our undertaking is to handle the freedom of the will; and we have to confess that we have written five chapters without attempting to say what we mean by it. The task can be no longer deferred.

To discuss freewill is essentially to discuss will. The addition of the adjective 'free' does not distinguish one sort of will (free) from another sort that is not. 'Free' is like 'proper', 'normal', 'healthy', and a string of other words which negate privations or exclude morbidities. A healthy body is just a body which does not happen to be sick. That in which health consists is simply the functioning of the body whose health it is; or, anyhow, the part of its functioning which is liable to go wrong. If you want to know what free breathing is, an investigation of the way we breathe will be nine tenths of your task. The remaining tenth will be to consider the ways in which breathing is liable to be cramped; if, indeed, this can be called an enquiry separable from the other. For by seeing what breathing is like, you can already see, in principle, how it might be hampered. From the mere observation that the expanding and contracting of the lungs draws air through the nostrils and expels it, you may deduce four types of possible trouble. The lungs may be faulty, so as not to pump; they may be confined from without, so that they have no room to expand; they may draw what is not air, but, let us say, water, through the head's being immersed; the nose and throat may be blocked, so that they cannot draw anything, whether air or not. In the same way we have only to enumerate the factors involved in voluntary action, to see in how many ways our will can be hampered.

An exact philosopher would wish to insist on the hybrid character of the word 'freedom'. It is always descriptive of a fact, at least in part; it is often in part evaluative. In denying the presence of obstruction, freedom denies something of a factual and describable sort; for instance, that there is any boulder on the railway line, preventing the movement of traffic. And yet no severely physical description would ever call anything an obstruction. Physical process as such is never obstructed; it acts as perfectly, it fulfils its principle as completely, whether the train runs on to Paddington, or crashes at Didcot. We call nothing either obstructed or free, except a sequence of action, or line of movement, whose fortunes we have selected as the subject of our special consideration. The progress of the train provides an example.

Our selection of such a subject may, but need not, attach a positive value to it. The point can be illustrated from a slip of the tongue, made by a first-aid instructor. A patient with an open artery, he said, could be saved from bleeding to death by a tourniquet applied at the right point; as soon as you tightened it, it would stop the blood from running out 'the way it should'. The absurdity lies in the substitution of an invariably evaluative phrase for an ambiguous term like 'freely'. It is enough for our attention to be fixed on the flowing blood, and we shall think of it as free if it runs, obstructed if it is staunched; we need not judge its freedom to be in the least desirable. Yet often 'freely' does imply 'as is to be desired' or 'in the way that it should'. Otherwise the good instructor would scarcely have made his verbal slip. Often, to say that something functions freely implies that it is a good thing it should do so; as in the case of that freedom from hindrances which constitutes bodily health.

In point of philosophical principle the gulf between 'freedom' with an evaluative implication, and 'freedom' without it, may be profound. But the distinction is much blurred in use, because we set on many patterns of function a value so unquestioning, as hardly to distinguish their nature from their worth. You can say, if you like, that the difference between a healthy and a diseased condition is evaluative only. Morbid and normal functioning are both functionings. We welcome the one, we deplore the other; that is all. Yet agreement on what is health and what is not is so entire, as to afford the art of medicine an unquestioned basis. Doctors disagree, but not about the aim. Medicine is not like morals; we debate the lineaments of virtue, we do not debate the picture of health. Medicine rests on a valuation; but the making of valuations is no part of the medical art.

How is it, then, when the freedom we have in mind is not the freedom of vital function, but the freedom of personal volition? We shall scarcely doubt whether the mention of such freedom carries a positive valuation of that which freely operates. But what sort of valuation? Agreed and instinctive, or conscious and disputable? The answer will turn on the way in which the action of the will is being viewed. We may view it as expressed in that conduct of life which is the matter of ethics; and then our implied valuations will be of the disputable sort. Suppose, for example, we are comparing the freedom of the monastic life with the freedom of life 'in the world'. The question scarcely makes sense, unless it is related to an appreciation of the *summum bonum*. Monks are free from hawkers and circulars; stockbrokers from the recitation of the Divine Office. To ask about the comparative freedom of the two lives is to ask which allows a less obstructed enjoyment of human good. As our views of the good differ, our answers will differ. We shall find ourselves asserting and defending rival valuations.

But we can think, and often do think, about voluntary freedom in a more formal way, in abstraction from the purposes to which it is put. The analogy of health will serve us again. Whatever a man does with his bodily powers, we think it good he should possess them; and this is the doctor's point of view. Whether the patient uses his recovered health to crush his wife or to support his children, is not his physician's concern. In like manner we take it that many mental powers are good to have, without pausing to ask what individuals do with them. It is a pity if a man cannot think, deliberate, resolve, execute, persevere. There is nothing contentious in the value we set on such capacities; nor in the consequent value we attach to freedom from their besetting hindrances.

The philosopher's question about the freedom of the will is understood to concern the liberty of volition thus formally considered. There is a valuation involved, but it is platitudinous. We waste no words on the man who affects to challenge the value of our ability to choose, or of our ability to do what we have chosen.

ii. *Willing and doing*

Freedom in general cannot be defined except negatively; it is an absence of interferences. Whenever we think of freedom as something positive, and able to be enjoyed, we have in mind a particular activity which we are free to exercise. 'How glorious to be free!'—'Ah, now my lungs can enjoy their freedom.' Well, but what do they enjoy? Just breathing. That the breathing is free needs no saying, the enjoyment implies it; for hampered breathing is far from enjoyable. Did not Aristotle give 'activity suitable to our kind, and unhindered' as the very definition of what causes us pleasure? We see, then, that talk about freewill may be talk about sheer volition.

To have established this point does not clear away our linguistic confusion; it merely dumps it somewhere else. For when we have decided that what we exercise as freewill is just will, we have to consider what that means. Is there something on its own, a phase of action called will, which I can nakedly enjoy? No, there is no such thing. 'Will' is action itself, in the full and personal sense of the verb to 'act'. But if so, why do we bother to have two words, 'act' and 'will', and why, when they are set side by side, do we resist the suggestion that they are synonymous? Because they denote the single fact under different aspects: 'act' emphasising what I perform, and 'will' my choice, energy or interest in the performance of it. We call nothing an exercise of will which does not constitute an act, though the act may be invisible and internal, say the registration of a decision for my guidance tomorrow. And conversely, no performance is to be called an action in the proper, or personal, sense, unless it is an exercise of will; though it has to be conceded that, in an extended sense, we may and do speak of the solvent's *action* on the dirt, and so forth.

Will, except as the auxiliary to the future tense, is in danger of becoming obsolete outside theoretical debate. This means that the linguistic enquiry, how the word is currently used, is liable to be uninformative. We should need to see first how it was formerly used, and then what words have been substituted for it in its several usages. We will not go through the exercise here, but merely ask that the consideration of obsolescence should be borne in mind. If it is not, it may be difficult to see what purposes the word serves; or why we trouble to distinguish 'will' from 'act'.

When we find a need for will (or some equivalent) as a distinct term, what concern have we in mind? Our interest may lie in either of two fields; we may be considering the direction of a man's will, or the degree of it. In the former case we ask what his will was, in doing what he did; the expression is admittedly archaic, but we have no difficulty in supplying modern translations. In the latter case we ask how much of will there was about his doing it. Here the sound of the language is not so much archaic as unreal, or theoretical. For we do not ordinarily ask how voluntary an act was, but whether it was voluntary or not; in the law court, for example. If it was voluntary, it is punishable, if involuntary, it is not. Yet the very process of assessing whether an action comes up to the legal standard of voluntariness, will quickly convince us that there are many gradations. Some acts are only just voluntary for our purpose, while others are unquestionably so. What makes the distinction absolute is the simplicity of the practical issue (to punish or not to punish). So the distinction between an eligible and an ineligible bachelor is absolute: either we invite him or we do not.

Voluntariness, as a variable quantity in action, is still an ambiguous notion. Sometimes it attaches not to the act the man saw himself as doing, but to the effect of it; what we are questioning is the relation between the two. Nathaniel Winkle's shooting was voluntary; but how about his shooting Tracy Tupman? Such enquiries, though capital sentences may hang upon them, are of small philosophical interest. Of more concern to us are enquiries into the act which, if he meant anything, the agent meant to perform. But did he mean anything? Not, for example, if he gave an involuntary start.

The involuntary start is an extreme case. There are obviously many gradations of voluntariness between such a movement and a deliberate choice freely made; made, that is, not under any sort of duress. Deliberate choice is the plain case, but not necessarily the strongest. What can be more voluntary than a project with nothing against it, immediately seized by the whole energy of our will; when, for example, on a day of leisure, we embrace an invitation to visit the person whom we love? The true middle cases are not simple, but sleepy, actions, say mere matters of routine; or, in a different area, actions on the borderland between intention and animal reaction, however lively.

The vanishing-point of will is the vanishing-point of action, in the full, or personal, sense. An involuntary start is not an action. What is it, though? Our vocabulary fails to serve us. We say it is something which the man does: '*He gives* an involuntary start.' But if he does it, it does not occur, or happen to him. Nevertheless, when we are in the mood to deny it the name of action, we shall probably be driven to call it an occurrence, or an event. And doubtless in the view of physical observation it is an event, whatever else it may be. But then, so are all actions; we have argued that in all of them something physical occurs.

When we have reached this point, we are in grave philosophical danger; one slip of the foot will all too easily follow another, and down we slide in a logical *glissade*. It goes as follows. 'All the things people are said to do are anyhow events. Some of them are mere events; others of them are events of a special class, called voluntary, and, on account of their voluntariness, actions. What does 'being voluntary' add to the notion of an event? According to the common opinion, it adds something which entails the event's not being the simple effect of ordinary causes. What can this something be, but dependence on an extraordinary cause? For surely no one supposes the voluntary act to be causeless; it is not any sort of fluke. What, then, is its extraordinary cause? What but a special mental act, which we may call a volition? But the supposition is perfectly useless, as can easily be shown. For all mental events are anyhow events, and indeed, as we have laboured to prove, physical events. And whatever they may be, one thing at least cannot be doubted—that they are voluntary. They fall, therefore, under the definition of voluntary events: the being caused by no ordinary cause, but by a volition. But that volition in turn must suffer the same analysis. It is evident, then, that according to this definition of the voluntary, an infinite regress of volitions is involved in the simplest voluntary action.

'We should conclude, then' (we are still sliding down the logical hill) 'that it is useless to connect the special character of voluntary acts with any singularity in the way they are brought about. Either it lies in the actions themselves, a flavour, a vigour, a consciousness about them; or else it lies in the type of event which is their natural cause; a thought, let us say, or a desire.'

Since we are convinced that there is something particular in the way voluntary actions come about, from which their voluntariness is inseparable, we look for the false step which betrayed us into sliding so far from the truth. It was where we introduced will, or volition, into action as its distinguishing mark; or rather, did not introduce it into the action (that was precisely our failure) but prefixed it as a cause. For acts of will do not cause events, they take shape in events; there is one thing, called 'action' in virtue of performance, and 'volition' in virtue of being willed. An action is what a personal agent does, or in which he acts. That is the special way it is brought about. To be able to recognise an act, is to see this. And some action is unmistakable, whatever difficulties there may be about borderline cases.

An equally instructive trail of fallacy runs through the province of will which covers the *direction* of our action. If the action was voluntary, we say, the direction was chosen; and so the agent could have acted otherwise. The apparent inference ('and so') is expository: a choice is no choice, unless it is the rejection of an open alternative. On 'could have acted otherwise' we may offer the gloss: 'Would have acted otherwise, had he wished.' The gloss obtains immediate assent, because, properly understood, it is an honourable tautology. 'Wished' is a vernacular equivalent for 'willed'; so all we are saying is, that the agent's performance took the shape it did, that being his will; and that if he had willed otherwise, he would have done otherwise; for the outside, so to speak, of the action would of course have varied as the inside varied. All the gloss amounts to, is that the action was an action.

But, having obtained for our gloss the acceptance which is accorded to tautologies, we may proceed to alter the sense, so that it is no longer tautological, nor self-evident, nor, indeed, universally true. This is done by giving 'wish' a new sense: it is not now the will expressed in the act, but is an antecedent state or motion of desire. The whole sentence will now read: 'Had his antecedent intention (or the like) been otherwise, he would have acted otherwise.' This is not true of all agents in all circumstances. Things that I do in accordance with certain antecedent wishes I should still do in spite of antecedent wishes of an opposite sort; and vice versa. To make the revalued sentence universally true we must add a fresh gloss. 'He would have acted otherwise, if his antecedent wishes had been so altered as to leave him no possible motive for acting as he did.' This is no doubt a truth: but not a very precious truth, nor one that will help the determinist cause.

The equivocation on the original gloss involves essentially the same false step as that which we detected in a previous fallacy: the wish or will determining the action is put outside it; so that 'determining' is given a causal sense, instead of the merely logical sense which in this connexion attaches to it.

The fallacy is easily exposed, but it is not without its importance. It is typical of many arguments, of which the common form is this: they trick us into stating personal-action themes in natural-event terms, and they proceed to force on us the consequences of our indiscretion. In the example we have considered, our conviction of alternative choice accepts the form of what the gods call a contra-factual, and mortals an unfulfilled condition. Had a certain condition been otherwise, the consequence would have been otherwise—Had the weather been worse, the holiday traffic would have been lighter—Had my wishes been different, I should have acted differently. But the grammatical form misleads. All we mean is that we could have acted otherwise, by simply acting otherwise, our action embodying, no doubt, an alternative intention. We are not giving what would have been the cause of our acting otherwise, by mentioning an alternative wish, any more than a child is giving a cause for doing what he does, by saying 'Because I want to'. 'Because I want to' means 'My act is an act of choice', and it implies 'Admittedly I could have done otherwise, only I have chosen not to'. That is why children who give such an answer get rebuked by their elders, and kicked by their equals.

The moral of our whole discussion so far may seem to be, that there is only one serious task before us, to examine the nature of personal action. To understand action would be to understand its voluntariness; and to understand how it is voluntary would be to understand how it is free. 'Free' and 'voluntary' seem nothing more than two formal aspects of a complex reality, personal action. We may write off the pair of them in a few definitions; whereas the modalities of action are an endless study—it is difficult either to frame a definition equally applicable to them all, or to pick instances typical of the whole range. If there are paradoxes about voluntary freedom, they are most likely to represent confusions over the general character, or the special varieties, of personal action.

So it may seem. We have still something to say about freedom, nevertheless, and in particular about the contexts in which it comes to be an issue. Meanwhile we do not wish to leave a philosophical reader in the air about action, or protesting that he has not been told what it is. So we will make two provisional remarks.

First, everyone knows the broad distinction between what is done (action) and what merely occurs (event). Second, within the province of what is done, some deeds are more ours, and more of actions, than others. Who hesitates to call a deliberate choice more of an action than a conventional salute? The salute, made almost unheedingly, seems to approximate towards being a mere occurrence. We may be content, then, for the present to think of actedness as a character distinguishing what is done from what merely happens, but more strongly exhibited by some of what is done than by other examples of it.

iii. Freedom enjoyed and freedom asserted

We have said that the freedom of the will can only be appreciated by contrast with the hindrances it excludes. To what hamperings, then, is voluntary action subject? Many of them are obvious and familiar: intimidation, physical constraint, hypnotism, obsession, neurosis. There are many more, some more subtle and out-of-the-way than others. To be unfree in one of these ways is not the same thing as to be unfree in another; and so to be liberated from any of them is a distinct sort of liberation. We could group them and catalogue them; but no philosophical issue (we suspect) would be at stake.

Here, however, is a philosophical question which equally concerns them all. If free action is defined by contrast with its impediments, why do we find the champions of freewill maintaining that where there is action at all, freedom remains, in spite of all hindrances? It is not difficult to see what these champions mean—A man subjected to intimidation is free, after all, to follow his bent if he likes, and wait for a dagger in the dark. We can hold out against bullying, restraint of liberty, or torture, so long as we remain ourselves. True, if the villain takes my arm and, by superior force, wields it against the face of my dearest friend, I have no liberty in regard to what is done; but then I do not do it—I do not strike my friend; there is no action on my part; the vanishing-point of liberty is the vanishing-point of action.

We do not, probably, wish to contest these examples. What we want to know is how freedom of action can be defined as freedom from impediments or constraints, if it is right to say that freedom remains in the midst of them. It seems preposterous to say that the most unfree action there can be, is still free. Or do we mean that the freedom is a diminishing quantity, never extinguished while action remains? That free and unfree are always relative, or comparative, like bright and dim? The analogy we formerly adduced of breathing, or of health, will bear this out. Breathing which is absolutely impeded does not breathe, and so is not even impeded. An absolutely unhealthy body is dead, and so not unhealthy. You cannot have an absolutely unfree act.

The solution seems entirely reasonable; or would, if it did not appear to conflict with some of the things we most want to say. If it is true that freedom diminishes with the increase of its obstacles, why do we find the shining examples of its exercise in resistances to extreme constraint? As when Christ at Gethsemane refuses to evade the ring of death closing upon him, and by undergoing crucifixion rather than recant, sets the Christian standard of a voluntary act. The paradox is taken to its limit by those who say that there are no genuine cases of free choice other than resistances to temptation, when we are under some sort of pressure.

The paradox rests on a confusion between the enjoyment of freedom and the assertion of it. When we are so free as to be unaware of constraints, we are unaware of our freedom; we simply exercise it. It is only when freedom needs to be asserted, that it becomes an issue; and the more burning an issue, as the constraint increases. To say that in assertion against constraint freedom becomes an issue, is not to say that the subject sees himself as asserting his freedom, but merely that he does assert it. Henley in his insufferable poem asserts himself, unbowed beneath the bludgeonings of chance. Christ in Gethsemane affirms his Father's will; but in so doing, he refuses to yield to the horror of death.

We can say, if we like, that we are not free to exercise moral heroism, except in face of severe constraint; and equally we may say that unless we are suffocating, we are not free to fight for breath. But freedom to fight for breath is not the same thing as free breathing, and freedom to be heroic is not the same thing as freedom of action. And the very use of the word 'free' in such a context is surely forced. It suggests that we go about the place spoiling for a fight with suffocation, and frustrated by lack of the opportunity, so that to find ourselves half drowning is a liberation. The man spoiling for a fight with the devil is a less fantastic figure; though not, perhaps, any better advised, if we are right to value the counsel 'Pray that ye enter not into temptation'.

Let us say, in conclusion, that there are two common occasions which throw freedom into relief, resistance to constraint, and escape from constraint: 'I *won't* choke' and 'Now I can breathe'.

iv. *Literal and notional constraints on freedom*

The libertarian philosopher may think of himself as asserting, or vindicating, freedom; but it would be highly ridiculous for him to masquerade in the armour and plumes of the hero. His battle is not against real constraint, his fight is with shadows; with fantastic, notional, or metaphysical constraints, which hamper not our action, but (anyhow in the first place) our thought about our action. It is this which (to change the figure) philosophical error persuades us to jam into tight shoes; that is, into the mould of some alien notion which does not allow it to be what it is, or (should we say) to mean what it means. For example, we are told that choice is the result of a collision of forces. We feel the notional pinch. 'No' we scream 'choice is free'; that is, choice is choice, choice chooses, which she could not do, poor thing, if she were the result of a collision of forces.

A subtler case of notional constraint is afforded by the imprisonment of one type of voluntary action within the definition of another type of voluntary action; for example, when choosing is treated as a complicated case of carrying on an accepted pursuit. 'No' we scream 'choice is free'; free, that is, from the limits of a presupposed pursuit. To choose may be to choose what one will pursue. The protest is perfectly justified. But we may become unduly obsessed with the distinction, or some other one distinction of the sort; and our obsession may lead us to narrow the meaning of *free* action, or volition, in a quite artificial way. We may find ourselves saying, for example, that an act of freewill, in the proper sense, is not any that is voluntary and unimpeded, but only one that escapes the limitation of a prescribed objective, and freshly chooses its own aim. Well, so long as we are not misunderstood, there is no great harm. But it is a perverse usage, surely, which withholds the name of 'free action' from the wholehearted, inventive and enthusiastic carrying on of a pursuit already adopted. Why should we regard it as aspiring to be a choice between alternative pursuits, and as unable, poor thing, to escape from being itself into being this other sort of act? We might as well commiserate the lack of freedom in a terrier racing on a lawn, because, poor thing, he cannot be a man, and vote in the election.

The protagonist of freewill, we have said, appears to himself to be liberating the *notion* of voluntary action from cramping confinement within the limits of a description foreign to its meaning. But why say 'liberate', 'cramped' or 'confined'? Is this language not mere rhetoric, the product of a comparison between the sage and the hero, the philosophical and the moral assertors of freewill? Apart from the influence of such a comparison, should we not be content to use less highly-coloured language? Say, that the philosopher is sorry to find the distinctive meaning of a term obscured or denied by inappropriate classification or description, and sets out to give it its rights. To speak of a notion as cramped or confined by misdescription is to use the rhetoric of personification; it is to suggest (as indeed we often say) that the subject defined revolts against the offered description of it.

But not all rhetoric is equally misleading. To say that the *definiendum* revolts against the offered definition is not simply to say that the definition won't do. It is further to suggest a mental revulsion on the part of someone who has the *definiendum* in mind, and feels the sort of interest in it which causes him to protest against so inadequate a definition. He feels how wrong it is, before he can get round to discovering just how and why it is wrong. As he goes about the task, he seems to himself to be untying linguistic bonds, against which the *definiendum* has already risen in revolt.

There is, perhaps, no definable notion in which someone might not acquire a proprietary interest; somewhere beneath the sun there beats the heart which will revolt against a misdescription of Marginal Utility, or of the Second Law in Thermodynamics. But revolt against the misdescription of will is a phenomenon far more general. For what is being misdescribed? What each of us takes himself to be, under a certain aspect; and the aspect in which he is most sensitive about himself. Tell me anything you like about the component factors in this psychophysical being that I am, and I will take it patiently; but put your finger on the point of life and action, touch the quick of resolution and I shall wince, if your description does not allow it the unique initiative, the creativity I find in it.

Well, what of it? And who cares whether I wince or no? What does my passion indicate but unschooled vanity, and an unwillingness to entertain unpalatable truths? Do not I wince when they tell me my very real faults? My wincing at accusation is the reverse of evidence for my innocence; and my wincing at a restrictive account of my voluntary power may be no evidence of my freedom from the imputed limitations. No, indeed; the revolt of feeling proves nothing alone. But when we look at the sequel, we see that the two cases are not parallel. Moral rebuke, however unpalatable, can be digested, if it is deserved; and once digested, leads to a liberation, not a frustration. The admission to myself of my irascibility sets me on my guard, and makes it possible for me sometimes to banish the tone of exasperation which defeats the purpose of persuasion. But the acceptance of a deflationary account of voluntary freedom never liberates, it only frustrates; if, that is, we try seriously to view the decisions we have to make in the light of it. The practical value of rebuke is this: it leads us to distinguish between things in which we are free, and things in which we are not. Rebuked for my irritability, I see that I shall hope in vain to manage a clash of purpose, or a wrestle against stupidity, without motions of exasperation. But I can hope (as Wooster advises Jeeves) to watch the tendency, and watching it, to check its effects. Whereas a determinist account of will in general appears to place everything in the class of what I cannot help. So far from making any useful discrimination, it appears to blur the distinction most vital to self-knowledge: between what I can help, and what I cannot.

The distinction is, of course, just as dangerously blurred by a lunatic libertarianism which denies anything we cannot help, and makes man, picking out his path on earth, as free as God creating earth and heaven. In opposition to such folly, determinism may have the practical value of a moral realism; a reminder that we have got our history on our backs, and that there is no certain limit to the determining factors we may have to recognise. For minds which can see only black or white, determinism may often be a more wholesome formulation than liberty. But the wholesomeness of the doctrine will depend on the imperceptiveness of those who entertain it. Once our mind is aroused to perceive that the formula of its creed determines and enslaves the very act which acknowledges and reckons with our enslavement, our determinism becomes a practical absurdity. It no longer makes any useful distinction between what we cannot help, and what we can; it simply belies the power and nature of action.

It is not to be supposed that a determinist philosopher will admit that his doctrine has so devastating or so paradoxical an effect. 'Those things which we can help' he will say 'are easily distinguished by a reasonable determinism from those which we cannot. Whoever doubts it, confuses predictability with constraint. What we cannot help, is what our decision cannot alter; what depends on the decision we make, still depends upon it, however predictably the way we shall decide follows from the previous situation within us and without us. The superstitious fatalist imagines an external force, invisibly constraining his decision to an appointed end, in spite of his apparent choice. The reasonable determinist is not bogy-ridden. Nothing, in his supposition, constrains his choice, either by way of force or of fraud. He chooses; only the process of his choosing conforms to a rule, and allows an ideal observer to foresee it.'

Our rejoinder to this defence is to concede that the determinist places no literal constraint upon decision; but to complain that he gives her none of her proper work to do. If you tell me that the children with the pencils are designing, and then I see that they are drawing over sketches faintly printed, I shall not protest that they are inhibited, but I shall deny that they are designing. You will plead in vain that their wrists and fingers are moving with a fine sweep; it remains that they are not choosing what to draw. A decision is not something we fulfil, it is something we create. And if we are told that in view of all factors or conditions, inward and outward, our decision is bound to work out in one (ideally) predictable way, we feel no literal constraint, indeed, but a notional, metaphysical, or figurative constraint. I, the decider, rebel against the implied definition of myself as the fulfiller, not the maker, of a destiny.

The determinist will retort that he proposes no peculiar description or definition of choice or of action. He is content that such ultimates should be recognised for what they are. He picks no quarrel with the noble tautologies, that doing is doing, deciding is deciding, making is making, and so forth. He merely asserts that the freest or most absolute choosing we can do has a principle or structure allowing of prefiguration in its antecedents. To say that such a prefiguration of it is incompatible with its being what it is, is mere libertarian dogmatism. As for the parable of the boys with pencils, it misrepresents the whole issue. The determinist is not like a man who denies that children can design. He is like a man who says that what comes out on their paper rises from a Freudian subconscious; the libertarian like a man who says it is invented, and that invention is just invention. The children are admitted to design, on either view; and so the voluntary agent chooses or decides, whether or no his decisions or choices are prefigured in their antecedents. Libertarians may feel a notional pinch, when they hear determinist doctrine propounded; but that is the effect of their libertarian prejudice. Determinists feel no pinch; and libertarians can be educated.

But is it true that only libertarians feel the pinch? In the moment of theoretical reflection, perhaps, but not in the posture of action.

No one, libertarian or determinist, can view the decision before him as destined to be settled in a way which antecedent factors prefigure. That would be to view what he will do as something to be discovered, or calculated; and he cannot both view it as such, and as something to be decided. If he endeavours to dovetail the two pictures he will suffer mental agony, he will feel the notional pinch right enough.

Since the determinist must drop his determinist thoughts at the moment of decision, he may be accused of double thinking. While he decides or acts, he must view himself as directing his way by a spontaneous reaching forward. But when he reflects on his action or decision after the event, he claims to realise that all the time it was determined from behind.

It is tempting to compare the predicament of the determinist with a predicament of Descartes, in the pursuit of his universal doubt. The apparent certainty of mathematical reasoning is the hardest nut the French philosopher has to crack; and he is obliged to admit that while he reasons upon it, it convinces him of its soundness; for the steps of the reasoning are acts of seemingly rational conviction, if they are anything. And yet, Descartes alleges, when he is not doing the reasoning, but merely recalling after the event that he did do it, it is possible for him to entertain the hideous hypothesis that, by the very constitution of his mind, the more he reasons, the more he errs, and the more convinced he is, the more he is deceived. Descartes cannot do his mathematics, nor the determinist make his practical choices, without supposing the activity he engages in, to be what it appears to be; neither can doubt except after the event. But there is this difference between them: Descartes's hideous hypothesis is erected to be refuted, for it turns out to be self-contradictory. Whereas the determinist stands by his second thoughts; he goes on believing that causal determination determines *ab ante* the act which is enjoyed and exercised as self-determining; and, what is more, determines that it should be experienced as what it is not.

Will a determinist philosopher admit the force of the Cartesian analogy? Not, surely, without a struggle. He will begin by observing that in Descartes's case there is a head-on collision between his first and second thoughts; whereas in his own case, if there is a collision, it is oblique. Descartes is talking about an act of which the very nature is rational conviction: to draw the conclusion in a mathematical argument is to accept its rational cogency. What he reckons to do in such an act, viz. to see reason, is precisely what the hideous hypothesis suggests he never can do. The clash in the determinist's mind is nothing like this. His subsequent and scientific reflection does not deny that he really made a choice, when he thought he did. A choice really took place, and it was really his, and really was a choice, according to all the ordinary rules of language for distinguishing between one man's choices and another man's, or between pieces of behaviour which are to be reckoned choices, and pieces which are not.

What, positively, is to be said about the incompatibility which the determinist must admit? How will he classify it? He will claim that it is no more than an incompatibility between attitudes. And surely we know that two attitudes, both legitimate, can be mutually incompatible. For example, it is a reasonable thing enough, to look at my friend's behaviour as a living illustration of standard psychological patterns. It is an even more proper and natural thing, to respond directly to what he is and feels, says and does. The responding and the psychologising belong to one mental world, and have something to do with one another; the responding furnishes data for the psychologising; the psychologising contributes understandingness to the responses. Nevertheless I cannot do the two things at once, or even, perhaps, in rapid alternation; there is an incompatibility of attitude between appreciating my friend, and psychologising him.

Why, then, should there not be a similar incompatibility of attitude between choosing, and studying the causes of one's choice? Both belong to the same mental world, and have a natural relation to one another; all that I am forbidden to do, is to practice them both at once. I may study the causes of other people's choices, or the causes of my own previous, or conjectured future choices, for the very purpose of helping myself decide what to do here and now. Only the decision I am now engaged upon is the living, subjective point; I cannot be studying it, as a thing already determined, while I am making the studies in view of which I am to determine it. For these studies are directed towards answering the question, 'What am I to do?' And to regard my action as predetermined, is to abolish this question.

We may agree with the determinist that mere attitudes may be incompatible; but we shall wish to insist on the point that the conflict is not between studiousness and choosingness simply—not between theorising about one's decision, and making it; but only between theorising about it deterministically, and making it. Admittedly all theorising distracts from the business in hand and delays the choice. But if, for example, I did some libertarian theorising, and said to myself, 'You are free to choose as you will,' delay would be the whole of the trouble; there would be no conflict, or mental confusion involved.

The determinist's comment on this will be that it is true, but without significance. For in his view, 'I am free to choose as I will' is no more than a tautology. 'Here I am choosing; the choice I make will be my choice.' The wonder would be, if so vapid a remark had enough substance in it to obstruct any mental process whatever. How could it be a cause of mental conflict, for me to tell myself that what I am doing, I am doing? What impedes the movement of choice is the act of mind which looks beyond it; which anchors it to its real place in the world, by relating it to its antecedents and its circumstances. Such an act of mind is a scientific judgement, and therefore, of course, deterministic.

Reflecting upon the determinist's defence against being bracketed with Descartes, we may feel that it has been fairly successful, on determinist assumptions. The determinist alleges that his scientific account of choice allows it still to be choice, whereas of course Descartes does not allege that his hideous hypothesis allows rational conviction to be rational conviction. But, in the eyes of the libertarian thinker, the determinist's allegation is a mere allegation; his scientific account denies the nature of choice, whether he realises it or no.

How, then, shall we proceed with the argument? Shall we make a frontal attack on the deterministic theory of choice? But what sort of an attack? Suppose that we test its adequacy by enquiring, whether it can explain why and how a conflict arises in the mind of a man both choosing, and thinking of his choice as something determined.

CHAPTER VII

A DETERMINIST ACCOUNT OF PHENOMENAL
LIBERTY

i. *The determinist story*

O UR general concern is with voluntary action. But at present we
are founding an argument on our consciousness of acting volun-
tarily. In so far as voluntary action is consciously such, it has the
form of choice. If I tell myself that I have my own action to make, I
tell myself that I have to choose it, even if the sole alternative is inaction. But if we are thinking of choice, it may be not unreasonable to concentrate on deliberate choice, or reflective decision, as
being the most explicit sort, and likely to prove the most informative. Let it be understood, then, that our determinist is called upon
to explain, on his own principles, why a deliberate choice cannot be
made in the lively and present belief that it is causally prefigured.

It looks as though the determinist were being invited to explain
the cause of an illusion; and perhaps we shall expect him to quote
those apparent but not genuine choices which specially concern
psychiatrists; those decisions really determined by concealed or
unacknowledged factors, while our most conscious thoughts go
through the motions of a face-saving parade. But there are genuine
choices, for the philosophical determinist, just as much as for anyone else; choices which are the real dénoument of a drama played in
the theatre of consciousness. He is not invoking any Freudian
abysses when he says that at the moment of choice (supposing
such a moment can be isolated) the factors then in play determine
the result. When he speaks of such factors he will be thinking of
purposes and objects set before the mind, or tendencies of the
mind in its concern about them.

The determinist imagines the figure of an omnipercipient observer, looking back on our decision after we have made it. Such a being would be able to make a complete analysis of it, and to see the result as following, in conformity with unvarying laws, from the elements converging at that point in the mental situation. The determinist will insist upon the time-factor; it is only at the moment of decision that the forces are in place which determine the result. Take any earlier moment in the process of deliberation, and the pattern of factors will not be the same. It may be that all the considerations, all the suppositions which will play any part in the decision, have already entered the field. But they have not yet taken up their final positions; their comparative degrees of urgency or relevance, their mutual alliances and oppositions are not yet formulated in the final proportion. And why not? Because, until the moment of decision, the subjective factors, the responses of the mind to what is before it, are not fully evoked.

It is manifest that the subjective factors in choice determine alone the relevance and force of facts, projects, or considerations. Apart from our subjective responses, nothing coming before the mind would have the least tendency to produce action of any sort. Even mortal danger, seen as a physical probability, would leave us unmoved, if we had no repulsion against death or bodily harm. Our abhorrence of these evils is so strong and direct, that our action in avoidance of them is often immediate and unquestioned. But in a situation calling for deliberate choice, the subjective responses are neither simple nor unopposed by others. Up to the moment of decision there is a measure of anarchy in the mind, a tolerance of conflict. Only the decisive moment braces and unifies us, forcing the subjective factors into that pattern of balance and subordination which produces the action. And as the subjective factors do not attain their effective deployment until the moment of decision, neither do the objective factors; for their relevance and force depend on the subjective. So, then, it is the total position in the last moment, and at no previous moment, which gives birth to the active sequel.

We have done nothing so far but apply to the deliberating mind a commonplace about causality. It is always the pattern of factors at the moment, and at no previous moment, which determines the effect. This limiting doctrine does not mean, of course, that we can never predict until it is too late. For each of the factors which comes into the determinative pattern has itself been determined to do so by the previous moment of its own history. So, by following streams of converging histories forward from moment to moment, physical prediction reaches the confluence of forces decisive for the future in which it is interested. And in like manner, according to our determinist's theory, the omnipercipient observer, from any moment he liked to take in our past, could have foretold the convergent and interlacing histories of factors objective and subjective, up to the point where their meeting produces our decision.

But let us have done now with the omnipercipient observer, and attend to the man whose decision it is. He is in no position to observe all the factors involved, as they progress towards the fateful *rendezvous*. It is not merely that the pattern is far too intricate; that to analyse the formation of a decision would take many hundred times as long as to form it. It is that one whole class of the ingredient factors, the subjective, is closed to him in principle.

This limitation of view follows from the very function of thought in the formation of any decision. The thinking we do in such a case is not an outsider's assessment of what is happening, it is a real link in the chain of events. What, in fact, is its job? The job of deliberative thought—we are still expounding the determinist thesis—is to evoke our subjective responses, and draw them into that final grouping from which action results. Such thinking, therefore, exerts a real causality. But for our so thinking, latent interest would remain unevoked, or would not take the direction that it takes.

It follows that the man who deliberates is engaged in an activity, which is not only temporally but functionally prior to the occurrence of the interest determinative of decision. Whatever he thinks about in such a posture of mind is either irrelevant, or else finds a place (he must say) 'in that description of my situation, to which I must respond'. We, looking at him, may say that he is engaged in marshalling the evocatives of his subjective response.

What happens, then, if you call upon a man, in the midst of his deliberative phase, to acknowledge that the decision he is working towards is already predetermined? He will endeavour to place the alleged fact you offer him in the only plane of fact which the posture of deliberation allows him to envisage—the plane of objective, and potentially evocative, fact. He will try to tell himself that there is a set of evocative factors before him which determine, by themselves, the resultant decision; and such a suggestion will be in violent conflict with what he knows himself to be doing. If he sets before himself any fact or any consideration, it is with no other purpose than to evoke a subjective response not yet made; 'So that I may see' he will say 'what to do about it'. He must find quite crippling any suggestion that this 'what to do about it'—this subjective response—does not need to be evoked, because factors of the sort which can be placed before the deliberating mind have already determined the effective result. The suggestion is agony, because in claiming that the decision is virtually made, it withholds us from taking the only step by which we could make it: the step, that is, of appealing to subjective response.

The explanation we have attempted on behalf of the determinist amounts to this: I cannot treat what has to be evoked as something determinate, I must view it as something still to be determined. For to evoke subjective response is to determine the form it will take;[1] and the function of my deliberative thought is to evoke it. To think deliberative thoughts is to think them as evocative and therefore as determinative. One cannot think such thoughts in the belief that they have nothing to evoke, nothing to determine. For then they would lack evocative intention, and it is this intention which confers on them the character of being deliberative thoughts.

[1] If, that is, I am deliberating; not if I am working myself up into the readiness to execute a preconceived intention.

The foundation of the position is that the emotional element in decision comes by nature, not by calculation. By the way I think out the situation confronting me, I may occasion or evoke the way I feel about it. But the way I feel about it is no part of my thinking it out, as it might be the conclusion of my argument. If I wish to decide, therefore, I must think in a way appropriate to evoke feeling; but I must let the feeling come.

It is easy to see how an attempt to think deterministically and predictively about the decision I have to make, will offend against the canon laid down. I cannot leave the element of feeling out of the calculation of my coming decision—that would be too unrealistic. I must count it in, then—I must reckon my existing feeling-tendencies among the causal factors. But to estimate one's feeling-tendencies is not, alas, the way to evoke them. The fact is notorious. Analyse the subjective springs of passion, and so far from evoking it, you dissipate it. It is not that some objects of consideration are liable to evoke feeling, while others are not; that to consider the situation before one's eyes evokes feeling, to consider one's own emotional nature does not. All objects of thought are probably able to evoke feeling of some kind, and certainly one's own emotional constitution is among the hardest things to view dispassionately. Who can reflect upon his capacities for sentiment, and stir no vanity, no self-pity or self-contempt, or at the very least, no painfully engaged curiosity? But the feelings stirred by reflection on our capacities for response are not the feelings which would constitute that response; they are a different set of feelings, at the best irrelevant, at the worst obstructive.

To summarise: a theoretical examination, after the event, may convince us that a certain pattern of factors, subjective and objective, gave rise to our act of decision. But a contemplation of this pattern, or anyhow of the subjective elements in it, undertaken at the time of decision, so far from helping to bring the decision about, is irreconcilable with the contemplation which would bring it about: bring it about, that is, by evoking the necessary response of feeling.

For reasons of simplicity we have talked of the evocable and subjective element as feeling. But the determinist explanation we are trying to state is in no way dependent on an overestimate of the part played in decision by emotion or 'affection'. On an earlier page we made use of the word 'interest'. Whether we choose to talk of feeling about . . . , interest in . . . , or concern for . . . , the case remains the same. If we like, we may cut away as inessential the whole gamut of mental attitudes, and view the evocable response as sheer appetite for action, or movement to- wards it. It will remain that the movement or appetite is stirred by the appropriate perception, or train of thought; but not by thought about that movement or appetite, nor yet about its roots in our appetitive constitution.

The deterministic explanation works with the distinction be- tween what comes by nature, and what is done by design. We carry on our deliberation by design; the response leading to action comes by nature, when the appropriate excitants have been brought into focus; it comes as the sneeze comes, when we have inhaled the titillating dust. For we sneeze by nature, though we take snuff by design. We know how to deliberate—not, of course, in a manner to satisfy Pericles, but in such fashion as we are able. We know how to think our situation out, but we cannot know how to feel about it, as it finally appears in the light of the deliber- ative process. For feeling, or active inclination, comes by nature, not by manipulation. We do not know how to sneeze, but only how to take snuff. The parable is, of course, inadequate, for though we do not know how to sneeze, we know roughly what form a sneeze will take. When we deliberate, we do not yet know what form our active inclination will take, when and if it comes.

It may sound as though the determinist made a quite unreal division of our mental life into alternate and mutually exclusive stretches, the active performances we know how to carry out, and the responses which come by nature: as though, for example, we began by feeling a concern about our situation, which led us to switch over into the performance of considering it; the conclusion of the consideration switching us back again into the responsive mood, so as to conceive active inclinations about the matter we have been considering. But in truth the determinist is committed to no such alternation of moods. He is free to make his own the dictum of Aristotle: choosing is an appetitive deliberation, or a deliberative appetition, call it which you will. There are, of course, occasions when an initial concern commits us to a mental performance in which concern plays no further part. If I am interested in a trip to the Antipodes, I am committed to a reckoning of the cost. The calculation is a routine performance, in which no further intervention of feeling is appropriate. At the most we may say that the interest which impelled me to begin, supports me in proceeding. Only when I have finished the arithmetic, is a fresh reaction of the heart called for. How do I feel about the expedition, now I see what a hole it will make in my purse? But arithmetic is no more than a move in the game of deliberation; it is not deliberation itself. In the typical deliberation fresh waves of feeling are constantly breaking upon us, bidding us to take one consideration seriously and to discount another, to pursue one path opening among our reflections, and to pass another by. The determinist's case is not that performance and sentiment alternate; he may hold, on the contrary, that they are natural partners; that their separation is exceptional, and never total. His case is that however conjoined and mutual their action, they act differently. Performance is what I know how to do; concern is the response of nature to what my eyes, or my thoughts, bring before her. And when I am thinking out that to which nature may respond, I cannot be thinking out what her response will be.

ii. *The great tautology of free decision*

So far we have simply been developing the determinist's explanation, allowing no libertarian objections but such as tended to draw it out. It is time that we gave the libertarian an innings, and propounded his most serious refutation. His line of argument is not to criticise the detail of the determinist thesis, but to reject it as *in toto* irrelevant. What, after all, was the determinist called upon to explain? The predicament of a man trying to make a decision, and at the same time to think of that decision as causally prefigured in its antecedents. And what has the determinist explained? The predicament of a man deliberating about a future action, and trying at the same time to think of that action as causally prefigured. And that is not the same thing at all. After all the deliberation in the world, a man may still be left with alternatives, between which he has simply to decide. Deliberation, by clarifying the issues, and evoking mutually opposed sentiments, may only make the difficulty of the choice more evident. My religion, or my country? My honour, or my love? My father, or my mistress? Such dramatic clashes of principle may be rare. It is more usual to find the interest involved on one side far the more important. Nevertheless, it may not be involved in so important a degree as its rival. Hence the almost hourly dilemma: 'That, if you press it, is my duty; but then this would be so great a satisfaction!' Such practical dilemmas are seldom solved by casuistry, or by any other intellectual technique. Nor are they, in the practice of honest men, solved by waiting for sentiment, or for undirected action, to commit us on one side or the other. We have to decide.

Whatever its causes, reasons or conditions may be, there is such a thing as the act of deciding, anyhow in the view of the agent. We may not often see ourselves as engaged in decision—by the time we are at it, we have little leisure for watching ourselves do it. A more typical occasion of self-consciousness, is that of having a decision to make. It is here that the determinist's evasion took place: for a man thinking towards a decision, he substituted a man thinking with the hope of leaving himself no decision to make. A man thinking towards a decision sees himself as clarifying alternatives between which to choose. But the man shown us by the determinist is thinking out his situation, in the hope of evoking a simple or one-sided response to it. If he began with alternative proposals, he means to end by feeling one alternative to be no alternative at all.

There is nothing unreal about the determinist's instance. It quite often happens that apparent practical dilemmas turn out on analysis to be no dilemmas. But such situations cannot be taken as typical of decision, or of alternative choice. We must take the man who, whether in deliberating or after deliberation, knows that he has a choice to make. The scales do not incline for him, he has to tip them: according to some maxim or principle, very likely; only not a principle formulating the way in which he, the scale-tipping agency, works, but a principle which he, by tipping the scales as he does, will adopt, adhere to, or even create. He may think of the principle as given, and as it were pre-existent. But he cannot think in this way of the decision by which, may be, he will range himself with the principle; he cannot think of it as being prefigured in existent facts, in such a way as to be bound to take the form it will take. It is the impossibility of the man's thinking thus, that we call upon the determinist to explain, and to explain on his own deterministic principles. Why is it, that a man with a decision to make thinks in a way incompatible with the simultaneous entertainment of deterministic ideas about what, in deciding, he will be doing?

The determinist must surely refuse the attempt at any such explanation. He can justly complain that the question we have now put to him involves a logical absurdity. To show what the absurdity is, we will first put forward an analogy and then apply it. Suppose that we have the same story or argument in two versions, one French, the other German. You can then fairly ask to be told how the matter expressed in French idiom demands, or justifies, the phrases used to render it in German. But you cannot ask to be told what there is in the French text, to account for the Germanicness of the German idiom in which it is alternatively expressed. To understand the relation between the two versions, you must begin by accepting the fact that there are these two languages, each with its own idiom. In the same way it has to be accepted that there are two ways of talking about the one matter, human conduct: the scientific, which analyses it in terms of factors, sequences and uniformities; and the personal, which employs the form of the subject and his acts. Now no one has ever supposed that life can be lived otherwise than in the personal form. The man making a decision is in his own view an 'I', acting; and since the acting is in this case a deciding, he must view his own work as his own decree. In so far as he is using the personal idiom, he cannot use the scientific; just as talking French is incompatible with talking German. And it is nonsensical to ask for a scientific explanation why personal language should be used. It is used because it is the expression, and often the vehicle, of personal existence. And as for personal existence—well, it exists. That a French text employs the French idiom, is an uninformative tautology; and so is the principle, that I cannot regard myself as doing what I view as done. Nothing material can follow from the logical platitude, that a man cannot set himself to decide what he views as decided, say by natural prefiguration, or causal sequence.

We may agree with the determinist, that the reason why he cannot explain that personal idiom which is incompatible with the scientific, is a logical reason. But are we to agree with him, that nothing material follows? He says that the personalness of the personal idiom is a tautology. Now admittedly tautologies are linguistic rules. When they were thought to be the most binding and unalterable of the laws of being, it was by men who took it for granted that correct and serious descriptions were exact reproductions of their objects; anyhow in such a manner exact, as to imply that linguistic necessities were also necessities of nature. We no longer think this sort of thing. We observe that there are often alternative ways, equally valid, of talking about the same matters; and so whichever way of talking we adopt, it appears, together with its linguistic rules, to be planted by us on the object, as a device for interpreting it. Even when we have only one way of talking about some matter, we are more inclined to attribute such a lack of variety to a limitation in man's linguistic resources, than to a compulsive self-revelation of the object. And so in general we say that tautologies reveal no more than the rules for a way of speaking. If they tell us anything about the object, it is only that it is such, as to allow a form of speech with these rules to be hopefully employed about it.

The suggestion, then, of the logical defence we are considering will be, that if I like to think about my voluntary act as something for me to decide, then of course I must think of it as open to decision, and so as undetermined hitherto. But such a way of thinking is just a way of thinking. I can equally well think about it in other ways, if there are any—and there are; for there is anyhow what we have been calling the scientific way, which interprets in terms of necessary sequence; and this, no doubt, will be the proper way to think for scientific purposes.

The force of the suggestion derives from an insinuation that the personal and the 'scientific' ways of mentioning decision bear the same logical relation to what they mention. The insinuation is, however, false. Contrast the example of a double description of vegetable growth, first in teleological, then in quasi-mechanical, terms. Under the teleological convention, we ask what vegetable nature was after (as it were) in the pushing of the roots towards water; under the mechanical, we ask what force, acting upon the vegetable tissue, caused the root-fibres to be built out or prolonged in that direction. In either case we are interpreting physical facts, revealed to us directly or indirectly through sensible phenomena. Nothing but such phenomena can ultimately justify or refute any particular statement made, whether in the one convention or in the other. So we say that the same logical relation obtains between either convention, and that which it is employed to describe.

But it is not like this with the 'personal' and 'scientific' ways of mentioning decision. The logical relation borne by the scientific account to that which it describes is, indeed, the same as the relation borne by both the rival descriptions of vegetable growth to that which they describe. The justification for saying that the causal ground of a decision lies in a certain complex of already existent states of affairs can only be found in observable phenomena. It makes no differences in principle, that some of the phenomena are observed by the witnesses in themselves; or, if you prefer another way of talking, that some of our evidence lies in the self-disclosures of witnesses. It remains that the scientific description refers to a pattern of sequence revealed by the evidence, and not to anything else. Contrast the claim or the admission of a man who says that an act he physically performed was also his deliberate choice. He states what he remembers having done. Moreover, the form of the statement has what we will call a logical continuity with the form of the deed stated. When he says 'I decided to do so-and-so' he is using a form of words which have only to be reset in the present tense, to constitute an operative form of decision. I can make a decision by saying 'I decide . . .', in answer, for example, to a question. 'Well, what do you decide?'—'I decide to stay in until the rain stops.' Though we more commonly speak or act decisively without saying 'I decide', everyone knows that the decisive use of words or movements may be equivalent with the operative use of 'I decide to . . .' and vice versa. Lastly (and this is the vital step in the argument) decisive speech or action, whether involving the use of 'I decide' or not, is that wherein the decision consists. For decision is a human act, the heedful and effective preference of a course of action to at least one alternative; and the act of plumping for what one prefers, whether by saying 'I decide' or not, makes the decision.

Thus any 'scientific' way to describe the coming about of a decision, is just one way of plotting a sequence revealed by the phenomena; whereas personal talk about deciding is a direct mention of the act wherein decision consists. In the same way you cannot understand what a statement is, unless you understand it as the act of someone stating, nor what a promise is, save as the act of someone promising. Statements and promises, like decisions, have their own logical conditions, as well as their own personal forms. I cannot affirm to myself what I see to be excluded by a fact I believe. I cannot take myself to be promising what I know to lie beyond my power. I cannot decide an issue which I take to be determined, whether by my own 'nature and constitution', or by anything else. These may be no better than tautologies, but they derive their tautological force from the characters of human acts.

If you do not choose to consider vegetable growth teleo-logically, you are let off saying certain things about cabbages, but the cabbages will get on as well as before. If you do not choose to view decisions as decisions, well, perhaps you need not; that is, perhaps you can avoid reflecting on what you do. But you will go on deciding, and your decisions will come about by the use of the form your reflection would have observed or stated. You can ask whether the growth of cabbages really has the structure which teleology diagrammatises. You cannot ask whether decision has the form which memory and foresight impute. The point we are making can easily be illustrated. If I draw a diagram to express, let us say, some concatenation of historical events, you may reasonably doubt whether the history has the spatial pattern of the drawing. But if I offer my diagram as a contribution to the growing body of abstract art, it is senseless to ask whether what I am drawing for you has the spatial pattern of my design. When we are deciding, we are not representing or stating anything; nothing is affirmed but the decision itself; a thought which may find its first expression in speech, but must find its last expression in execution.

Thus the form of decision—the form of determining the as yet undetermined—is not a way of thinking about what is done, it is the way of doing it. If this is not done, if what is done has not this form, then not only is there no decision, there is not anything to which decision-language could possibly be applied. And so there is a good sense in saying that our so-called 'scientific' retrospect of the decision, reducing its occurrence to factors and causality, is not the account of a decision at all, but only, let us say, of events in which the decision took shape. If a retrospective account is to mention the decision, it must mention it not 'scientifically' but historically; it must contain the sentence 'I decided' or some honourable equivalent for it.

When we say that a rule is only a tautology, we seem to be claiming an option; not the option of accepting or rejecting it, but the option of employing, or not employing it. To think about vegetable growth teleologically is to employ certain interpretative conventions; but we need not think about vegetable growth teleologically. In the case of human acts, the option is simply to indulge in such forms of act, or not to indulge in them. If I play chess, I must play by the rules; but I need not play chess. If I promise, I must employ the form, and stand by the conditions, of promise-making; but perhaps I can get through life, or we could all concur in getting through life, without making any more promises. It would, surely, be very awkward to do without statements; and hardly less awkward to do without decisions. Is it possible that we should always leave it to feeling or impulse, after taking, impulsively, a good look round? But if we had always done this, should we be men? If we were to start doing it now, we could succeed only by the painful and unrelenting exercise of an insane option: the option never to opt; and is not that a contradiction in terms? For we can scarcely suppose that natural motives, and a mere drifting with the tide of feeling, would keep us to so self-destructive an abnegation. Descartes saw that nothing but an exercise of sovereign will could carry out the experiment of not believing; and equally nothing but an exercise of arbitrary choice could keep up the experiment of not choosing. But it would be an experiment of little value, for proving the separability of choice from the continued enjoyment of human existence. To all intents and purposes, then, the tautologies about choice are rules for being human, or (which is the same thing) laws of human nature.

iii. Argument from regress in explanations

Really, says our determinist, you have made a great noise about nothing, and proved the obvious with much contention. I am somewhat deafened, but not at all confuted. Do I wish to deny that men must make decisions, and make them in form? Of course not. The rules of decision are the rules of decision, as the rules of explanation are the rules of explanation. The function of decision is to decide the issue, not to explain itself; it is a practical, not a theoretical activity. But there is also a theoretical activity, whose function it is to explain. The idiom of explanation is foreign to the business of decision, just as the idiom of decision is foreign to the business of explanation. But that is no reason for denying that the explanation, when it comes, really can explain the decision; or for asserting that there is anything in the decision which is in principle withheld from explanation. While decision is deciding, she holds explanation off; but after the event, she becomes the *corpus vile* of explanatory dissection, and can offer no resistance to her anatomist. While I decide, I may see myself as an unaccountable creator; but having decided, I may call my supposed creation to account. Explanation has the last word.

No, says the libertarian, she has not. The act of explaining is itself personal and voluntary. Explaining, admittedly, is not deciding, but it is the expression of will—the will to explain, rather than to engage in any other form of activity. The sense in which all conscious reasonable behaviour, and not critical choice alone, is choiceful, would require careful definition, and we must for the present defer the attempt. But you must anyhow admit that explaining is a personal activity, of which the 'scientific' cause in any given case is not self-evident, but needs to be established. My explanatory act can never become the *corpus vile* of its own dissection; it calls for another act to anatomise it, and that other again for another. Explanation never has the last word.

Your appeal to an infinite regress, rejoins the determinist, proves nothing that is to the point. I can never see my own eyes by direct vision, but that does not prove that they are not directly visible; another's eyes can see them. The same thing is true of him in turn; he cannot see his own eyes, but another can; and so *ad infinitum*. The last seeing eye we consider is always invisible to itself. Yet the conclusion we draw is that people's eyes are directly visible (though not to them), and similarly we should conclude that acts are open to causal explanation (though always in a further act).

The libertarian will not let the moral pass. Whatever your parable proves, he will say, it certainly does not show that the seeing eye looks to have the visible qualities it has, to anything other than a seeing eye; nor, if we are to argue from analogy, can it suggest that any personal act ever exhibits the pattern of causal uniformity, to anything but a person exercising a further personal act. It is only because there are people exercising themselves in a certain sort of thinking, that there are causal explanations, whether of personal acts or of anything else. Even if explanation could have the last word, personal action would be having the last word, for explanation is personal action. Can we ever have a better reason for admitting the uniformities which causal explanation claims to establish, than we have for admitting that personal agency is what it experiences itself to be? If it sometimes seems otherwise, it is because we fall into a sort of unconscious Platonism, and assign an objective or impersonal subsistence to mental entities like causal explanations. Then indeed the last word will seem to lie with your explanatory truth; that the truth cannot be caught, or known, or stated, except in the act of a person, will then seem accidental, or immaterial. But such a Platonism is nonsense, surely. Explanations are not properly said to be known, or found, but to be made, or offered. The truly revealing verbal form is not 'I know the explanation' but 'I explain the fact'. Only the fact, or perhaps we should say, the state of affairs, is simply there, whether to be known, or to be explained. Explaining, like knowing, is a personal business; but unlike mere knowledge (if there were such a thing) explanation is a lively procedure, the exercise of a self-articulating activity.

It is no use saying, then, that because attempted causal explanation may overtake everything in the end, the claims of active self-consciousness to vindicate its own causal inexplicability are overridden or extinguished. For nothing can do any explaining except a person; and the person experiences himself personally and self-determinatively, even when he explains. Everything, including personal action, is open to whatever degree and sort of explanation its nature allows. But in judging the character of personal action, and assigning the explanations proper to it, how can we refuse the evidence offered by the form of consciousness through which it comes about?

What is the upshot of the discussion? Let us retrace our steps, and recall the starting-point. We were considering the predicament of a philosopher, who admitted that he shared a universal human weakness: that the mood of decision was for him a mood of belief in undetermined power to determine choice. But this man thought himself well-founded in the subsequent and retrospective judgement, that his decision must in every case have been prefigured by states of affairs existing within and without him, before he made it. Our question was, whether such a man, in his retrospective mood, could not take a further step, and show, on the grounds of his general causal hypothesis, why decision had to be made in a mood exclusive of belief in its own determination according to causes. A causal explanation of the cause-blindness of decision would add greatly to the strength of causal determinism. But the impossibility of such an explanation, an impossibility we hope we have demonstrated, does not refute the determinist doctrine. All we have done is to establish two stories in parallel, a 'scientific' and a 'personal' story, each with its own idiom. If the stories conflict—and on the determinist's view, they seem at least to do so—we have still to strike a balance. Is one false, the other true, or are both partially false? We have done nothing, so far, to settle the question. We have merely entered a plea that both witnesses should be heard, rather than that one should be ruled out of court, because he does not speak with a theoretical, or truth-telling, voice.

The question remains to be judged; and how strong, how plausible after all the determinist case appears! How likely it seems that in deciding, in the heat of action, we all of us suffer from an inevitable limitation of view, an inability to get outside our own skins; whereas in the cool hour of a detached reflection we can hope to view ourselves as though from without, as unprivileged items in the uniform structure of a contemplated world. Is it not this detachment of view, sometimes pompously described as self-transcendence, which dignifies us above the beasts, and properly deserves the name of reason? Does not the mood of decision share the self-obsession of appetite, while the mood of scientific reflection resembles the impersonality of justice? If we are bound to decide in the warmth of a libertarian belief, ought we not to think and to reason with a deterministic detachment?

CHAPTER VIII

CONDUCT AS UNDERSTOOD AND PREDICTED

i. *Meaning of conduct and meaning of speech*

W E resume the discussion on a new basis. We allow that the idiom of decision-thinking, and the idiom of causal construction, are different idioms, and that the first cannot be reduced to, or explained from, the second. It remains to delimit the sphere proper to each. For the purposes of our new discussion, we define determinism as a doctrine which restricts the idiom of decision as closely as possible to the sphere of action, libertarianism as a doctrine which extends it into the realm of theory. The libertarian, that is, takes the way we think in the mood of decision as evidence for a theoretical belief, belief in a sort of agency undetermined by natural law. The determinist disallows the inference; in his opinion, our action exemplifies natural law as much as anything does; only the mood of decision employs an idiom unable to express the thought of its own subjection to laws.

Having entrenched our disputants in their respective positions, let us see what they have to say for themselves. The libertarian is a man of feeling; his conviction, he is inclined to think, needs no defence, beyond the exposure of unnatural sophistries advanced against it; he fumbles for a positive argument. Meanwhile his opponent, a rationalist to the finger-tips, with his batteries of logic all in order, opens fire. The ground, he says, for barring decision-thinking from the realm of theory is plain enough. It is that such thinking is theoretically impotent. There is no way to understand the occurrence of anything, save by rules uniformly determining effects. To say that a person simply chose to do what he did, makes no contribution to the understanding of his choice. If we are to make any advance, we must place the occurrence of his act under some scheme of natural uniformity. But then we have abandoned the decision-idiom for the scientific.

Our libertarian is happy to be provided with an occasion for his chosen manoeuvre; now he has something to counter-attack. He opens his assault in the following terms. Have you not overstated the scope of the scientific method, by saying that there is no way to understand the occurrence of anything, save by rules uniformly determining effects? Unless, of course, you mean to prejudge the issue by putting your own definitions on the terms. If asking how the occurrence of an event is to be understood, is defined as meaning, 'What was the cause of it?' then none but causal answers will serve. But it is not true that every demand for explanation is a demand for causes. If one of our neighbours acts in a way which, while unexpected, is, we think, deliberate, our curiosity need not take the form of asking 'What caused him to do it?' We may just as well ask 'What is he up to?' If we do ask 'What caused him to do it?' we shall expect an answer in terms of the circumstance or occasion which set him the problem, or afforded him the opportunity, in face of which he acted. And if an answer on these lines satisfies us, we shall be supposing, rightly or wrongly, that our friend's act was a routine affair, and that the situation being what it was, he had virtually no choice. But if an account of the occasion for his action still leaves us wondering why he acted as he did, and not otherwise, we shall pursue the enquiry by asking 'What was he up to?' And it is only if this question, or some equivalent for it, seems appropriate, that we can be said to be interesting ourselves in our friend's action, as an action.

The answer to the question 'What was he up to?' will not take the form of assigning a cause; but what form will it take? Should our reply perhaps endeavour to state in third-person language what our friend might be supposed to tell himself, in first-person language, about his intentions; supposing, of course, that he were to take the trouble, supposing that he were entirely honest with himself, and supposing that his self-knowledge left nothing to be desired? 'Supposing . . . supposing. . . .' There are a lot of supposes here, and none of them, even if they are granted, casts any light on our reading of our friend's behaviour. For though he gives himself the most candid and perspicuous account of his plans, I have no access to his silent discoursings; if I do give a representation of them, I shall have to make it up for myself. And from what evidence am I to construct it? From what my friend visibly does and publicly says; sometimes from what he does, alone. But if I can anyhow interpret what he does, sufficiently to found upon it a story about his intentions, then it seems simpler to say that the story I give is my interpretation of what he does. Why introduce the reference to an imaginary perfect story he might tell himself about himself, but probably does not bother to tell himself; or, if he does, tells himself most inaccurately, and with a strong bias to self-justification?

But how is my seeing what my friend does, to give me the understanding of what he is up to? A key to the mystery may be found in our common understanding of speech. We tried the linguistic key just now, indeed, but we mishandled it, substituting for the true object of our enquiry (our friend's behaviour) a mythical linguistic object (what he tells himself about it). That is not how the key of language works—not by substitution, but by analogy; by showing us that the understanding of behaviour, though direct, is analogous to the understanding of speech. The analogy is helpful, because speech is the typical case of what is intelligible; if behaviour is intelligible as speech is, then it is intelligible indeed. The analogy is close, because speech itself is but a specialised form of behaviour, and the intelligibility of speech is nothing but the intelligibility of behaviour made artificially clear.

Consider the series: behaviour, emphatic behaviour, informative pantomime, speech. A simple story will illustrate the transitions between these four forms of intelligible action. The shipwrecked sailor lands on a savage coast, only to discover his fatal omission—he has brought pipe and tobacco with him, but left the matches behind. He stumbles upon a kraal of Hottentots, and sees, to his immeasurable delight, a little man making flame with a fire-drill. He grasps what the little man is up to, but he is not master of the process at a single view. The accommodating and perceptive Hottentot appreciates at once his interest and his frustration. He goes through the process again, but this time with emphasis, acting it at the sailor. Once more the flame kindles, and is caught on a reed. The grateful mariner withdraws, and sets about the making of his own apparatus. He finishes it, he works it, confident of a happy smoke. Alas, the drill smoulders, it will not burn. Back goes the sailor to the Hottentot, with his tail between his legs. The benevolent savage, at that moment discussing with his family an appetising joint of man-flesh, presses the sailor to dine. The sailor is eager to explain that hunger is not the occasion of his visit. But how explain? He falls into a pantomime of fire-making. The clouds gathering on his host's dusky brow are scattered by the light of understanding. He rises from the festive board, he fetches the fire-drill and kindles flame, describing the process, as he performs it, in the simple language of his mother-tongue. Alas, how hard it is to teach a new dog old tricks! The sailor's fire-drill fails again; but his memory for a euphonious vocabulary holds. Once more he puts Hottentot hospitality to the proof. But this time he has no need of pantomime. 'Bomba-bomba mulamba bu!' he exclaims, and is understood directly.

The moral of the fable is, that if simple behaviour were not intelligible in principle, it could not be made intelligible by emphasis, nor could it be put across in pantomime, nor, at the final stage, formalised into speech. The introduction of emphasis adds a secondary purpose to action: to inform one's neighbour, as well as to achieve one's act. In pantomime the informative intention survives alone, and passes over from pantomime into speech, when shorthand vocal signs are substituted for the tedious elaboration of mimetic action.

Now suppose you are listening to a delightful story with an unpredictable dénoument, and suppose that the narrator is inventing as he goes along not, perhaps, the actual plot, but anyhow the manner of introducing the points, and of contriving the crisis. You can almost see the bright bubbles of invention rise from the deep bottom of the mental cask, as the epigrams, the whimsical phrases, are thrown freshly out. If you have a friend who can give you this kind of pleasure, I do not think that, while you are under the spell, it occurs to you to ask what causes him to go on like this. If you did ask, you would be content to say that he is moved by the desire to please you, by delight in the exercise of a charming gift, by just a tincture, perhaps, of pardonable vanity. These are his motives for talking, and for talking his best; but they do not determine what form that *best* should take, nor does it occur to you to concern yourself with such a question. Your wits are concentrated on seeing what he is up to, and guessing what he will be up to next.

What is our purpose in recalling an experience of this kind? Not to show that there are pieces of speech-behaviour free, in their small detail, from determining causes. Nothing we have said will prove anything of the sort. Those bubbles of invention, for example, which rise from the bottom of the mental cask, may have escaped from a sediment about which Freudian or Jungian psychologists have a right to be heard. All we have wished to show by the evocation of the situation is something less ambitious —that there is plenty for the listener to puzzle at, without ever raising causal considerations. To you, in such a posture of mind, the explanation of any stroke in the verbal picture is its contribution to the design. Of the whole thing, there is no explanation; it is what your friend makes up, it is the triumph of his wit. It would be the same if you watched him miming, with genius, a dumb charade. And it will be the same if you watch him extricate himself, by clever improvisation, from a difficulty of real life.

No doubt when we come to real life the part played by determining causes is greater and more pressing .The flutter of fancy is a sweet diversion; the day's work is not a brave invention extemporised by us. It is a response to pressing needs and inescapable claims; to forget them is to reckon without the host. The value of free fancy is the value of a pure case; when we compare it with the mixed cases, it helps us to see one element that goes to the mixture. The inventions, the extemporisations, the decisions of real life may be sternly commanded by the exigences they meet; but to acknowledge the stringency of their occasions need not stand in the way of our taking them for what we invent, extemporise, choose, decide; and this, indeed, is how we do take them.

ii. *Several workings of analogy*

It may help us to see more exactly what we are saying if we examine a somewhat obvious objection. It runs as follows. 'You are attempting to distinguish' says the determinist 'between two methods for interpreting trains of events. On the one side you **want** to put explanation in terms of causal uniformities, on the **other**, understanding in terms of active purpose; and your whole **drift** is to suggest that they are markedly different. But are they? When I am said to have a direct understanding of what my neighbour is up to in his action, or of what he means by his discourse, what then is the nature, or the structure, of the understanding I enjoy? I observe the several moves he makes, and the things he successively says, in extricating himself from a practical difficulty. And I am to understand it; that is, I am to see how one action leads on to another. For if his course of conduct remains for me a series of disconnected events, then I precisely do not understand it. I must grasp the connexions; but what connexions?

'If Henry follows up action A with action B, I must be able to see that it is in general human, or more in particular Henrician, to act in such a sequence. But what is this to say, except that I am interpreting his conduct by uniformities, whether belonging to the human character, or to the Henrician? And what else do I do, when I interpret trains of physical events by physical causality? Since Hume's time, we have not wished to place on causality any stronger sense than conformity with a rule of uniform sequence; such sequence being taken to express either the character of physical nature in general, or that of some more restricted physical kind. If this is what we mean by causal interpretation, then our reading of our neighbour's conduct is also causal interpretation, whether we call it so or not. And the equation is confirmed by a consideration of the conditions for success in the two cases. In commonsense causal interpretation (since technical science does not here come into view) the prime necessities are relevant experience, and a just feeling for analogies; and what else do we require in making personal interpretations? What else but previous experience of our fellows, and a nose for analogies between situations, persons and passions?'

Such is the determinist's case for breaking down the distinction we have been erecting. What are we to say to it? There is one very neat reply, but it is not ultimately the most effective. We will state it as a step in the direction of a more decisive answer. The neat reply is this. There is a factor lacking from personal interpretation which is vital to physical-causal explanation. If I call A physically the cause of B, I am taken to have isolated an event-pattern A, and to be claiming that whenever it recurs, a formally constant consequence, B, accompanies it. Thus the proposition that in any given case A is the cause of B can be refuted in two ways. First, it may be shown that the A and the B before us are not really an A-and-B in the sense intended by the causal rule 'A produces B'. Or second, it may be shown that in any other single case observed, an event-pattern answering to the A defined by the rule failed to produce a B as defined by the rule. By the first refutation we refute the applicability of the rule to the case, by the second we refute the rule itself. Either refutation will overthrow the statement that (in virtue of the rule) A causes B in the given instance.

Now in the exercise of personal interpretation the first of these refutations might be allowed, though with a rather different context; the second not at all. Suppose you tell me that Henry's conduct is inexplicable, and I reply, 'Not in the least; people are always doing B as a follow-up to A.' You may perfectly well rejoin: 'True enough; but what Henry has just done isn't really a case of B, and I am not even sure that the antecedent of it was a genuine case of A, either.' But you cannot get away with the rejoinder: 'You say people are always doing B as a follow-up to A. Nonsense. Last Tuesday week George, having been led to do A, did not follow it up by doing B, or anything like it.' If you said this, I should make short work with you. 'Don't be tiresome' I should retort. 'You know perfectly well that "People are always doing X" means at the most that there are always people doing it, and implies no denial of there being also people doing otherwise. All I meant by my use of the phrase was, that there is abundant analogy for such a line of conduct; that it is one among the admitted human possibilities.' By such a retort on my part you would, I trust, be silenced. And what would your silence admit? That to intepret an action by general human analogy is to interpret it merely as possible, not as necessary; and this is not to interpret it as caused; for the operation of causes is necessary, by definition.

So much for what we have called the neat, but not wholly cogent, reply to the determinist's contention; not wholly cogent, because it can be set aside as resting on an accidental effect of human ignorance. For, it may be said, probable effects are, admittedly, not sheer effects, nor probable causes sheer causes. Yet probable causes are probable *causes*, and probable effects, probable *effects*; and where there are neither causes nor effects, there are neither probable causes, nor probable effects. A probable cause is nothing but a cause, stated as a likely guess; and to guess at a cause is to believe there is a cause which, but for our ignorance of detail, we might with certainty determine. Now it may be that, in personal matters, our common ignorance of psychological imponderables condemns us to put up with probable causes, probable effects. But our interpretation will still be causal, so far as it is an interpretation.

If we do not wish our argument to be brushed away by this rejoinder, we shall need to introduce a further point. We shall have to say to the determinist: But your story falsifies what we know ourselves to do. When we say: 'He reacted thus and thus to such and such a situation, and there is plenty of analogy for people doing so, though admittedly they sometimes do otherwise' we are not stating a probability at all. The evidence we cite establishes in our eyes not the probability, but the certainty that it is often a genuinely open choice before human beings, to act in the way we mention; and the contrary evidence which we do not cite, but admit, establishes that the opposite line of conduct is often a choice equally open. As to Henry's having embraced the choice he did embrace, that was not a probability either—he did embrace it. It is true, of course, that our interpretation of our neighbours in general is seldom indubitable, so that, if you like to say so, 'probability' is scrawled all over the picture. But, having admitted the consideration in general, we discount it in particular. It may be that we are only talking probably; but we are not talking about probabilities.

An open choice is, no doubt, a possibility of a kind; but it is possible not by relation to our ignorance; it is possible by relation to a man's power of choice. To call a choice possible is not to say that the situation, so far as we can define it, allows of several human responses, but that the further degree of definition which would eliminate alternative possibilities, eludes us for the present. It is to say that it is open to the man to do this if he likes. Choice, by definition, lies between alternatives. That an alternative is genuinely and psychologically open to choice, can be supported by the observation that people have chosen it. That people have sometimes failed to choose it, has no tendency to show that it is closed to choice. 'Genuinely and psychologically open' contrasts with 'theoretically open'. It is theoretically open to a sane and happy bridegroom to hang himself upon his wedding-day; but evidence and analogy do nothing to support the real openness of the choice. Example confirms that it is open to a bridegroom to take his bride on honeymoon to France; the fact that many bridegrooms take their brides elsewhere, is no evidence against the real openness of the French alternative.

We will now take up a question posed above, and still unanswered: the question how it is, that we see in our neighbour's conduct a firm transition from one act to another, if we cannot exhibit it as the instance of a binding sequence-rule? For in the province of physical explanation, what we mean by a firm transition is one taken to exemplify an invariable consequence. What, then, takes the place of necessary sequence in the interpretation of behaviour? The answer is, personal action. The sequence was not necessary, for the alternatives were open. But by his personal act, our neighbour adopted one alternative and rejected the rest. That is how we think, and what in our ordinary descriptions of his behaviour, we are taken to affirm. But how do we come by our thought? How do we justify our affirmation? Through what an old philosophy conveniently called *connaturality*. We are ourselves, as active beings, *connatural with* our neighbours, in other words, we are of the same nature as they.[1] The making of choices, the active decision between alternatives, are things we do ourselves. Without this clue we should be as powerless to give a subjective interpretation of our neighbours, as we are to give a subjective interpretation of physical phenomena.

Although it should be clear to any reasonable mind that we understand our neighbours by connaturality with them, it is notoriously difficult to talk about the process without falling into glaring unrealities, and lying open to philosophical attack. It will not do, for example, to say that we know our neighbours by analogy with ourselves, for we draw no such analogy; the interpretation is immediate. If we must use figures, we may perhaps say that our own active nature serves us less as a standard to which we refer our neighbour's conduct, than as a sensitive organ in which we feel it. It will not do, either, to say that we understand our neighbour by thinking what we would do, if we were he, or by putting ourselves in his place. We do, indeed, sometimes make such an effort of the imagination; but that is a special exercise, and quite unlike our ordinary construction of our neighbour's action.

Here is a comparison which may prove more illuminating than some, and less misleading then most. Consider two cases of my understanding you. In the one case you are describing to me places I have not seen, and events in which I have not participated. In the other case you are expressing your intentions by your handling of a situation; not expressing them at me by acting at me, or with emphasis; but merely acting without any attempted disguise.

Now to take the first case: how do I understand your descrip-

[1] Never mind how we come to be so, whether by identical constitution, common education, or mutual infection.

tion, I who have never been through, nor witnessed, what you describe? Everyone will agree that I form a mosaic of my experience, in response to the suggestions conveyed by your words. I have not seen a tropical forest; but I have seen a forest. I have seen tropical pictures, and so forth. Besides, previous writers and talkers have prepared the way for your story by telling me about the jungle. And so, many of the combinations I require for understanding you are prefabricated in my mind; whole figures of the mosaic-work are ready assembled, and only need fitting into place. All this mosaicking is somehow carried out; but it is done by the nature of the mind, and not by the will. All I do wilfully is attend to your words, and make the general effort of understanding. I do not rake my memory for experiences to supply the pieces I need; the pieces simply come.

And now to take the other case: how do I understand your conduct, I who have never lived your sort of life, nor handled such situations as I see you handle? Shall not I make a mosaic of small pieces from the active experience I have had—not this time from my past seeing or hearing, but from my past doing, feeling and thinking? And will not it be as true here, as in the other case, that many of the combinations I require, even though unrealised in my own previous action, will be ready to hand, prefabricated in the course of my construing other men's behaviour, and above all, no doubt, in my construing of your previous behaviour? Here, as in the other case, the mosaicking is all effected by the nature of the mind, not by the will; all I wilfully do, is attend to your words and actions.

We had better admit that the language of 'mosaic-work' is, in either application, a pretty violent metaphor. What we are talking about is in neither case the coming together of a composite object, but the enjoyment of a simple power, the power of understanding what is heard. But the achievements of this power are limited and conditioned by the previous experience, or the previous activity, of the agent. It is only by referring the several elements of that achievement to their several sources, that we pulverise the work of the understanding into a mosaic. The appearance of mosaic-work is produced by an artificial mapping of the control exercised by our past over our present.

The degree and stringency of such control is by no means equal in the two cases we have considered. When we understand a description in visual, tactual or auditory terms, we are far more tied down to our sources in previous sensory experience, than when we understand conduct in terms of action. To explain the distinction we wish to draw, it may be convenient to accept a somewhat Cartesian account of sensation. Let us say that the qualities of sight, hearing, touch are all subjective, a paintbox of sensory colours with which Human Nature is provided. With these she paints her pictures of the world; but, by an inscrutable dispensation (the Cartesian philosophy assures us) our Nature is prohibited from bringing forth or spreading any of her colours, except on occasion of the physical presence to her of the object, for which that colour is conventionally appropriate. And indeed, Cartesians or anti-Cartesians, we all know that we can neither see nor hear when and what we will, but only what is there to be heard or seen, and when it is there. Imaginary objects will not evoke the senses; only real objects will do it. Imagination herself is tied down to the rearrangement of sensation previously enjoyed.

But now (our Cartesian story proceeds) Human Nature is provided with further innate resources: passions and emotions neatly stoppered down in phials, compressed springs of intention and initiative ready to be triggered off. What sort of object is needed to evoke these powers? And how must the object be placed, relatively to the person in whom the powers reside? Is it not plain that the presence of the object to our senses is in these cases quite inessential? New qualities of awe, and of aesthetic delight, of compassion or of sympathetic indignation can be evoked on hearsay; and, what is more to our present purpose, new ingenuities of action can be invented by us, for dealing with situations which exist, so far, in our imaginations only. It would be awkward for us if it were not so; we should never be able to see how to meet our difficulties until they had overtaken us.

But the power we have of making novel reactions to imagined

objects on our own account, is equally available to us for the purpose of understanding our neighbours' conduct. We can understand in them attitudes and intentions which we have ourselves
never experienced or exerted; anything we could conceive ourselves to do or feel, we can see them do or feel, and even more;
the possible range of our reaction and invention being more
widely stretched by the otherness of our neighbours' lives, than
by the conceivable variability of our own. This fact is as evident in
the case of speech, as it is in the case of conduct. To understand a
talker is to appreciate what he says, both as a possible use of the
common language, and as a possible thing a man should want to
say. But it need not be anything I can conceive myself ever wanting to say, nor even anything I could of myself have invented for
my neighbour to say. My power to conceive is not in such a case
extended by its own inventiveness; what stretches it is the perceptible process of my neighbour's conduct, the audible voice of
my neighbour's speech.

The discussion we have been indulging arose out of a deterministic objection. There is no great difference, said our determinist,
between causal explanation and personal understanding. To explain
an explosion is to appreciate it as what, under such circumstances,
dynamite does. To understand our neighbour's behaviour is to
appreciate it as what, under such circumstances, a man does. This
was the objection; and what has been our answer? First we
showed up the formal falsity of the comparison. 'What dynamite
does' means 'What dynamite *always* does'. 'What a man does'
means 'What we can conceive a man's doing, and what, in the
present instance, a particular man (Henry) is seen to do'. We
proceeded to turn our attention on this 'Is seen to do,' and asked
ourselves how it works. We answered, 'Through connaturality
between persons'; and in developing the meaning of connaturality, we have uncovered a fresh formal difference between personal
understanding and physical explanation. Analogy plays a vital
part in each, but it is a different part. In physical explanation we
analogise between one observation and another. In personal
understanding we do not analogise at all. We make a direct

employment of powers which are *de facto* analogous with our neighbour's powers, and which, if they were not, would not serve us for understanding him.

That is the basic contrast; and the contrast holds good, even when we proceed to admit that the act of analogising plays a subsidiary part in our understanding of our neighbours, whether before or after the moment of comprehension. Before I manage to understand my neighbour's conduct, I may draw analogies from his previous behaviour, or from other men's. Such reasoning gets me into position for my act of understanding; but when I make the act, it is not the perception of an analogy, but the appreciation of an intention. It is not: 'So his acting thus was the instance of a rule X,' but 'So that is what he was up to!' Equally well, after the moment of comprehension, I may question my understanding of my neighbour's behaviour, or you may question it; and either to you or to myself I may justify it by invoking analogy. 'Why not?' I say, 'People often do', or 'Last year on a similar occasion, Henry himself...' or 'After all, didn't the Emperor Napoleon...?'

Analogies like these, so far from weakening our case, confirm it. For what is appealed to is one example or more of a personal conduct which has itself been directly understood. If we did not rightly appreciate Napoleon's intention, or see what Henry was up to on the cited occasion last year, the analogy will cast no light on the present case. We analogise from the clear to the dubious, not from the instances supporting a generalisation to the new example of it. And such analogising as we do employ is neither essential nor conclusive. I can be sure, and rationally sure, about my reading of my neighbour, when I can quote no close analogy in my support. And to take the opposite side, I may cite all the analogy in the world for my view of him, without rationally obliging you to accept it.

My power to understand my neighbour is not exercised as a spelling out of determined uniformities; it is exercised as voluntary action is exercised, as something I can do; though what I do in this case is to keep up with what my neighbour is doing, in his use of a power which he exercises as self-determining. It is because my own reaction to circumstances is potentially self-varying over an amazing range, that I can keep up with the turns and twists of my neighbour's intention, under the guidance of the visible signs his behaviour affords. You can hold, if you like, that both my neighbour's behaviour and my own are determined to the last detail by universal principles, which an adequate science would unearth. What you cannot hold is that my ordinary understanding of my neighbour's action or speech is a deterministic understanding. It simply is not true that whatever sense we do make of our neighbours' lives we make by bringing them down to uniformities. And this is all we undertook to prove. The ultimate validity of the common form of personal understanding is still under judgement. We are simply refuting the contention, that there is only one way of understanding any train of events, the scientific. The personal way of understanding, and the causal, are both ways of understanding. It makes sense, therefore, to weigh the contributions they respectively make to our thought about the occurrence of human actions. We cannot ban the comparison on the ground that the idiom of decision is purely pragmatic, and incapable of fulfilling any interpretative function.

iii. *Prediction of free acts*

We have made our determinist listen to a lengthy exposition. What will be his reaction to it? 'I am glad to observe' he may now remark, 'that you still do not suppose yourself to have disproved our principal contention. For anything you maintain so far, it may still be true that an account in terms of natural uniformities will cover human conduct to the last detail. All you pretend to show is that another sort of account is possible, and that it does, indeed, serve the purposes of our common social intercourse. I can allow all you claim, and still assert that a more minute and difficult account, couched in what you have been calling scientific terms, must take precedence in any seriously theoretical context. It is one thing to get on with one's neighbours; to understand the pattern of nature in the production of human conduct is quite another thing.

'Such is my view, but if I have understood you rightly, it is not yours. You establish a lacuna in nature's uniformity, and make it the field of something called freewill. Faced with the objection that your freewill is an unaccountable power, whose operations defy construction, you help yourself out by crediting to it an order and intelligibility all its own, not scientific or natural, but personal. The story is plausible, but the gain is not great; for you run yourself into a dilemma. Have you forgotten the ground on which you build your whole libertarian faith? Is it not that the man in the posture of decision cannot regard the decision he is trying to make, as being prefigured in states of affairs already existing, or as liable to be certainly forecast from such states of affairs by an omniscient observer? But now, seeing the absurdity of a mere chaos in human conduct, you allow decision to be subject to a sort of rationalisation; and I cannot for the life of me see how you are to get rationalisation without readmitting prediction. Here, then, is the dilemma I propose to you. Either your purposive, or personal interpretation of free volition is such as often to support prediction, or it is ineffective as interpretation. If it is ineffective as interpretation, it fails to perform the function for which you invoke it; whereas if it supports prediction, it is inconsistent with the ground of your position, and no less so than the "scientific" interpretation you abhor.'

How are we to meet this dilemma? We had better begin by clearing up a preliminary point. Prediction is not the stumbling-block in any case; the offence lies in the grounds of prediction. To put it picturesquely, effects not yet actual, but predictable on grounds of natural law, are felt to be already 'sleeping in their causes', so that the part of decision can be only to awaken them into act; and if that is all decision does, decision is not decision. The question to be settled, therefore, is whether prediction on grounds of purpose involves this sort of predetermination by the antecedents of decision, or not.

That prediction as such is innocent, can be seen from the supposition of time-slip clairvoyance, a supposition which some of our contemporaries are prepared to take seriously. An examination of what fortune-tellers and other queer folk are apparently able to do, suggests the drawing of a fundamental distinction. Some of the seers' successes look like subconsciously inferential guesses from present facts; facts themselves, no doubt, appreciated by an abnormal sensitivity. It often looks, for example, as though the general lines of a young man's career have been forecast from a clever reading of his character, circumstances and ambitions. But other equally successful predictions have not this sort of look at all. Their whole form is different; they present such things as isolated scenes of fear or delight; vignettes without a context, of which neither seer nor enquirer can at the time interpret the bearings. If they are horrors, we do not know how to avoid them; if they are joys, we cannot run to meet them; for we do not know in what direction to go. In such cases, some do not hesitate to suppose that the clairvoyant mind has made a raid on the future, and returned with a fragmentary capture.

The accepted paradoxes of relativity-physics make so bold a supposition almost intelligible. For if we say that the clairvoyant mind has raided the future, what are we saying, but that it has run ahead of contemporary fact? But the contemporary object is now defined by us in physical terms. To say that I can see what is contemporary only, is to say that nothing is now visible but what lies in the path of a ray now striking my eyes. And in general, the limitation of sensory awareness to the contemporary, is simply the limitation of it to things effectively geared with the nervous system by lines of force. Now suppose clairvoyance; suppose a sensitivity of the embodied mind to bodily facts not joined to her by bodily lines; and you suppose a perceptivity which has jumped the system of physical rails, by reference to which contemporaneity is defined. There seems then no reason why the clairvoyant mind should seize an object contemporaneous with her act of perception—on the contrary, it is pure accident if she does. The past and the future lie as open to her as the present. The limits of her range are set, not by the rigid boundaries of the contemporaneous, but by the fluctuating confines of the interpretable. What she can make nothing of, she will not effectively apprehend.

We do not mention this speculation as deserving of credit, but simply as presenting what would constitute the extreme case of a prediction unembarrassing to freedom. For on this, it may be fantastic, hypothesis, the ground of the seer's prevision is simply the event he foresees, in the very futurity of its occurrence. It is an object to his knowledge for no other reason than its happening there; as to what puts it there, a free decision will serve as well as any other process, power or cause. The free decision is then the reason for the event, and the event is the reason for the seer's prevision of it. It is clear that in such a case prevision cannot embarrass freedom. Let all the angels, or all the gipsies in the world foresee my choices; they have only foreseen them because I make them.[1]

We have taken an extreme example, but it will suffice to show that our sense of freedom is not undermined by prediction as such. The offence begins when prediction has its ground in states of affairs already existing, before a supposedly free decision is made; for then it must seem that the effect of decision is 'sleeping in its causes' before we decide upon it. But what now are we to say about our ordinary predictions of our neighbours' conduct, or theirs of ours? These are no sort of crystal-gazings, or hariolations; they are based on no psychic raids into the future, but on practical inferences from the present or the past. Is it any less embarrassing for us to think of our unmade decisions as 'sleeping' in already formed purposes, than it is to think of them as 'sleeping' in existent causes? Is there, indeed, any difference between the two suppositions? Since we have agreed that a reasonable determinism will find the causes of our decisions in our purposive being itself, reacting to the circumstances of the time.

To start with the last point—there is certainly a difference between the two suppositions. Both find the ground of prediction in

---

[1] But suppose the gipsies tell me their foresight, and I see the means to disappoint it. Am I free to do so? The puzzle is merely verbal. Previsions are not guaranteed by that solidity which invests physical perceptions. They are no more than imaginative phantasms, presenting themselves with a certain spontaneous force, and in a certain mental context. They cannot be known to be foreknowledge except by being fulfilled. If I frustrate them by heedful avoidance, they are thereby made to have been forewarnings, not foreknowings.

something labelled 'purpose', but they view this thing in different ways and make different forms of inference from it. Causal analysis sees purposes as states or processes squaring with general descriptions and coming under general rules. Personal interpretation sees purposes as intentions entertained by men; the abstract 'purpose' being here a mere shorthand for Tom or Dick purposing so-and-so.

It is obvious that we often have good reason to suppose a man will persist in a line of purpose once adopted. Johnny, for example, has come to the fair. He has a shilling to spend. He deliberates at length how to lay it out. Rejecting the swings and roundabouts, he plumps for the coconut shy, and gives his shilling to the man. We shall now predict with confidence that he will have his shillingsworth. He will take up the wooden balls, and do his best with each of them. We shall be much surprised if he leaves off in the middle of his turn, unless, of course, he suffers an accident; say his first throw dislocates his shoulder, or his second knocks out the showman. Otherwise he will finish the course.

What is the basis of so confident a prediction? No more than this, that every decision takes some time to execute; by making a decision we bind ourselves to see it through, over a tract of time. Such binding is no bondage, it is the mere condition of any achievement whatsoever. And if people predict our behaviour on the strength of it, they are not denying our act of decision; they are assuming it to be effective. Johnny decided for the coconut shy; that is why he will throw the fourth ball. But it is important to understand the nature of his commitment. It is not as though his giving of his shilling to the man had put down a pedal in his mind, from which the throwing of the four balls mechanically followed. If he makes one throw after another, it is only because he continues in the purpose he initially adopted.

He need not, of course. We have suggested accidents which would unquestionably remove his will to go on throwing. We may suppose a more interesting case. No sooner has he thrown the first ball, than he remembers the girl at home, and his promise to buy her a bunch of blue ribbon, to tie up her bonny brown hair. On the one hand, he is impelled to go on with the game; on the other, to surrender his remaining three balls to Harry, for the price of sixpence. If he goes on throwing, he upholds, or re-enacts, the statute of his first intention; if he gives up, he repeals it, to make room for another; that of adhering to his promise, by recovering sixpence for poor Jenny's hair-ribbons. Whether he plays the game out, or changes his mind, we shall, in our common way of thinking, impute his action to his simple choice.

But let us return to the original supposition. No second thoughts occur to Johnny; he has his shillingsworth without re-flection, and justifies the expectations of the onlookers; expecta-tions which are unlikely to become vocal, but if they did, might take the form, 'He will throw the fourth ball, because he has chosen' (to play the game). 'Because he has chosen' in such a case does not exclude, but rather implies, the complementary form 'Because he chooses'. For 'Has chosen' means that the choice remains in force; he chose to take up the game, he chooses to play it out.

Johnny himself feels the force of the onlookers' expectation, as they see the champion of All-Muggleton reach for his fourth ball. He knows what they expect him to do, and why—because he has chosen, because he still chooses. Their expectation squares with the form of his choice, as he is aware of exercising it; he cannot pos-sibly feel that their foresight either questions or insults his liberty. It would be otherwise if they were to say to him 'You will throw the fourth ball because you are so constituted that, in the given circumstances, you will want to throw it'. For then they would be claiming to divine a necessity governing his way of choice; whereas all they actually do is to see that he has chosen, and not changed his mind.

The example we have taken is both plain and trivial; but we will dare to extract a common principle from it. A prediction from present or past facts will not call freewill in question, if it is based on previous and standing choice.

The principle is easy enough to formulate; it is not always so easy to see when it applies. That a man who has paid his shilling at the coconut shy should have a standing choice to throw until the balls are finished, affords the simplest sort of case; the case in which the period of standing choice is short, continuous and engrossing. There is nothing else on hand, the player is likely to feel, between paying the money and throwing the last ball. Take by way of contrast a man who has bought himself a partnership in a firm of solicitors. He may be fairly credited with a standing choice to practice his profession in the office of Sharp, Sharp, Sharp, Downey and Sharp; but the choice is in practical abeyance while he eats dinner with his wife, or plays golf with his friends. When it comes back into force, it seems to revive of itself, unbidden; you might be tempted to compare it with hunger, toothache, and other unwished-for visitations. As the impression of the original choice fades with the passage of the years, our friend will come more and more to see his professional work as something incumbent or inescapable, which periodically asserts its claims. But the fading of the original choice will have the compensatory effect of throwing more weight on daily choices. The less he acts by the impetus of his original decision, the more decisions he must make, to keep himself in action. Work is in a sense inevitable, zeal is not; he keeps tipping the balance this way and that between professional activity and the care of his family, his garden, or what you will.

By many gradations, a policy of action may come to be voluntary in an altered sense; it is no longer the uninterrupted prolongation of an unrevoked choice, but it is constantly reaffirmed by many particular choices and, in being reaffirmed, is redefined. The solicitor's effective policy is not simply to practice his profession, though the sky falls; it is to give it a certain place in his life, along with many other interests and claims.

As we continue to advance in this line of development, we shall find ourselves crossing the boundary between chosen policies, and policies of choice. To be a member of the firm was, originally, a policy chosen. But it may well be that our solicitor never at any point laid himself down a line of action, determining the relative claims of his firm and his family. He found himself making *ad hoc* decisions, and treating them as precedents for further decisions;

and so he acquired a policy of choosing, which had never been a policy chosen.

It is all too easy to assimilate policy of choice to involuntary habit; the boundaries between the two are often hard to determine; but in principle the difference is absolute. A man who, met by new circumstances, adheres to a line of choice implicit in previous decisions, is not the victim of his past, as is the slave of a habit. If you think he is, you must be supposing that our living choice would always change direction, were it not for the constraint of our dead deeds; and the supposition is manifestly absurd. Changes of front are the exception, not the rule, because our normal attitude must be one of confidence in our previous decisions. We should not get far in any direction, if we never took for decided what we decided yesterday.

We make many predictions, which appear to discount choice, but suppose it in fact. 'If Johnny remembers his promise to the girl, he will not empty his purse at the coconut shy' may seem to bear comparison with 'If the grease gets between the points, the car will not start'. But Johnny would not feel that your prediction was treating his action as the working of a necessary law. He would take you to be reasoning on the supposition that he is courting Jenny; or that his policy is to keep faith with a lady, whether he loves her or not. But go on to suggest that his policies work in him like natural forces, or that causes comparable with natural forces have simply produced them; insinuate that his devotion is all fatal passion, and none of it active fidelity; deny him any absolute or personal power to determine priorities between sportsmanship and amatory attachment, ribbon-buying and shying at coconuts; then, if he understands what you mean, Johnny will knock you down. Policy and principle are not reckoned to be fate; we view ourselves as each sovereign in our own republic, acting on the line of self-imposed decision, and competent to revise our edicts when we see fit.

'But you will not, surely, revise your policies without occasion; and the occasion may then be called the cause of the change.' No, it may be called the occasion of it. It is platitudinous to say that the sensible man will not change his mind without occasion; but it is contentious to claim that, granted the constitution of his mind, the occasion determines the form of the change. Anyhow when we are thinking in the personal mode, we suppose that the occasion gives us matter for a decision, but that the decision itself is *made* by us. Hour by hour, in the occasions of life, we are forced to re-assess at least the relative importance of our aims or policies; and in this constant balancing of the scales, the voluntariness of our total conduct may be said to lie.

It is obvious that we are not making brand new decisions every moment. But at every moment we act in pursuit of objectives, in obedience to principles, or in execution of policies, themselves resulting from decision and liable to be re-decided. Our conduct may be called freely chosen in so far as we so act, but no further. Not all the principles which motive us express decision. We can decide against instinct, we do not commonly decide for it. I may choose self-destruction, or the mortification of natural appetite; but in a normal state of consciousness I opt neither for self-replenishment nor for self-preservation. It would be mere clowning on the part of a hearty eater, if he said he had decided to satisfy the recurrent demands of hunger, so that he might continue to be of service to the human race. He may decide on any day when, where, and what to eat; but by forbearing to resist appetite he does not adopt a policy of ingestion.

iv. Determinist argument from human dependability

It is a convenient working principle with psychologists that all personal policies have their roots in instinctive urges. The common man, engaged in personal interpretation, either forgets this piece of technical wisdom, or accommodates it to his everyday assumptions. No one can act, he will agree, except in the execution of certain grand policies, dictated, as it were, by Nature herself; but he will claim for mankind a free option between various possible interpretations or developments of Nature's policies. He will take men to be amative or curious by nature, not by choice; but allow Henry and John to act out their curiosity or their amativeness in the way each of them chooses. He will be puzzled, however, to define where natural policy ends, and chosen policy begins; and so he may find it difficult to deal with the determinist argument which fuses them.

The determinist will point out to us that we depend on the consistency of human choice, as confidently as we do on the consistency of human nature. Dependability, he proceeds to argue, supposes systematic predictability; and systematic predictability, natural uniformity. But this hypnotising incantation of abstracts, dependability, predictability, uniformity, masks vital and concrete differences. Dependability needs breaking down into a variety of grounds we have for confidence in the regularity of our friends' conduct; and predictability into a variety of degrees in the regularity we look to find.

The Parry-Joneses come to call. We rely on Uncle Peter and Cousin George to rise to the occasion. There are many things we are sure they will not do. They will not talk across to one another, and ignore the Joneses. They will not go on reading *Country Life* and the *Sporting Times*. They will not insult the Welsh character. But these are negatives. What will they do? Our reliance on them to act characteristically may involve very different expectations: about Uncle Peter the sickening certainty that he will tell the anecdote of the two Irishmen; about Cousin George, that he will sum up his company in the twinkling of an eye, draw them out, pick up the points of their interest, and lead them on into one of those charming conversational games, in the invention of which he has an inexhaustible fertility. In fact, we rely on Uncle Peter to do, alas! exactly what we expect; and with an equal confidence we rely on Cousin George to do what we don't expect. Our expectation in the one case fills in the whole picture; in the other it defines the merest frame, with 'something ingenious and polite' written under it.

But the grounds of our reliance are as various as the degrees of our ability to predict. Sometimes, when we depend upon people, we formulate rules for them: 'I am sure Henry will keep what amounted to a promise'—'Henry would never keep a lady waiting.' Here the ground of our confidence is Henry's presumed concern to observe these very rules. Now as we know from our own case only too well, there is nothing automatic about the keeping of rules; to maintain and strengthen our observance of them may be a matter of constant aspiration. We may be steady—we assume that Henry is—in opting for the rules; but that does not mean that there is no alternative we might be opting for. We attribute to the libertarian an absurd philosophy indeed, if the free choice in which he believes can never point steadily one way, but must always be jibbing about.

At other times our confidence in Henry bears upon what we call his attitude. Men do not easily change their whole way of feeling or reacting; and we, for all our concern about our own liberty, would not wish to be always changing our own. We would like to change it, certainly, once for all to something better and more humane; but having once effected so salutary a change, we would be content to leave well alone. It never occurs to us that our social attitude constrains our free choice; it provides the occasions upon which we make free choices. From a knowledge of a man's attitude you do not predict what he will do, except when there is only one thing to be done. You predict merely that what he does will be of some general character, or point in some general direction. Or, to take another type of situation, our confidence in Henry's line of action may be based on a particular interest which he might perfectly well lose, but which, for the present, we suppose him to maintain. If he is in love with Kate, he will not throw away obvious opportunities of pleasing her; but he might fall out of love with Kate, and take up with Anne or Jane; especially if Henry is the Eighth of that name. After such a change of heart his way of behaving will begin to be quite different.

The last case we will mention is the only one which has any determinist flavour: the case of a set habit. We can get stereotyped reactions out of some old men by pressing (as we say) the right buttons; and other routines they go through anyhow every day, without our pressing any buttons at all. We may set our watches by their motions. It may still be that a sufficient occasion would break the habit—it is not an irresistible compulsion; but if there is no interfering cause, it simply acts. Since no one supposes that these little set ways are expressions of free choice, our confidence in relying on them is no argument against libertarian belief.

All that is required to refute the deterministic argument from commonsense expectation is to distinguish, as we have been doing, the several grounds of such expectation. It is only when we confuse them, and see them all as manifestations of a single principle called predictability, that we raise a metaphysical nightmare.

Viewing the argument more in general, we may see how unpromising it always was. It invokes commonsense against commonsense: commonsense expectation of dependability, against commonsense conviction of free choice. The burden of proof lies on him who alleges that commonsense is thus at war with itself. Of course commonsense language employs apparent absolutes, talking at one time of unqualified predictability, at another of unqualified freedom. But it is false philosophy to take these contrasting absolutes at their face value and set up a real contradiction between them. If we want to know how these absolutes are meant, we must see how they are used, or in what activities and attitudes they find a place. If we adopt this method, the contradiction disappears. Commonsense neither supposes a man in a given situation to have as open a choice as God creating the world; nor yet supposes that the predictability of conduct is uniform and entire.

We have discussed in this chapter the intelligibility and the predictability of conduct. These have been our themes; but in the course of pursuing them we have defined the scope of choice, a corollary of sufficient importance to call for separate statement. Choice, properly so called, is the making up of one's mind between alternatives; deliberate decision being the most highly-wrought example of it. We are not always choosing, let alone deliberating; we are often doing something quite different. But in so far as our behaviour expresses a persistence, or even an acquiescence, in lines of choice already chosen, it is still what we choose to do. And one very useful sense of the word 'voluntary' is coextensive with behaviour of the kind.

CHAPTER IX

THE ANALOGY OF PHYSICAL NATURE

i. *'The world' and 'the known world'*

IN the preceding chapter we have argued that it is possible to understand why men do what they do, without bringing their actions under any rule of natural uniformity. We do not abandon the attitude proper to the making of our own decisions, when we turn to the interpretation of our neighbours' conduct. Common-sense thinking about the consistencies of human behaviour is not a veiled or inchoate determinism. There is a 'personal' way of thinking which has its own sort of systematic articulation, and covers a wide field of social observation.

'Wide?' says the determinist. 'Width is relative. Wide, no doubt, compared with the area of a single choice; but narrow enough, when compared with the sweep of physical investigation.'—Here is an opportunity to stitch a purple patch on our threadbare argument; let us incorporate a piece of deterministic declamation.

'The scientific or contemplative mind ranges through the whole body of fact, the world of nature, and everywhere understands its object by finding in it the lineaments of uniformity; that is to say, of causal sequence. No supplementary principle is required; for though explanatory hypotheses are many, they are but so many formulations of different and complementary uniformities. In one corner of the field the mind encounters man, dust on the dust of the stellar heaven, real in his insignificance, artificial in his prominence, through the accidental circumstance that he houses the contemplating mind. How infinitesimal a part of things is man; and again, in this minute being how few are the moments of practical decision, compared with the moments of passivity, of observation, of routine performance, of actuation by simple desire! In the moments of decision, and of deliberation preparatory to it, it has to be conceded that we meet a singular phenomenon: an unbreakable attachment of the agent to the supposition of un-caused self-determination. How much more natural, however, to treat this phenomenon as what it manifestly is, a singularity of belief, than as what it pretends to be, the awareness of a singular fact; and of a fact so singular as to constitute the only surd in the whole arithmetic of nature!'

In this piece of declamation the colours of rhetoric are so laid as to suggest a proportion of importance between apparent freedom and acknowledged uniformity. Importance cannot be deduced from hard fact, and yet it is a tautology that importance is impor-tant; to bring it out is one of the legitimate functions of rhetoric. But the rhetoric of importance must somewhere touch on facts, and these at least it should not falsify. In the determinist declama-tion we have just delivered, there are two touches on fact which cry out for scrutiny.

(a) It serves the purposes of the orator to see the maker of the scientific survey as mind-in-general, a pure contemplative power, a power merely happening to be housed in that foolish human creature, which practises decision under the form of causeless liberty. But surely this apotheosis of a contemplative or cognitive mind-in-general is utterly foreign to scientific naturalism, and to all our experience of mind and of man. Instead of saying that the contemplative mind happens to be housed in the human animal, we might with better reason say, that the human animal happens to stray into the fields of dispassionate contemplation. 'Never mind' it may be rejoined: 'however rare the true students of Nature, and however few their studious hours, it is by such men and at such times that Nature is explored; and it is on this explora-tion alone that we build, when we discuss apparent voluntary liberty, or any other subject of rational enquiry. The hours, the moments of study may be few, but it is in them, not in the moments of wilful decision, that truth is descried.'

(*b*) The rejoinder only serves to uncover the second of the two rhetorical falsifications we spoke of. The instinctive claim to a voluntary liberty is not confined within certain odd moments, the moments of decision. It is with us whatever we do, not least when we are scrutinising Nature. Our study of her is nothing like exposing to the world a photographic plate. It is sometimes the setting of physical traps to catch experimental fact; and when it is not that, it is talking, at least to oneself, about what one has observed. And talking is activity. Try turning the scientist's attention on his activity of discourse, and persuading him that he does not frame it in any sense which excludes its being framed by causal factors; does not either ask questions or reply to them, otherwise than as they arise of themselves and elicit their own answers. You will find that he is as unable to think this way about his work, and to get on with it, as a man is to deliberate in the belief that his decision is determined. To experiment, to speculate, to pick the fruitful point for examination—everyone engaged in such endeavours regards them in practice as free activities.

So, then, the whole mass of natural fact, as we men have put it together, is the product of an enterprise which knows itself as free. The mass may stand there with the granite solidity of a mountain; but its contours and outlines would be totally unknown to us, but for the free play of exploration, trying the surfaces this way and that, extemporising with native wit the machinery of ascent, or the instrument of mensuration. So far from the natural conviction of our freedom's being confined to occasions of heroic choice, it covers the whole area of that activity through which we sample or construe our physical environment. The world is not known but as the playground of human thews, and human thoughts; were there no free play, there would be no knowledge.

When theology develops the idea of a divine mind, she conceives a knowledge of things as they are in themselves; as though divine spirit had the same insight into the whole being and action of physical nature, which we have into our own most perspicuous voluntary performances. But theology is well aware that such a suggestion, however expressible in words, is unrealisable to imagination. Physical knowledge, for us, means the knowledge of our physical playground, as it reveals itself by conditioning our play. And this is so, even though much of the play is designed for no other purpose, than to explore the features of the field. To talk about the field, indeed, is not to talk about the play which explores it; and yet it is an arrogant pretension of divine knowledge, to suppose we can know things simply as they are in themselves, and in perfect abstraction from our ways of sounding them. Berkeley's error was not so much his refusal to prescind the object from the mental act, as his failure to admit the embodied condition of the mind.

Let us strike a balance. If we talk about *the world*, we talk about a system in which the points or moments seen as claiming freedom for themselves are infinitesimal and few. If we talk about *the known and knowable world* we talk about a system which bears in every part an intimate relation to freedom-claiming action. Both ways of speaking have their proper use. For practical purposes we purify our abstraction of the world, ignoring the observer. But for certain philosophical purposes we think the other way: not about the world, but about the known world. Which way of thinking, then, is proper to our present enquiry? We are asking how seriously we ought to maintain the instinctive claim of action to undetermined self-determination, in face of the great analogy of cosmic order. The question cannot be, What is objectively the case? for no one doubts that the stars are moved by rule; even he who said that they were moved by love, made an entire conformity to law the thing they both coveted and attained. The question must be, how do we know? How know such facts as the astronomical and nuclear on one side, the mental and spontaneous on the other? And the answer is, that in all our knowledge we are knowing each through the other; however much we may disattend on any given occasion either from the world or from the mind. Everywhere we experience a world-conditioned spontaneity, and a world spontaneously explored. It is hard to see how our assurance of order can be greater than our assurance of freedom;

or why the indifference of illimitable spaces should intimidate the survey which sweeps them.

ii. *The libertarian's world includes natural necessity*

The conclusion we have just attempted to establish is that no knowledge of physical uniformity can be more certain to us, than our assurance of the mental freedom through which we acquire it. But, we were inclined to admit, if we take the cosmological rather than the epistemological view, and think about the universe as objective fact, there is no gainsaying the loneliness of freedom in the vast ocean of uniformity. And, say what we will about the vulgarity of an imagination which allows itself to be intimidated by quantity, the loneliness of personality in the universe weighs heavily upon us. To put it somewhat quaintly, it seems terribly improbable that we should exist; and from this it is a short step to suspecting that (since after all we do exist) we cannot be as improbable as we seem: that is to say, that we cannot stand out so startlingly as we supposed from the great uniform mass. And the first move towards assimilating ourselves to our environment will be, to jettison our faith in undetermined self-determination.

We can scarcely help allowing that reason has a genuine interest in unifying the picture of nature. We can ask with our lips, 'Why shouldn't things be infinitely anomalous? Why should we believe this to be any more the tidiest than the best of all possible worlds?' But though the question sounds well in the lecture-room, we cannot make the mood last any longer than the discussion. We cannot always be pronouncing to ourselves antimetaphysical incantations; and with the fading of the incantation the charm dies, our instinct for unification revives.

How difficult it is, in philosophy, to advance! After hours of discussion we find ourselves just able, by hard running, to catch up with our starting-point. The problem presented by two pictures, one 'personal', the other 'scientific', was the subject of our opening chapters. We quarrelled with a fashion which was content to juxtapose the two; we insisted, for our part, on establishing a relation between them; and we supposed that in the sequel we had done, if not all that man could do, anyhow all that we could do, towards a unification. Having consolidated the position, we advanced to conquer fresh worlds; and ever since, we have been marching hard. An obstacle rises before us, which it seems vital to reduce. We move in upon it, and are dismayed by a feeling of familiarity. Have not we been here before? Are we to debate all over again the duality between a 'scientific' and a 'personal' account of things?

No; the question we initially discussed, and the question we are attempting now, have a family likeness, but they are not the same question. Our old puzzle concerned the human individual, and two ways of regarding him, the physical and the personal. It was axiomatic that the physical man should be understood physically; the question was, whether conscious action was a mere phenomenon, thrown up by self-sufficient physical process; or whether the factor of consciousness did some real work, and made the event other than it would else have been. We settled that question, right or wrong, by deciding that consciousness does real work. But how is her work done? This is the question we are now engaged upon. And in the course of pursuing it we have encountered the suggestion, not that the action of conscious persons is merely physical, but that it is paraphysical; analogous, that is, to physical process in its sequential orderliness. For though we have agreed that personal action is no mere part of the physical system, we have still to place it in a setting which, so far as we can tell, is purely and overwhelmingly physical; and it seems only reasonable to interpret it as a sort of extension, or special modification, of physical nature, exhibiting the same basic form of order, and of predictability.

Those who follow this line of reasoning do not, therefore, deny the real efficacy of personal intention or choice; they give a paraphysical account of the way it works. The object of such an account is to get rid of dualism; but unhappily, as we have been at pains to show, the dualism breaks out in a new place. You get the waistcoat and the trousers to meet, only to open a gap between

the trousers and the socks. You may seem to reduce the gap between 'body' and 'mind' by interpreting the workings of 'mind'
in a bodylike manner. But only at a price—you open a hiatus in
your thought about the mind itself. There is an area which the
paraphysical story cannot be stretched to cover: that intimate
province of the person which each of us is, going about its own
business according to its proper manner of proceeding. The paraphysical account proves to be at best a diagram we make of mind-
at-a-distance; it can never close in upon its object, or coalesce with
the mind's own way of thinking itself.

Here, then, are the two pictures we are at present trying to
accommodate with one another: a 'paraphysical' picture of mind,
and a 'personal' picture of it; the paraphysical being a sort of
extension to the out-and-out physicality of our accepted nuclear
and stellar universe.

The more the paraphysicalist struggles to absorb the personal,
the more he convinces us of its irreducible personalness. This at
least (we may, by reaction, feel) is a certainty; and if we are to
believe Descartes, nothing can in the nature of things be more
certain. If, then, there is to be a unification of the whole picture,
should not it be done by turning the tables on the determinist, and
asserting not that all is physical or paraphysical, but that all is
personal or somehow person-like? It will cost us no great effort of
invention to develop the suggestion; so many wits have been in
the field before us. Indeed, we have an embarrassing number of
cosmic personalisms, or pampsychisms, to choose from. There is
subjective idealism, which makes things somehow the creatures of
our dream. There is pluralistic mentalism in the manner of Leibniz, alleging that the forces which strike us as physical are in themselves a sort of elementary consciousness. Or there is pantheism,
according to which they are all the manifestations of a single
action, multiform and divine.

There is no dearth, certainly, of cosmic personalisms, but a sad
dearth of philosophers ready to believe them. To take them one
by one, and expose their incoherences, is a gymnastic for students;
but the issue of the exercise is foregone from the start. No such

system achieves the initial plausibility which suspends disbelief. We feel it as outrageous to erode the physicality of nature, as it is to sap the personalness of persons. 'Let everything be itself, and not another thing.'

It is a waste of time to swing the pendulum between physicalism and personalism. If the libertarian thinker allows himself to be drawn into so unprofitable a game, it must be through ignorance of his own resources. He could be doing better than this. To unify the picture without sacrificing the personal, he is under no necessity of transsubstantiating the physical. All he need do is develop the personal picture. He will find it to include the physical world without denaturalising it.

The libertarian's citadel is the predicament of the agent. Here am I, I who have to do something about the situation in which I stand. And if so, then there are two truths equally certain; that I have to embody personal decisions in my actions; and that there is a situation in view of which I have to decide, or act. What is meant by saying that there is a situation . . . ? Surely that there is a necessity. To say that I am in a situation is to say that things condition or affect me. And neither 'conditioning' nor 'affecting' has any sense, unless what I suffer is the regular or necessary consequence of what environing things inflict. These things need not be things usually so-called; they may be persons; and what they do to me may be the expression of free choice, not the outcome of causal necessity. Even so, the relation of what I suffer to what they do cannot be understood except as necessary. If I am a small boy, and a bully is twisting my arm, he twists because he will; but granted that he twists, the displacement, pain or damage follows in me by a natural rule. My reaction need not follow by rule; it is difficult to be brave, but I *won't* scream and I *will* go on kicking his shins. My courage or my cowardice equally presupposes inescapable pain. I may lessen the agony by successful resistance, but that too will be in accordance with a necessity of nature. If I force my arm back into a less constrained position, the pain will of necessity be less.

It may be possible to imagine a physical environment for every free agent, entirely composed by the bodies of other free agents; the generalised form, as it were, of the situation besetting a man forced into the air by a milling crowd, who keeps his balance in a sea of arms, heads and shoulders. What we have to conceive is a hurly-burly in which all the participants suffer the fate of the man in the air. No one has his feet on the ground; the whole struggling mass is somehow suspended in free space. According to this fantastic hypothesis, everything that any agent does is freely chosen; but their capacities for affecting, and being affected by, one another are still determinate, and so are the actual ways in which the movement of any one affects any other. Every agent can make another suffer, but none can make another act. Necessary sequence, in such a system, is limited to the following of suffering on action; it does not extend to the following of action upon suffering.

It is obvious that this fantastic world is little like the real, and (what is more to our present purpose) that it offers anything but an ideal field for the exercise of free decision; a truth which has its classic illustration in Carroll's description of Wonderland crocquet. If my swinging of the mallet-head will never assure its hitting the ball squarely, because it is free to writhe its neck; and if my hitting of the ball will never assure its rolling in the line of my aim, because it is free to uncurl hedgehog-wise, and make off on its feet; then the decision to produce an indirect effect like the passage of a ball through a hoop, will lead to little but disappointment; and in an existence of which Wonderland crocquet was typical, the very idea of producing indirect effects would have remained unborn.

In a world where we could produce no indirect effects—could make other agents suffer, but never make them act—the scope of human activity would be so reduced, that it would scarcely be human at all; a conclusion which squares with the well-known thesis, that a physical ability to use tools was decisive for the evolution of the *animal rationale*. For if the thesis is sound, human consciousness has been bound up from the first with the ability to produce indirect effects, or make other agents act. Apart from this power, we should not hold together the system of action, nor exert the articulation of purpose, which either calls for human mentality, or employs it.

Philosophers have often insisted that a uniform natural world is the condition of intelligence, for the reason that no causal chaos would offer sufficient objects to the mind. It seems more in accordance with the order of cultural history to start from the pragmatic end, and correlate the growth of intellectual power with the ability to extend our action through subordinate agents. A predictable regularity in nature is the condition of our imposing effective decisions; and so it is not alien from the picture of a free man's world, but intrinsic to it.

iii. Pattern and action in nature

Yes, no doubt. What determinist thinker would wish to deny that the libertarian faith is parasitic on necessity? What he denies is that it is consistent with the necessity it supposes. Man, full of the conceit of his freewill, begins, gaily enough, by congratulating himself on the predictable regularity with which his instruments execute his chosen purposes. He goes on to ask why they do so, and sees that it is because they are parts of a system having a certain structure throughout, the structure of natural uniformity. He pulls the trigger, the displacement of the trigger is followed by the release of the spring, and that again by the detonation of the cartridge. Step by step, through an inevitable sequence, it comes to the death of the deer. The philosophical marksman considers what is meant by the following of one event upon another in the executive series, and concludes the principle of succession to be no other than the uniformity of nature's operation. With such an ally, there is no limit to the remoteness of the effects he can hope to produce, or to the dreams of voluntary control which he can entertain.

To make sure that he has not deceived himself in so delightful an arithmetic, he proceeds to count the sum backwards from the death of the deer. He swims up the causal stream against the current, passing from each condition to the condition conditioning it, till he reaches the pulling of the trigger. And what was the condition of that? A complex situation, no doubt; yet one in which a mental element played a decisive part. And why not? We long ago agreed to accept mixed histories, physical and mental. A mixed situation can be a condition within the terms of the argument; that is to say, an antecedent upon which its consequent necessarily follows, in accordance with the uniformity of nature.

But necessarily? And in obedience to a natural uniformity? If so, what has become of free decision; for is not the transition from mental antecedent to decisive action now a determined one? Whereas if it is not so, how can the antecedent be the condition of the consequent, according to the meaning of 'condition' which the argument prescribes?

There is surely something the matter here. Yes, says the determinist, but no matter for tears. In tracing the sequence of our action outwards from our bodies into the series of our instruments, we are able to view it objectively, and to isolate its serial principle. Turning homewards again, we realise that the same principle applies *de jure* to our 'inward' action, even though we experience a *de facto* difficulty in seeing the application, because of our inability to get out of our own light.

No, says the libertarian, the trouble is more serious than that. We have fallen into a confusion of logical levels, or shall we call it a category-mistake? It is true that uniformity-thinking excludes any other determinant but uniformity, on its own level. But then it is equally true that active force, such as that of a personal agent, excludes any interagent on its own level other than a comparable force. To contaminate the levels causes nothing but confusion; our business is to see how they supplement one another.

Let us endeavour to expand the somewhat oracular remark we have just made. The libertarian's own account of the accusation brought against him will be something of this sort—that he is proposing a sequence of determinants and determinates, which begins with the action of a voluntary agent determining a correlative 'passion' in a 'patient', but from there continues as a chain of causal situations, each link determining the next by a rule inductively established. Such a sequence, he agrees, is an absurdity, for it jumps from one level to another without remarking it; it starts on the level of action and proceeds on the level of pattern.

He who studies uniformity-rules is studying order, pattern, or rhythm. But of what? Of action, without a doubt. On the level of action, we can always say that some action reacts to ours, and another to that, and so *ad infinitum*. On the level of pattern we can always ask what pattern (of action) must be assembled, if (an action of) a given pattern is to follow; and so on to the end of the world. When we are on the level of pattern, all action, including that of our own free will, must be seen under its patterned aspect. It will, indeed, be axiomatic with us that the account of our own action in terms of a patterned uniformity cannot sufficiently explain the form it takes; nevertheless, there will always be something to say about it in such terms. What we do, however freely, in a given situation is at the very least an action of the human type, such as arises out of the organisation of our living, bodily person. And of course we can draw the limits *a priori* within which the pattern of any free choice will fall, a good deal more closely than that.

Our ordinary speech does not confine itself to one level at a time; it combines the two. We talk about a complex of actions and reactions, but a complex which exemplifies certain uniformities. We commonly combine the two levels; but we do not pay them equal attention in every part of our discourse. In the area of our own or of our neighbours' conduct we commonly attend to action, and take for granted the conformity of its pattern with certain generalised expectations. But the further we stretch into a remoter field, the more we view events under the aspect of pattern and of uniformity; we take pretty much for granted the action which supports the scheme.

The emphasis of our attention shifts from one level to the other without our noticing it. Take the example of a statesman wrestling with economic embarrassments. He begins from where he is; he considers the action to be taken by himself and his colleagues, and how the opposition leaders will react to it. So far all is stated in the mode of agency. But as he proceeds to consider the broad effect of his proposals, he falls into the generalisations of political and economic thought. He talks about patterns of mass-action, statistically established, and arising, in obedience to uniformities, out of antecedent situations; situations which it is the purpose of his measures relevantly and salutarily to modify.

Suppose now that one of his colleagues protests against so soulless a strain, so much talk about the bank-rate, the rise and fall of shares, the recession or the expansion of business. 'Do you realise' he says, 'that you are talking all this while about the actions of suffering mankind?' 'Certainly I do,' replies the Chancellor of the Exchequer; 'but for the purposes of our present calculations, it does no particular good to recall it.'

What such an example as this may serve to show, is that the net of patterned uniformity can be extended over the privileged domain of action, human conduct. But what needs to be shown, for the credit of the libertarian argument, is the opposite—that the field of action extends all under the network of brute physical system. However much, in an overall view, we disattend from the particular actions of men, we know well enough that they act. But however severe an attention we bend upon the activities taken to underlie what we study as physical pattern, can we ever claim to descry them? We do not, if we are wise, attribute to the forces of inanimate nature either the consciousness or the purposiveness which we know in our own conduct; and can the idea of action, once stripped of these qualities, retain any character, to distinguish it from sheer occurrence, or event?

The difficulty of abstracting physical action may be brought out by a parable. Suppose we were to land on a foreign shore, and find ourselves surrounded by dusky men, whose words, faces and gestures we could not read at all. But what became evident to us after a short acquaintance was that they were punctilious ritualists. When we approached a party of them, they went through an etiquette of motions, repeated to the last detail exact, and leading to some consequence like withdrawal, or the production of food. Our only way of understanding the performance in detail, would

be as the fulfilment of a rule; we should not see what they meant
by it nor, as we say, what made them tick to such a rhythm. Yet
we should not suppose, any the more for that, that we were confronted with a mere shifting of the scenes of perceptible nature, in
an order which analogy had led us to expect. Nor should we be
content to say that we *perceived* a shifting state of affairs, and
imputed activity to the agents in it. We should say that we *perceived* activity, and *imputed* a purpose we were powerless to
interpret.

Now to apply the parable: in the case of physical nature, we are,
similarly, limited to uniformity-thinking if we wish to explain,
or predict, in detail what occurs. Yet we should say that what we
perceive to be uniform is a real activity on the part of the physical
elements; though in this case we do not, as we did with the
mysterious negroes, impute purpose at all.

But is not this just the difficulty? For though we cannot understand the action of the negroes, we have often understood the action
of other men; and when we see the negroes, it does not take us
long to reflect that they also are men, and are therefore presumably
up to something, though we do not know what. Moreover, while
their purposes may be unintelligible to us, their motions are not.
If I see them swing their legs, I know what it is to do that. The
chorus did it in the musical comedy last year, and (though less
liquidly) I can do it myself. A fellow-countryman of my own,
suitably darkened with burnt cork, could be slipped into the place
of any one among the mysterious beings before me; but a man
cannot be slipped into the place of a machine, nor vice versa. The
comparison fails, because it is one thing to suppose a purpose unknown, another to suppose no purpose at all.

Let us try another fable. Two rustic youths were wasting time
in the barn. They picked up the end of a long rope and began
having a tug of war with it. The boy who had the loose end of the
rope made a great pantomime of it, leaning back, groaning and
shutting his eyes; of which the result was, that he did not see what
was going on. The old donkey at the other end of the barn had
been left harnessed to a revolving shaft which wound the rope on

a windlass, for an agricultural purpose we will not here particular-ise. Waked up by the boys' antics, the beast began to pull and tautened the rope. The inside boy let go, and stood back to watch his antagonist, with screwed up eyes, pulling against the donkey and the leverage. The donkey won.

That is the outline of the plot; but what concerns us is the thoughts of the boy with the screwed-up eyes. 'Here I am, pulling against Tom, and I can feel him pulling against me. Ah, now he's trying a long, strong pull; I'll have him over when he relaxes. . . . But how he's keeping it up! By Jove (opening his eyes) it isn't Tom, it's the old donkey!' Pulling is something the boy does, it isn't anything that just happens; and the same is true of Tom's contrary pull. And when the donkey is found to have taken over, there is no sudden metaphysical transformation, no turnover from an agent pulling, to a law-abiding alteration in the perceptible state of affairs. The old donkey doesn't know what he is up to, he is virtually sleep-walking, but he is pulling all the same.

Well, but a man might sleep-walk as well as a donkey, and between donkeys and men there is a degree of analogy which is sometimes frighteningly close. Granted; but all you have to do is to substitute a donkey-engine for the donkey. You can make up your own story why the engine suddenly began to turn; my invention is exhausted. But turn it does, for whatever reason; and, turning, takes over the pull from Tom. Does it make all that difference to his antagonist, to discover that what is pulling against him is not a donkey but a donkey-engine? Surely his own pull, and the engine's pull, remain somehow *in pari materia*; there is a real exertion of force on either side, though the one is exerted with purpose, and the other according to natural uniformity.

To obtain the moral of the fable, all we need do is to generalise. Our whole physical existence is an interaction between our exerted efforts, and an environment which interplays with them, resisting, co-operating and invading. We have no power to think of this environment otherwise than as *in pari materia* with our active bodies and our exerted efforts. To analyse the forces or agencies we meet into their real components is, of course, a task beyond commonsense; and commonsense, having talked to a few physical scientists, suspends judgement about the analysis. But neither commonsense nor science doubts that there is real agency there to be analysed, whether the analysis can be carried through or not.

David Hume, having imbibed the folly of his English predecessors, and accepted sight as typical of the five senses, complained, and very justly, that he could not *see* the force by which one state of affairs produced another. But being an honest man, and not willing to brush away a universal human conviction as of no account, he felt it his duty to discover the root of belief, even if belief proved to be illusion; and so he claimed to discover in the mind the source of our idea of physical necessitation; accounting for our reading of it into nature, by that tendency to project the mental into the physical which is, indeed, a fertile and widespread source of deception. Hume is subtle, as always, in the account he gives; but how steadily does he turn his back on the obvious! If anyone wants to know whence he derives the idea of that constraint, by which one event constrains another to take place, he may shut his eyes, if he likes, and observe how, with his hands, he himself constrains physical events to take place; or how physical events from time to time constrain him to give place to them. And one day, constrained by one force from the front, and by another from behind, he may slip out sideways, leaving them to exercise their constraints on one another. Being no longer there to feel the constraint, he will not be directly aware of it. But his eyes will give him sufficient tokens of the effect produced, as he sees one body slowed down by the resistance of the other, and the other giving place to superior force.

iv. Anthropomorphism and physics

There is little mystery, then, attaching to the origin of our belief about a real action in nature. What is less clear is the content of the belief. I have no doubt that I am acted upon by natural forces, or that I interact with them. If I am acted upon, something acts; if I interact with something, something interacts with me. But what do I mean by saying that it acts? Surely that its action is somehow *in pari materia* with my own. But I do not suppose it to be voluntary or conscious, as mine is. What then do I suppose?

Perhaps it is misleading in such a connexion even to speak of supposition. We take physical action for granted as something directly experienced; for interaction with 'nature' is part and parcel of our action itself. If we attempt theories about the intrinsic character of that which interacts with us, they will as likely as not be very foolish. We are likely to oscillate between extreme positions. We may begin by suggesting that natural ener-gisings, being somehow *in pari materia* with our own actions, are a sort of conscious life themselves; only not very alive, not very conscious. *Omnia sunt quodammodo animata.* Then, quickly revolt-ing from our own absurdity, we run into a denial of all natural action whatsoever. Nothing acts, we say, but ourselves; we do not experience interaction, but merely a succession of phenomenal conditions for our own action; the appearance of nature's action being a mirage, produced by the imaginative attribution of a con-tinuous activity like our own, to the series of its phenomenal con-ditions. But this second position falsifies our experiences of pressure, resistance and the like, by assimilating them to forms of sense-experience from which they are utterly diverse—the 'mere' phenomena of hearing, seeing, and so forth.

What are we to say, then? It will be prudent to begin by allow-ing that the experience of interaction has its own dose of pheno-menality, though not the phenomenality of sight or sound. Things look coloured; events, such as the banging of gongs, sound noisy; and in an analogous way, forces feel constraining, support-ing, or resistant. Colour and noise are what they are, in relation to our organs of special sense; constraint, resistance, support are what they are, in relation to the body through which we act. Interaction does not deliver up to us the very being of nature-in-itself, un-coloured by the form of our response, or of our interference. Nevertheless, the phenomenality of what we experience through interaction is not so absolute as that of the so-called secondary qualities. The man-relatedness of the experience affects, but does not create, the apparent characteristics. To talk of things as looking green to one another, is to talk nonsensically; to talk of natural energies as constraining one another, is merely to talk anthropomorphically.

Must we acquiesce in a full-blown anthropomorphism? Cannot the man-likeness be strained out of our talk about natural energies? But what shall we strain out? We might start by discarding the most absurd, or inapplicable feature of the human model— voluntary intention. Tom was trying his hardest to pull his antagonist over; the donkey-engine to which he has now transferred the task is doing nothing of the sort, nor does Tom suppose that it is. It is pulling, though; but then a man can distinguish in his own action between the exertion of force and the willing of the intention. The simplest way to exhibit the distinction may be to take an activity like running. The whole complex action may be willed intensely (the runner is all out to win the race) but the separate parts of it are not (he does not plant every step by a distinct intention). Yet the taking of every step is an exertion of force; and so the intention to run is exercised through many exertions of force, not each distinctly intended. We need find no great difficulty, then, in conceiving the physical energies with which we interact, as the actions of a force governed by no intention, but just blinding away.

It may still be objected that the several actions of force by which I run are only known by being felt; and surely I am not going to attribute sentience to the donkey-engine. The objection appears to be nothing but Berkeley's grand fallacy breaking out in a new place. If I feel the wall with my hand, I feel the wall; I do not feel a feeling; and if I feel a muscular exertion, it is not a feeling that I feel, but the exertion. I attribute to the engine no feeling of a force exerted, but simply the exerted force. It is felt, indeed, but by the boy, in interacting with it; in trying, that is, to pull against it.

We may come so far, but we cannot go the whole way in ridding our minds of anthropomorphism, when we talk of the physical forces we encounter. If we strip away intention and

THE ANALOGY OF PHYSICAL NATURE

feeling, and leave action alone, the action is still animal action; and we cannot suppose it is the same thing for physical forces to act, as for organised bodies to act. When, therefore, we speak of a physical action as interactive with our own, we think of animal action, but allow an indefinable discount. It is (animal) action, only of course not animal.

How absurd, you may say; and yet it is a sort of absurdity in which we are deeply involved. Turn back again, for example, from mere action to full-blown intentional action; and let it be the action of an ancient Egyptian king, whose mind, in acting as he did, we endeavour to understand on the evidence of his inscriptions. This man, we can see, did not think as we do; yet we have no means to understand him but thinking for him, or after him. When we have gone as far as we can to meet him, there is still a gap. We allow an incalculable discount. How unable we are to reckon it up or pay it off, may be judged from the strange unreality of historical novels, written on scenes so remote from us. Pages of lively anachronism interleave pages of dead archaeology.

Looking at kings, especially at Pharaohs, is an occupation we can easily economise; but what about looking at cats? None of us supposes cats to be automata, let alone patterns of obtainable phenomena. We cannot doubt that their anger is anger, their pleasure pleasure, and their fear fear. Yet we cannot make the discount which would reduce these passions or affections from the human form in which we experience them, to the feline form in which we ought to impute them. What then do we do? To psychologise cats is a silly occupation, and the insistence that they should be 'understood as people' is a sentimental heresy. Commonsense cuts its losses, and is content to take the perceptible behaviour of the animal with that tinge of emotional or voluntary interpretation which it immediately suggests. We are content to see her anger in her claws and eyes, and not to ask what sort of anger it is, beyond what her action defines. We hear her pleasure in her purring, we feel it in the relaxation of her muscles. Yet pleasure can no more be heard in purring, than cold can be seen in ice. There is an associative imputation of emotion, and it borrows

187

from our own bosoms. It seems safe to say that the cat is pleased. After all, pleasure has a wide range of levels in ourselves; yet we are content to claim pleasure, for the most part, without particularising it.

The case is much the same when we interact with physical force, and think of it as active. We tie ourselves down to the perceptible effect, the way in which the encountered activity conditions our own. It is crushing, constraining, overbearing, yielding, sustaining or the like. Our thought of its activeness is merely that it so acts, as to be or do these things to us. And yet we think that it acts, that it does these things. If I fail to make headway against the blowing gale, it is not that walking becomes first painful, then impossible; it is that a contrary force pushes me back.

The attribution of action becomes more careless and progressively less emphatic, as we look further away from the personal focus of our field, and observe the play of forces upon one another, not upon us. Even so we do not, in our common speech, abandon the idiom of activity, or begin to talk mere diagrams of natural uniformity. We continue to use the same sort of verbs, and often identically the same verbs, about natural events, as we do about personal actions.

Let us take an extreme case, and consider the double sentence: 'The sun rose at six-fifteen, but I did not rise until seven.' The language suggests that as I climb out of bed, so the sun climbs the heavenly road. We may feel rightly disposed to deny it; but we would do well to get clear what it is we wish to deny. There are so many senses in which the suggestion can be rejected, and it is worth our while to distinguish them. In the first place, it may be denied that the sun goes up; it is rather that a point on the earth's surface revolves downwards. In the next place, even granted that the sun's active contribution to the relative change of position we are considering is secondary, we may be taken to be denying that the sun is a single unit of active force, or an organic whole, either. The sun is a mere conglomerate; it is more like a swarm of bees, than like a bee; its total movement is the mere resultant of the conjoint forces of many minute elements, all pulling the same way. Then thirdly, we may be taken to deny that the active verb, with its personal associations, can properly be used of the exertion of force by the molecules, or whatever other elements are conglomerated in the sun. It is not by any sort of pushing or pulling on their part that the sun gravitates. Such language is nothing but the survival of an always bad metaphor. We ought to limit ourselves to saying that movement takes place, and that its doing so under the given conditions accords with rules of physical uniformity established by other evidence.

It is only the third denial in which we are interested—the entire discounting of the active sense of active verbs, in their application to physical agents. Now we have seen that, in one definable way, we do discount it. In explaining or predicting physical happenings we do not attempt in any way to feel the nerve of the action. We content ourselves with viewing what perceptibly happens, as the case of a known or supposed uniformity. Yet in another way, a way less easy to define, it is gravely to be doubted whether we have any power to discount the active sense of the active verb, when it is used of the physical; whether we can, or should, take a physical happening to be a mere alteration in a state of affairs affecting our senses, rather than a real exercise of force by some of the physical elements upon others, or in relation to others. If we say that some of the physical elements *do* something to others, or, indeed, that they all mutually interact, then we are still using the washed-out analogy of action to interpret the physical world; to interpret not its modes of behaviour, as it were (uniformity-thinking takes care of those) but merely to give content to the general idea that it does act.

We may put the issue in a convenient light by turning to history. Once on a time, it will be agreed, men used to personify natural agents in a more or less full-blooded manner; and in those days no natural agent was held to be understood, unless it had been seen what it was up to, much as if it had been a person. Not quite a person, since the naturalist conceded the appetite of physical agents to be simpler and less diversified than that of man; which is what all of us, as a matter of fact, think now about the appetite of brutes. Such was the ancient creed. But then a revolution set in, of which the effect was that teleology was expelled from physics, and nothing was studied in natural agents except the uniformity their action exemplified.

Having followed the story so far, we may be inclined to ask: Ought the reform to stop there, and leave us with a real action in nature, of which we can (admittedly) study nothing but the uniform pattern; or ought the reform to be pushed further, and to expel the very ghost of real action, leaving us with nothing but uniform sequences of alteration in a perceptible state of affairs?

To make the issue clear, we have expressed it rhetorically and, indeed, politically. 'How far is the revolution to be carried?' Yet to put it in such a way is to falsify it. We have no real option; we cannot press the revolution home, if that means ceasing to read real action in natural events, when we are interacting with them. It may be otherwise, no doubt, when we measure them, and make formulae on the basis of our measurements. So the issue can be put in this way: Is it hypocrisy to pretend to discredit what all the while we take for granted; or is it atavism not to discredit what plays no further part in scientific calculation?

Measurement and interaction are two ways of sounding our environment, and they tell us different things about it. I can experience my brother's weight by lifting him in my arms, I can measure it against my own by sitting on the other end of a seesaw. I can feel the trajectory of a ball by catching it; I can time it over a distance against the beating of my heart or (more conveniently) against the second-hand of my watch. Measurement alone is scientifically fertile; but what it tells us is only the quantitative relation between one thing or event and another; it casts no light on the question, what it is that we are measuring. Formally, of course, we know that we are measuring (let us say) weight, which we define as the tendency of something to depress the scale. But what tends to depress the scale, what real constituent of the world, unless it be a self-exerting force? A force, or forces; we make no pretence, if we are wise, to resolve physical activity into its component acts. The diagrams of the scientists certainly suggest a minute atomisation; but they, by their own admission, are not minute enough.

There is, then (to conclude), a mensurational diagram of the world, and a world of interactional experience, both in principle complete, and covering one another without remainder. The world of live interaction can be described, with pardonable exaggeration, as the extension of my body in all directions; the radius of sight extending the optic nerve, and my sensitivity for impact being extended by bodies through which a shock is passed, as far as the source of the shock. We have said that in principle this way of knowing the world covers the whole diagram of cosmic measurement; but it is in principle only. The 'extension of our body outwards through space' is not effectively felt beyond a moderate depth in any direction. Outside the range, our world may strike us as virtually a mensurational diagram; we merely impute to the more distant reaches of the universe an active or substantial reality, which nothing but a felt interaction could experience.

The vast disproportion between the effective areas of our interactional and mensurational explorations may create *malaise* in the imagination, and cause us to say that self-directive action is a stranger in the world. It is not a stranger in its own world, but only in a world viewed under the aspect of measurement alone. No one feels intelligent action to be a stranger among the brute interagents in its directly encountered environment. Brute they may be, but they too are active; they provide the only sort of field in which we can conceive our action as being exercised.

CHAPTER X

CAUSAL LAW AND MENTAL CASUISTRY

i. Three attempts at an agreed compromise between causality and freedom
W E will take it as granted that physical events are no mere
measurabilities or lawabidingnesses attaching to the sequence of
our sensory phenomena; they are a sort of action, however mysterious in its nature. Hume's puzzle about causation arose through
a failure to admit two distinct levels for interpretation—the
activity of force, and the perceptible pattern of its action. Only the
first yields the idea of a constraining necessity, or real power; only
the second yields us any causal laws. In the preceding chapter, we
used the distinction for the purpose we there had on hand—to
give our voluntary action a physical setting, in which it could find
a natural home. But cannot we, perhaps, draw a more important
consequence from the same distinction? Cannot we use it to
explode the whole problem of freedom and necessity?

The problem is supposed to lie in an apparent discrepancy between the real action we claim to exercise, and the assumed subjection of our conduct to causal interpretation. But now let the
scientist (for example, the psychologist) view us as naturalistically
as he likes, and reduce our behaviour as nearly as he can to the type
of physical occurrence. It will remain that the uniformities he
claims to establish will lie on the level of pattern; they will
discount, or take for granted, the energy which throws or enacts the patterned sequence. But it is for this energy that the
voice of our personal being claims to speak. In lifeless nature
no voice rises from the level of action; because it says nothing
for itself, we have nothing in particular to say of it. In man, we
have the privileged instance; action speaks, and tells us that

it acts; what conceivable ground can we have for contradicting it?

It has been advanced against the causal interpretation of conduct, that if a personal act takes shape in a pattern prefigured by antecedent patterns, there is nothing left for the person to do; pattern does everything. The objection is now seen to rest on an absurdity. Pattern does nothing. Only agencies act; though of course in a patterned, not in a chaotic, way; and in the case we are considering, the agency is a personal one. It thinks it acts, and it says so. We are doers, in our own eyes, if we are anything. And how right we are! But as for what we do, and the pattern we throw, all that is fair game for the scientist, the hunter of patterns.

What then? Have we finished the question? Shall we exchange congratulations, and go home? It would be premature. For the claim of the personal voice is not only to do what it does, but to decide what it will do; and it still seems a cheat, if whatever we think we have freely decided is found to have been bindingly prefigured in antecedent actions or events. We do not, or rather cannot, regard our action as limited to the setting in motion of a prefabricated process. How strange it would be, if all the people who thought they were painting pictures were found to be colour-printing, and merely striking off what was set up for them in the press!

Our question, then, remains with us. But need it remain with us much longer? Surely we have hit upon a hopeful method for disposing of it: the method which makes room for freedom by ridding our thought about causal uniformity of all exaggeration, all metaphysical superstition. Our first attempt along this line has proved too simple for the complexity of the issue; but cannot we go further and fare better? Cannot we hope for an agreed solution, showing that whatever causality can meaningfully claim, liberty can cheerfully concede?

We will mention first, if only to dismiss, a topic too abstract or general to afford us much consolation. A strong case may be made for the intrinsic absurdity of supposing that the operations of nature can be exhaustively described as conformities to natural law, however completely or subtly the prescriptions of such law may be drawn. Events are never mere paradigms of the rules applicable to them; there is an element of the irreducibly singular, not only in the fact of their occurrence, but in the arrangement of their structure. The argument is logical, but it can be supported empirically. The most exact of natural sciences is found to admit an ultimate irrationality in its subject-matter; an irrationality which physicists labour by various methods to discount.

In so far as every actualised pattern has a touch of the singular in it, it must defy prefiguration by its antecedents; and we may feel inclined to say that the energies active in the event must, as it were, give their pattern its singular twist for themselves. 'As it were,' we say, speaking of physical energies; but speaking of our own voluntary action, surely we can leave the qualification out. We can cheerfully claim that whatever, in the shaping of our conduct, is additional to the causally prefigured, is the creation of our act.

Such is the outline of the argument. We would develop it in more detail, if we thought it capable of doing us any good. But, as we began by saying, the principle it claims to establish is of too general an application to help us with so particular an issue as freewill. The uniqueness and uncausedness it asserts, it asserts of all events, even of those which are our proverbs for predictable regularity; eclipses of the moon or revolutions of the clock. To claim for our own actions the power of self-variation we allow to such motions, is not to claim anything much. But the disappointment may teach us a useful lesson—not to trouble our heads over the general nature of causal thinking, but to look for features distinctive of its development in narrower fields.

May not the distinction we want lie between an area of event-sequences reducible to mathematical form, and an area of event-sequences not thus reducible? the determinism of modern scientific thought is not, after all, the child of the causal axiom, but of the mathematical method. In fields where arithmetic does not apply, we may have no better reason to be determinists than had the pre-Galileans.

The cruciality of mathematics to the question before us can best be exhibited by a somewhat general discussion. It is a common-place nowadays that theoretical science has ceased to look for *the* cause of any event. If we define a cause as 'that event, upon which a given event follows, in accordance with an invariable rule,' then it must be confessed that there are no causes in nature; for no single antecedent ever suffices to determine a consequent. When, in a practical science such as medicine, we ask for *the* cause (say of the disease), we are taking for granted an enormous complex of operative factors, both constitutive of health, and hostile to it. We look simply for the event which upset the balance, and let the enemy into the camp. It would be plainly ludicrous to treat the one event as by itself capable of producing a diseased human functioning. It would have to begin by producing a man, and that is beyond the powers of (let us say) a sudden sharp fall in the temperature.

Every consequent, then, follows upon a complex of ante-cedents, in accordance with either a variety of sequential laws, or a variety of applications under some one sequential law. How are we to work out the mutual interferences of so many causalities, and reach a single result? Shall we, with Aristotle, invoke accident and the incalculable? No, we will invoke arithmetic and calcula-tion. The typical case is that of a gravitating body, under attrac-tion from every quarter of the heaven. How do we determine its path? How dovetail our plurality of causes? We begin by stating them in a way which makes them relative to one another. We do not, that is, say that such and such an attractive body, having such and such a mass and being placed at such and such a distance, will draw the body we are considering with such and such a speed; and then lament, because the contrary attractions of other bodies prevent this very proper speed from being attained. No, we say that each of our attractive bodies, in proportion to its mass and distance, exerts a certain pull. Then we sit down and calculate the movement from the balance of pulls. Our ability to make the calculation depends on our ability to interpret by a common arithmetic the forces involved. Otherwise we should be rendered helpless by the plurality of causes.

But what is to happen when we apply causal reasoning to a field into which mathematics will not accompany us—the field of immeasurables? Nothing in human psychology is more like a force than is a passion. Yet anger is not measurable. Its physical concomitants may be; but the effect of the anger in a man's conduct is not proportioned to such measurable quantities. We may lay it down as a general rule, that when a man is angry, he. . . . But there is always plurality of causes for his behaviour. The person with whom he is angry is one whom he also fears, respects, despises, loves or hates. Several of such attitudes at once will have their influence, and none of them any more measurable than anger is. It is likewise to be supposed that the man who feels the anger is more or less observant of various customary restraints; and the force of these cannot be measured, either. So how are we to add the whole situation up, and get the answer?

The difficulty we are investigating attaches to psychological determinism, not physical. If we accept epiphenomenalism, and write off consciousness as an inefficacious play of shadows cast by the action of our nerves on an interior screen, then we can reduce —or rather, can dream of reducing—the causes of human conduct to a common arithmetic. But we have quailed before the enormous paradox of making consciousness a sheer luxury in nature, a something, or shall we say, a nothing, which does no work. And so here we are, considering the application of causal reasoning to sentient and thoughtful self-direction. Arithmetic fails us; what do we do? We have recourse to casuistry. That is to say, we draw up complex secondary rules, to tell us what will happen when two or more of our primary rules are in opposition or conjunction. But of casuistry, as our moralists have pointed out to us in their proper field, there can be no end. It cannot provide for all possible conjunctions, all possible situations; and in endeavouring to do so, becomes too particular to serve as a rule, and too disorderly to pass for a system.

Our plan of amiable compromise seems to have broken down. We had hoped to show that once the formal character of causal thinking, as applicable to personal acts, was understood, the libertarian might cheerfully concede whatever the determinist could meaningfully claim. But our present conclusions seem so to ruin the determinist case, that it hardly advances a claim of any kind. We must try again, and see if we cannot do it ampler justice.

ii. *Restatement of Aristotelian naturalism*

It is unfashionable nowadays to employ historical topics in philosophical discussions. Nothing annoys us more than the Crocean dictum, that philosophy and the history of philosophy are identical. Are we to rake over the old pile for ever, and never make a direct attack on living subject-matter? Does not 'the way we think' offer an abundant material for investigation, and excuse us from a continual harping on the development, by which we got to think the way we do? Nevertheless history sometimes gives us hints so clear and serviceable, that it is stupidity to neglect them. So far from wasting our time, they shorten our labour; they place us at a point of discovery, to find which we might otherwise beat an extensive field. In the present case we cannot help observing that the psychological determinism we know is, historically speaking, the child of mathematical physics. Having seen that the inapplicability of measurement to mental phenomena calls in question the very meaningfulness of the determinist thesis, we can hardly repress a curiosity about the state of philosophical discussion, before Descartes had theorised Galileo or Newton corrected Descartes.

During the scholastic age, the bogy of strict determinism was most familiar in the philosophically uninteresting form of astral fatalism. But apart from the spurious science of planetary influences, there existed the elements of a psychological naturalism, a system which represented one side of Aristotle's own thought. The nature of the human person was thought to be determinate, the essence of Man being the same in all men; and the essence determined the action. This it did through prescribing the character of various active principles, incarnate in several faculties and organs. These principles would determine the subject to act, when suitable objects or stimuli were present in the environment. An exhaustively naturalistic account was offered for the behaviour of animals; the behaviour of men was lifted above mere nature, by the presence in us of divine or infinite faculties of reason and choice.

Such was the orthodox position; but it was an obvious temptation, to reduce the anomalous infinite powers to nothing more than a refined and complex working of finite natural principles. An Aristotelian naturalism along these lines was always a possible deviation, to say the least. Modern critics of Aristotle have sometimes claimed more, and contended that the Philosopher had only to follow his empirical, anti-Platonic bent to its logical conclusion, and he would have been a simple naturalist himself. If, then, the analogy of our mathematical physics proves a misleading guide to the causal explanation of conduct, should not we do well to start again from Aristotelian naturalism?

It is easy, of course, to wave the old naturalism away, on the ground that Aristotle's explanation of human action formed part and parcel of a system of nature, and that we can no longer entertain his account of natural events in general. We no longer see around us a universe of passive matter, diversely actuated by substantial forms, each form being credited with a characteristic appetite for self-realisation through appropriate action. And so we may find it hard to take for granted the presence and operation of similar principles in the animal man. But Aristotelianism is not so easily exploded as that. For it may be fairly rejoined, that the Philosopher's account of inanimate nature was anthropomorphic; and that to have expelled anthropomorphism from physics is no good reason for imposing physiomorphism on anthropology.

The Aristotelian theory of nature is rejected by us, on the very ground that it projected mental or linguistic form upon the inanimate world. Where we should say that the perceptible facts justified or invited the application of a formula, Aristotle would wish to say that the perceptible facts exhibited the corresponding formal character, as the principle of their being and operation. Indeed, the reality covered by any correct formal description was in his view nothing but the corresponding formal principle, actualising a suitable mass of corporeal matter. To our minds, the doctrine is sheer intellectualism, the formula or diagram by which we think the things having been made the substance of the things themselves. This is the very absurdity which Berkeley exposed— the supposition that 'ideas' or 'forms' could have the same sort of life and being in an inanimate matter, as they have in the active spirit.

That ideas, formulae and so forth are the essential forms of our thinking acts, and confer upon them whatever logical efficacy they have, is, on the contrary, a truism, and probably an actual tautology. There is no absurdity, then, in holding that formal principles constitute and direct our thought, in a way in which they do not constitute or direct the physical world. Language, unlike physical matter (for anything we know about it) is a medium of which all but the formal aspect can safely be neglected. A sentence means what it means, whether written, printed or spoken; for the purpose of those who utter it is to make it simply the vehicle of the meaning it carries. Granted that people are talking, we have only to consider why what is said is said, rather than anything else. And we find the reason we seek in the action of formal principles; the meaning of what is said, and so, what is said, being determined by the meanings of things previously said; or by the meaning of descriptions given for perceptible facts, and suggested to us, as we say, by those facts.

To see why people say what they say is, then, at least in large measure, to observe formal principles at work: a statement which does not commit us to overestimating the rationality of our talkers. So long as they shape their sentences in response to meaning of any kind, they are responding to form, for meaning belongs to form; and the response they make is formal, if it is speech at all. They may have done their formal exercise badly, but it is still a formal exercise; and if there is a mistake, it is the formal elements involved that give occasion to it.

Our present concern is with the thinking embodied in, or leading to, decision. It may be true that many decisive actions are not thoughtful nor even reasonable in the least. But when freewill is defended, it is not the caprice of madness nor the blind impulse of brutality that is in question. It is the decision of the reasoning animal; and the processes of thought, of internal and external speech, have something vital to do with it. In many decisive acts we assert habitual preferences without justifying them. But that is because we see no present occasion for the justification. There are conceivable circumstances which would put any preference upon its defence; and he is a very irrational man whose least challenged preferences do not draw their strength from many harmonising options, and from a wide view of the facts.

In what does an Aristotelian naturalism consist? In tracing back to inarticulate roots the principles which give shape to our articulate decisions. Formal principles may not (we have already conceded) really actuate the physical processes which our verbal formulae diagrammatise; but then there is neither identity of subject nor continuity of action between the gyrations of electrons, and the construction of those equations in which the physicist endeavours to plot them. Whereas between sheer appetite and proposals for dining, there may be both identity of subject, and continuity of action. The appetite is my appetite, and the proposals are my proposals; and though the proposals embody conscious choices and acquired preferences, they implement the demands of simple appetite, and are largely motived or inspired by it. My intention, in dining, is mainly to satisfy physical need; although, on the side, I solace myself with reasonable gastronomic delights, take occasion to enjoy the society of my friends, and rest my brain from the composition of Gifford Lectures.

If we say that there is continuity of action between dumb appetite and articulate decision, we may run against a strong prejudice, or well-entrenched linguistic habit. People may have been accustomed to set their most conscious and thoughtful level of life on one side, as personal or intentional; and to set everything else over against it, as brute fact in view of which they think, decide, and act. According to such a way of dividing our world, subjective passions and objective situations are bracketed under one description; they are the two sorts of brute fact in face of which we take conscious action. For example, I may have two facts to consider: that I am hungry, and that such and such a substance is dubiously edible.

It is certainly possible sometimes to look at things in this manner: to externalise, or objectivise, our instinctive responses, and to deliberate on a total situation, inward and outward. Yet such a way of thinking is secondary, and artificial. If I succeed in putting my desires among objective facts, I do so by putting myself—the self which desires—among objective facts. And while it is true that I can think of myself as though from without, and through the eyes of my biographer, I am myself, all the same. It is not as though there were something specially objectifiable about my desires—as though I could take a biographer's view of them, but not, say, of my thoughts or speeches. The objectification of thought may often be the easier of the two; I do it all the time when, in composing this book, I read over the page I have written, and make my own reflections the objects of my critical scrutiny. Yet it is I who thought the thoughts, and thought them on a principle essentially similar to that of my critical reflections about them. In like manner it is I who am hungry, and I who arrange to eat. In this case the continuity of principle is certainly not so plain—to do philosophical criticism, and to criticise philosophical criticism are more nearly the same thing, than to be hungry, and to see about some dinner. Yet there is continuity here also, a continuity about which two things at least can be said.

First, the principle of appetite, impulse or desire can be, and normally is, taken over by deliberate action. The instinctive concern for food, which is hunger in operation, is adopted as a principle by the man who starts seeing about some dinner. He makes it his axiom, that he must have nourishment; and this axiom remains the soul of his practical deliberations, or deliberate actions.

Second, the transition from mere action upon impulse, or on appetite, to deliberate action is so gradual, that we often do not know where to draw the line. When am I to say that my hunger turned my eyes towards the menu in the restaurant window, and when, that I looked to see if that would be the place at which to dine? When does sexual attraction cease to be the pull of appetite, and begin to be the young man's selection of promising company?

The primary distinction drawn by our linguistic philosophy is between occurrences directly or indirectly present to us through our senses, and our talking about these occurrences. The question then arises, where to put our intelligent and deliberate conduct; is it more a sort of talking, or more a sort of (brute) occurrence, to be talked about? And the correct answer is, as we have elsewhere argued, that it is more like a sort of talking. A deliberate reaction to our environment is a sort of comment upon it, and a decisive action is a sort of practical conclusion. But the question does not end there. We have still to ask on which side of our primary division to set instinctive behaviour, the reaction of impulse or desire; and what we are now suggesting is that it too should fall rather on the linguistic side. The sea-anemone makes a universal comment on what floats within her reach; she divides it into the assimilable and the unassimilable, by either repelling or ingesting it. So much for her theory; and as to her philosophy of practice, she stands by the general principle that the one sort of stuff is to be ingested, the other repelled. Let no Lockian deny her the power of generalisation; it is the singular that escapes the notice of this scientific beast.

It seems that what used to be called ideas, but are now called meanings or intentions, the senses carried by our words, are a sort of things which cannot be accepted by us on an independent basis —they must be seen as the sublimations of something else. Aristotle might view them as sublimations of the sensible, re-expressed in an intelligible form; as a sort of refined noble relatives to perceived physical groupings. The view persists in the curiously Aristotelian anti-Aristotelism of Locke: mental ideas are, as it were, the abstract form of sensory images. This strikes us nowadays as the most elementary of philosophical mistakes. To us, meanings are the principles or forms of self-conscious, symbolising acts, and, as such, are a sort of special refinements from the principles of animal actions, or reactions, in general. Our abandonment of Aristotelian physics, so far from undermining the

Aristotelian type of psychological naturalism, should tend to consolidate it. For the more the continuity of 'ideas' with their physical objects is denied, the more the continuity of them with their animal roots will be thrown into relief.

The assertion of such a continuity will have its effect, if not on our reason, anyhow on our imagination, in assimilating to one another the terms between which the continuity is said to obtain. We shall tend to think of appetite as a sort of intentional policy, and equally to think of policy as a sort of rationalised appetite. And since we have a prejudice in favour of what is simple, determinate, and clear, our tendency will be to credit either with those features of the other, which most strongly exhibit these favourable characteristics. We shall credit appetite with intention, and policy with givenness; thereby ridding our minds of what is most puzzling on either side. The most puzzling thing about policy is that it is self-made; and the most puzzling thing about appetite is that it is blind. What a comfort, then, to think of policy-making as a self-adjustment or self-specification of our given natural appetite through the instrumentality of conscious processes; and what a comfort to think of appetite as a preconscious, unadopted intention! These mutual borrowings once negotiated, the stage is set for Aristotelian naturalism. No further preliminaries are required; the determinate direction of appetite, instinct and so forth can without more ado be set up as the parent of deliberate choice.

We continue to use 'Aristotelian naturalism' as a convenient label; we do not burden ourselves with period furnishings. We do not, for example, tie ourselves to the antique doctrine of an unalterable essence, the ground of an invariable pattern of powers, appetites and aptitudes in every human being. We are content to say that at any given time, the instinctive and dispositional state of a man is what it is; never mind how it became so, by whatever processes, evolutionary, environmental, cultural or historical. The cause of dispositions will be a headache for another occasion. It will, very likely, be a philosophical problem of some nicety, how we should describe the causal joint between physiological conditions and psychical tendencies. But for the present purpose we take the psychical tendencies for granted, call them the nature of the man, and derive his conscious decisions from them.

iii. Application to the problem

We have now given some sort of account, impressionistic, it is to be feared, and logically slipshod, of an Aristotelian naturalism, and of the reasons which might seem to make it acceptable in our own day. It is time that we recalled the purpose which led us to bring forward such a system. We had fallen into difficulties over an attempt to apply the model of mathematically manageable causality to the explanation of conduct. Deprived of arithmetical aid, we found no satisfactory method for defining the joint effect of several uniformity-rules, all applicable to a complex situation. The difficulty was the more formidable, since simple situations hardly arise; or, if they do, hardly call for decision. And unless we could see how to define the joint effect of competing uniformities, we scarcely knew what we could continue to mean, by claiming that the decision in which their competition takes effect, is prefigured in its antecedents. The only device we could propose was casuistry: the provision of secondary rules for the conjoint effect of primaries, of tertiary rules for the conjoint effect of secondaries, and so *ad infinitum*. And the device seemed inadequate to support a serious deterministic theory; for either our rules would be too wide to cover their instances, or they would be too narrow to deserve the name of rules. Distressed by our predicament, we turned to a consideration of Aristotelian naturalism. Well now, has our consideration of it put us in any better case? Can we at least see now what a deterministic claim could mean?

At first sight, it seems that Aristotle has done nothing for us. The subject-matter offered by thought and conduct is no more amenable to measurement or calculation, for being looked at with Aristotelian eyes. We have proposed to think of policy-making as a self-adjustment or self-specification of our given natural appetite. But how is appetite to be understood to apply, particularise or formulate itself in special policies; and how are these policies to adjust themselves to singular situations? If such language means anything, it means casuistry. We credit the casuistry, indeed, to the operation of unreflective appetite. But if we are looking at human conduct, and pretending that it is explicable by causes, we are surely claiming that either we ourselves, or at any rate some conceivable observer, could draw nature's casuistry out, and state it; and that such a statement would be a watertight explanation, telling us why each thing that was done was done, in preference to any alternative there may have been. If such an explanation is not claimed as at least ideally possible, no deterministic hypothesis at all is being advanced. But it is not possible, not even ideally so, unless the fatal and admitted weaknesses of casuistry can, by some logical miracle, be remedied. Has the Aristotelian any greater logical resources than any other casuist? No, he merely has a greater effrontery. We tell him that his casuistical explanation is an explanation full of holes, and he replies, 'What of it? My casuistry is a tracing over of Nature's own, employed by her in determining the conduct which I explain. The *order and connexion of ideas is the same as the order and connexion of their objects*, let the order on both sides be as rickety as it may.'

Has the Aristotelian any defence? If he has, it must depend on his proving a genuine access to 'the order and connexion of his objects', that is, to the workings of appetite in the mind. In the case of a physical hypothesis it would be indeed laughable to say: 'I admit that the formula is too loose either to account for, or to predict, the occurrence of what occurs. But then I happen to know that the things themselves (say, the electrons) work to this formula, helping themselves out with an *ad hoc* casuistry as they go along.' An absurd claim to make, since we know nothing of the 'things themselves' independently of the hypotheses we may frame about them. The very name 'electron' is part of a hypothesis; it has no meaning outside it. And the hypothesis itself has neither sense, use, nor justification, unless it enables us either to account for, or to predict, or to control, the occurrence of particular events. Let us say that a physical hypothesis must be logically fertile of veri-fiable deductions. The case of a psychological hypothesis is surely different. It is a hypothesis about myself, as much as about any other man; and there is no getting away from the significant tautologies that I am myself, and that no other thing is I. The person 'I' is never a bunch of electrons, but the person 'I' is often a hungry creature; he may therefore reasonably claim a direct perception of hunger at work, independently of any subsequent reflective attempt to formulate or diagrammatise the working of hunger. And so it may not be absurd to protest: 'I am sorry—I know it is unsatisfactory, and logically slipshod, the way hunger works; but it just does work so; it's a terribly thoughtless, unscientific passion.'

Surely there is nothing out-of-the-way in such an avowal. Scientific thinking, with the scientific conduct which supports it, is the expression of a special effort; we are holding ourselves to the observance of certain standards. It would be quite unplausible to suggest that when we think unscientifically, and merely as the thought comes, we are thinking crypto-scientifically, and do not know it. Still more unplausible, if we take an activity less articulate than thought: the working of immediate recognition, or of appetite. Let us take recognition first. A scientific observer will allow no description of an observed fact to stand, unless it can be scientifically justified; tests are prescribed, which will determine whether the fact deserves its description, or no. But immediate recognition does not stand upon forms. We recognise or accept our object as meriting a certain description, by an unreflective, hit-or-miss reaction of the mind. This is brown to us, that is yellow, but neither object is a standard shade of either colour; 'brown' stretches a point, and embraces the one; 'yellow' stretches a point, and covers the other. Yet it will not do to call our recognition of qualities, or (which is the same thing) our assigning of names, a purely haphazard affair. There are principles at work, which are the standing values of the names.

It may well be that a long explanation could be produced, showing why a given observer at a given moment favoured 'brown' rather than 'yellow', as the label to assign in a dubious case. But the possibility of such an explanation is immaterial to our awareness of the fact: we do describe or name; the process is animated by certain principles, the meanings of our words; and the principles are applied with much elasticity. Moreover, if we look into the explanations offered for the directions in which descriptions or names are stretched on given occasions, we find that all such explanations are casuistical. 'Red' stands for a standard shade of colour, and for any neighbouring shades over which no rival standard colour exerts a stronger claim. That is the general rule. But there are special cases. If the object of vision is a chessman, it will be seen as red, even though it is more of a purple; and a man on the opposing side as white, though it is more of a yellow, or buff. There may, however, be a conflict of case-law. Viewed as a chessman, it is white, but viewed as an antique ivory, it is yellow. We shall need a further rule, to tell us in which way (under given circumstances) it is likely to be viewed. Such is the casuistry of recognition-habits.

It is much the same with appetites. Perhaps the blessed word 'disposition' will serve to bring appetites and recognition-habits under a single bracket. It would be going too far to call recognition-habits themselves a sort of appetites; as though the urge to recognise things for reds or for whites were straining at the leash in us, and hungry for appropriate objects. The opposite exaggeration would be just as great; if, that is, we called appetites a sort of recognition-habits, dispositions for recognising the edible or the lovable when we saw them. For appetites are not motived by interest in the objective character of things; they are set to gratify particular needs. But exaggeration apart, there is an important analogy between recognition-habits and appetites; and among the features common to the two, we can place the casuistical way of applying. An appetite has a principle, sure enough—the pursuit, let us say, of nourishment. But then there is a wide stretch possible in the range of what anyone will regard as edible or appetising, and an elaborate casuistry about the occasions, circumstances and places which allow us to attack an edible substance with a knife and fork. The case-law of animal appetite, like that of perceptual recognition, begins to work at an unconscious level—there are many things potentially edible which it never occurs to me to regard as my food; I look in certain types of directions when I look for my dinner. The casuistry of appetite becomes conscious, when I begin to deliberate where, what, when and with whom to eat. But so does the casuistry of recognition, when I begin to ask myself which of several epithets will be the *mot juste*.

Let us concede to the Aristotelian, that the working of a loose casuistry in the mind can be experienced; and that a man who speaks of being determined by appetite at work in him through casuistical applications, may be talking sense, independently of his ability to exhibit the case-law as a watertight system, or even independently of his belief that it ever could be exhibited as such. So much we can grant; but we must go on to ask what is meant by the word *determine*, when it is said that, through its principle and helped out by its casuistry, appetite *determines* our behaviour.

We will make the question more precise, by applying to it the grand distinction with which this chapter began: determination by force on the one hand, determination by rule, pattern or natural uniformity on the other. Are we, then, to say that determination by appetite is determination by force, or determination by rule, in the view of our Aristotelian naturalist? We must answer, 'By force.' The answer may look paradoxical, since an appetite is nothing but a self-imposing rule, and the casuistries it employs are rules also. To understand the answer, we must fix our attention on a single point—how it is that the working of appetite imposes itself on our belief. A law of nature, in the physical sense, wins our acceptance by being uniformly verified in our experiments. The law of appetite, with its secondary rules attached, imposes itself on our belief by no such evidence, but by our finding ourselves to be actuated by it. We do not constate the invariant regularity of it, we feel the occasional force of it.

According to Hume, the mind's feeling of being actuated by its own custom is the source from which our very notion of necessitation, or real constraining power, derives. We have already denounced Hume's doctrine as a paradox. As the common use of words suffices to show, force is primarily felt in the exertion and the undergoing of constraint, as between the embodied person and his physical environment. If a man is said to feel the force or constraint of appetite, 'force', or 'constraint', is being used in a transferred sense. Take the case of two starving men, who struggle for a loaf of bread. Neither sees himself as forced by his appetite; each, indeed, identifies himself with appetite, and acts in the line of it, while he exerts force upon his antagonist, and encounters an answering force. How comes it, then, that our actuation by appetite is felt as constraint? By contrast with choice. Choice is exercised by us, appetite comes upon us; comes upon us, like a giant who surprises us sleeping—the very phrase implies comparison with an extraneous power or person. We find ourselves overtaken by hunger. We can do nothing about that. But being so overtaken, we can choose what we will do about the gratification, or non-gratification, of our hunger. Not only is there this contrast between the occurrence of appetite and the exercise of choice; there can be an actual conflict between the two—I choose to defer the satisfaction of appetite, but the stimulus of hunger goads me still, bringing force to bear, as it were, against a line of policy with which I identify my intention; against me, therefore. The fasting man sees himself as wrestling with appetite for the control of conduct, as one starving man wrestles with another for the possession of food.

The mere contrast between choice and appetite may be appreciated in a moment of quiet reflection. To justify the contrast, appetite need not provoke our resistance; we may bracket it with other 'customs of the mind', and view it as 'a gentle force'. In the moment of mental conflict, when we are fighting appetite, 'gentle' is the last epithet we are likely to bestow on it.

To say, then, that appetite determines, is to say that it befalls us, and imposes its rule; thus contrasting with choice, an act in which we adopt the rule or policy which we will follow. And Aristotelian naturalism is a doctrine which holds that every adoption of a rule by choice has its whole motive in principles laid down by appetite, or by some urge equally constraining, whether working nakedly, or through the casuistry of custom. The same thing is said in other words, if choice is called a working out of appetitive casuistry through conscious process.

It is true that the determination of choice by appetite works with an effect not exactly calculable; but, the naturalist holds, that need not involve the intervention of supplementary determining reasons, independent of appetite; unless you wish to make an additional determining reason of the desire to render appetite effective, by supplying the casuistry required. The judges in our courts of law are faced every day by facts not precisely foreseen in the letter of statutes, and nevertheless falling within the scope of those statutes. It is for the judge to make the application which fails, as it were, to make itself. Unless he makes it, it will remain unmade; yet when he makes it, he need have no other guides but law on the one side, and circumstance on the other. He argues his decision, he does not simply pronounce it. Every argument, however, is an appeal either to fact, or to law. A logician will point out that judicial reasoning is not mathematically cogent; it contains an element of unreduced analogy, and analogy can always be challenged. But not every argument that can be challenged, can be challenged successfully, and judicial reason may attain moral certainty, excluding a persuasive contradiction. It may be, on the contrary, that the judge's decision is wrong, and his reasoning bad. Even so, it need not be that he has been carried crooked by the intervention of extraneous motives. His intention may have been simply to apply the existing law, only he has not done it well. The casuistry of appetite, whether conscious or unconscious, is often enough no miracle of reason; but even if it leads to the frustration of the very principle which motives it, it may still have no other motive than the principle it frustrates.

We have no more than sketched Aristotelian naturalism, but sufficiently, perhaps, for our purpose. We wanted to see whether it would give us a determinism so chastened, that all it could meaningfully claim, the libertarian might cheerfully allow. Is the 'agreed solution' in sight? But what are the suggested terms? Presumably these: the libertarian can have his real act of decision, applying the principles to the case; and the determinist can have the principles. The man of liberty can comfort himself with two reflections: that but for the personal act of accommodation, the principles would fail to take hold of the situation; and that there is no predicting decision, by rule of thumb—one has simply to judge how a given man in given circumstances is going to decide. The friend of Necessity can be happy in the assurance that human actions are never motiveless; and that any motive we can ever state, whether natural or rational, will turn out to express a principle already present in the agent, and now in some way awakened, or called for, by the situation which confronts him. The principle in question may have been fixed by casuistical formulation on occasions of previous decision. Even so, that formulation itself was motived by principles already in the agent at that time. So back and back we go; but we cannot go back *ad infinitum* in a finite biography. We must come to principles either instinctive in the animal, or inculcated upon the child. These, then, will be our root-causes, the parents of all our decisions.

Well, and will such a division of the spoils satisfy both parties? It will not content the libertarians. They will put in their claim for a share of the Principles. They will agree, of course, that many principles are simply given, or natural—hunger, for example— and that acquired principles can become a second nature. But they will assert that many principles expressed in decisions, and constituting the motives of them, are not given, but made. The Naturalist has conceded that new decisions make new rules; but such rules he regards as a casuistry applying old principles, and finding in those principles their only stable motives. The Libertarian is not satisfied with such an account. He wants to say that new rules, and even new particular projects, can be their own motives; that we adopt either general plans of life, or projects of particular action, because we wish to realise them. If we are asked to explain ourselves in such a case, we need allege neither existing states of affairs, nor accepted principles of taste and liking. We may simply dilate on the project, as what we want to do, or the form of life, as what we wish to see actualised. No doubt our plan, if it is to attract us, will have to lie within a range of objects touching upon existing preferences. It must have analogy with what a given tendency or principle recommends. But there is no warrant for claiming that the interest it excites is proportionate to its pull on any such principles or tendencies. The new acquaintance, from whose friendship I hope so much, must be capable of exciting and retaining regard; the interests I look to share with him must be capable of delighting a human mind. But these are platitudes. I take them for granted, and in explaining why I am after this friend, rather than any other possible friend, I state what I take to be unique characteristics, and sketch what I take to be singular hopes. I should think it inadequate, irrelevant, or downright absurd, to commend him as embodying the character of the Good Friend, or even the good friend for me; to praise up our proposed common activities as proper to please mankind, or a man like me, or even a man whose life has been what mine has been.

The Naturalist will hold that existing tendencies determine our new preferences by their imperceptible casuistry, whatever we may think. The Libertarian retorts that the Naturalist cannot prove it, nor can the man engaged in action and decision think it. Against naturalistic Aristotelism he invokes the authentic Aristotle, and reasserts the potentially infinite faculty, the god in us. Our practical concern, according to his view, may share something of the open range proper to our intellectual interest. If pure speculative curiosity is to be accounted a human appetite, it is an appetite for nothing narrower than what there is to know. Our animal nature limits our range of experience, and limits what we can make of it; it does not dictate the directions of our enquiry. Other beings, remote constituents of the world, can intrigue us by their very otherness, or remoteness from us; our attention is drawn simply by what they are in themselves, so far as we can know it. Yet the most abstract speculative interest is itself a practical concern, for it commits us to a difficult investigation; and this single truth would suffice to prove our contention in principle. But it is scarcely possible to stop there, and extend our claim no further. The sort of practical concern we may have with an investigation of the galaxies is admittedly austere and cool, when compared with our interest in the things we can alter or invent, cooperate with or profit by. But there is no evident reason why sheer objective interest should cease to be a motive, when the patterns of action which concern us are such as we mean ourselves to weave; whether we weave them in free space, as it were, or round existent beings who enter into our designs. Why cannot we be motived, in either case, by the character of what we propose to make, in abstraction from its appeal to set habits or finite appetites?

The idiom of spiritualising Aristotelism is, perhaps, somewhat stilted and antique. The libertarian may take a less unfashionable level, by merely attacking that assimilation of rational decision to animal appetite, on which we saw naturalism to be based. The self-application of instinct or appetite to various circumstance can be sufficiently described as a sort of unconscious casuistry; but justice is not done to the distinctive character of reasonable decisions, by making the casuistry conscious, and more elaborate or refined. Reason introduces a concern with the object, the product or the action, each for its own sake. Decision advances into an open future, and chooses what it will create, for the sake of the creation. Human decision does not create *ex nihilo*, like the divine; and if the necessity of a pre-existent matter is all the determinist claims, Liberty herself will shake hands with him. But our determinist is a naturalist; he wants not only a pre-existent matter, but (to load him with the Aristotelian jargon) a total prefiguration of the formal cause.

iv. *Argument from accumulation of innovations*

Philosophers have been taught by Descartes to divide their subjects and work upon the limited, manageable instance, confident that it will disclose the principles needed for a more general explanation. The maxim is salutary; and yet there are areas in which it does not apply, and where (to speak with the vulgar) we may miss the wood by scrutinising the trees. If we wish to estimate the plausibility of naturalistic determinism, the microscopic view is not the best. Take for your field any single decision, or voluntary action, and you can hope to represent naturalism as sturdy commonsense, libertarianism as high-flown metaphysics. Survey the history of human culture, and things take on a different aspect.

About any single decision, the naturalist can always challenge us to prove a negative: a debating-point which will have its usual effect. 'Of course you feel' he says 'that you interest yourself in the simple, and it may be unique, character of the friend, the project, or whatever it is. You no more see the subjective beam of determinate appetite gilding your objects with a borrowed light, than you see the sun at midnight illumining the moon. The interest is seen as dwelling on the single object; the project you devise appears to be an unique creation—but then you have no insight into the recesses of the mind, which supply the principles shaping it. How could you possibly prove that the very flexible formula of natural casuistry will fail to explain your particular choice? Would omniscience be floored, by the demand for an exhibition of considerations both sufficient to motive your decision, and exclusively drawn from the interplay of your standing tendencies with your environmental perceptions? How could you hope to prove anything of the kind?'

Well, perhaps we cannot. But look at the total fact and history of culture. If the naturalist is right, the whole frame of human things was virtually contained in the animal instincts of the luckiest among apes, taken in conjunction with the characteristics of his physical environment. If the conclusion does not make sense, we shall have to admit a power in the reasoning animal, to create the objects of his interest, and to interest himself in his creations. No contributions from the several polyps, no coral-reef; but there is a coral-reef. No deviation in each millimetre from the standard red, and the spectrum will never get to orange; but see, here it has reached a pure orange; so whether we can show a perceptible colour-change within a given minute range, is not the decisive argument for or against innovation. The power of sheer novelty centred in the human being is evident in the whole body of his history; so anthropology joins hands with intuitive conviction.

To summarise the argument. The attempt at an agreed solution between Necessity and Freedom has broken down. By reducing the meaningful claims of deterministic explanation, we have failed to produce the story we had hoped for: the story which concedes Liberty all she can sensibly assert, while still allowing choices to be somehow the outcome of natural process. No, what Liberty still claims is in contradiction to anything that could pass for a deterministic formulation.

CHAPTER XI

MOTIVE AND CHOICE

i. 'Every choice requires a determining motive'

OUR latest discussions have been somewhat loose and general. It may help to give greater precision to the issues, if we take a single argument and analyse it with some degree of exactitude. Here, then, is a determinist who has nothing to say to our wide and luminous considerations. He restricts his survey to the view he thinks we are bound to take of our choices themselves, as soon as we reflect. A moment's thought, he says, will convince us that we cannot choose without a motive; and that if we have a motive, the motive determines the choice.

There are supposed truths which seem more evident to a moment's thought, than they do to twenty minutes of reflection; and in the suspicion that this may be a case of the kind, we will set the argument out at greater length. We will formulate it in four lines or steps; and we will comment briefly on each, before we go on to the next.

The first line is this. No one acts without a motive. This is a sort of tautology. For though we may make bodily movements which are motiveless, we should not call them acts of the moral person; and they are of no concern to the theory of freewill.

Such is the first line of the argument, and we may as well concede it. If our object were to waste time, and talk the motion out, we could make a long protest on the ambiguity of the word 'motive', demanding the concession of one distinction after another. It would be a disingenuous defence. For there is a large sense of 'motive' easily stated, and sufficient to justify the formula that no one acts motiveless. To see what this large sense is, one has

merely to reflect that there is a virtual infinity of possible objects
for our attention, and of possible projects for our action. What
makes us attend to any one object, or start on any single project?
We may say that the object, or the project, appeals to us, or makes
a claim upon us. But this is metaphor, and the metaphor misleads.
Projects and objects reach out no hands, they raise no voices. The
movement starts from us; something in us goes out to them.
Motive, then, is whatever in us moves us towards an object or
project. And if motive is defined like this, it seems right to agree
that apart from a motive none of us would act; for all projects
and all objects would be indifferent to us. So much, then, for the
first line of the argument.

The second line says that a motive, unopposed by any conflicting motive, takes effect. This cannot, obviously, mean that no
interest we conceive in anything even fails of its effect through
petering out unopposed; it is too evident a fact of experience that
interest dies, without being killed by anything that can be speci-
fied. No; when it is said that motive, unopposed by motive, takes
effect, it is being assumed that the motive of which we speak is
alive and moving us. And what is being said is that it takes effect
in our action; we act upon it, unless we also have a different motive;
a motive for acting contrary to it, or for refusing to act at all. We
concede this, and pass to the third line of the argument.

The third line is as follows. Where there is an opposition of
motives, one of two things will happen. Either the man 'does
what he feels like most'; allows, that is, whichever motive can, to
capture from its rival the machinery of action; or else he makes a
decision between the courses recommended by the rival motives.

Shall we allow this dilemma to pass? Is the first half of it
genuine? Can a man abdicate the seat of judgement, and let his
motives fight it out between them? Is not what is called 'just doing
whichever one feels like most' the making of a lazy and incon-
siderate decision? On these questions there is scope for much
debate. Perhaps, however, we can afford to waive it here. For
supposing that there is the case of 'the motives fighting it out' it
will not be claimed by libertarians as a shining example of free

choice. We can afford to leave open the question, whether there are such cases or not. So let us accept the third line of the argument, merely rephrasing it, so as to rob it of its apparently empirical form. Let us say that, where there is an opposition of motives, there are only two things that we could suggest as possible. Either the man undergoes the arbitrament of war between the opposing forces, or he imposes an arbitration on them: that is, he makes a genuine decision.

To proceed, then, with the fourth line, which develops the dilemma of which the third has laid the foundation. If the motives fight it out between them, then, in his resultant conduct, the man is determined by the preponderance of motive, and the thesis of the argument is proved. If, on the other hand, he imposes a decision, his decision is a further act in its own right. Now we have agreed that no one acts without a motive. And since to make a decision is to act, no one decides without a motive. Now either the motive for the act of decision is unopposed by any other motive, or it is opposed. If it is unopposed, then it takes effect; for we have agreed that unopposed motives take effect. And so the decision is determined by the motive. If, on the other hand, it is opposed, we have the same situation as before—a conflict of motives; and the same dilemma will arise. Either the motives fight it out, or a fresh decision is imposed; and so *ad infinitum*. The conclusion is, that no agent will ever reach a decision, unless one of two things happens: either a simple motive takes effect, or a battle of motives fights it out. And so all decisions are determined by motives; whether it be by one motive unopposed, or by a preponderance of one over another. And that is the conclusion of the argument.

But the argument is a sophism. The sophistry lies in disguising the distinctive character of decision. Decision is treated as simply another personal event, like the initial taking of interest; it is not acknowledged to be a personal event of a different order. According to the sophism, decision is distinguished from the rival interests between which it arbitrates, by having, like them, its own motive; and the part played by motive in decision is taken to be the same as the part played by motive in causing initial interest. Both these positions are false. Decision responds to motive in a way quite different from the way in which initial interest responds to it; and this difference in the manner of response to motive is, of itself, sufficient to mark off decision from the initial interests between which it decides; there is no need to assign a new motive to the decision, if we are to make of it a distinct event. Let us exhibit these two points in order.

(1) The argument we are criticising takes the innocent assertion that no one can act without a motive, and interprets it to mean, that every act requires its distinct motive. But there is no self-evidence in the interpretation. All that is evident is, that we cannot act without a motive, or motives. But when we try to decide between interesting projects, whatever may embarrass us, it is not a lack of motives; we have all too many: enough not for one line of action only, but for two or three. We may, of course, pull in fresh motives to help us decide. For example, a man who feels a direct interest in rival lines of action, may also be anxious to gain the good opinion of a girl; and so he may ask himself which way of behaving will impress her more favourably. But even if he does ask himself this, he still has to decide for pleasing the girl by the one action, in preference to securing, by the other line of action, whatever it would secure.

And so, for the purpose of grasping the character of decision as such, the introduction of extra motives is a red herring. It is more convenient to stick to the case in which the motives remain the same throughout. A tutor wonders whether to give his old pupil a testimonial. Before he reaches a decision, he wants to do for the young man an office of friendship. And if, in the upshot, he decides to write the testimonial, friendship is still the motive of his action. Only now he has satisfied himself that no motive excluding it is of greater importance to him. On the other side, he was initially reluctant to deceive the young man's prospective employers. And if he decides to withhold the testimonial, it will be for no other reason than this. Decision is not made to be decision by the intervention of a fresh motive; it is made to be decision by deciding between whatever motives there are.

But surely (it will be objected) if a man, who was not previously engaged in making a decision, sets about the making of one,
he enters upon a new form of activity; and he requires a motive
for so doing. Yes; he makes a change in the form of his mental
action, and he requires a motive—but only a formal motive. An
old-fashioned philosophy would have said, perhaps, that the
motive was a concern for unity of consciousness, or for the man's
own humanity—finding himself caught in a conflict of desires or
aims, he needs no other motive for resolving it, than the axiomatic unsatisfactoriness of such a state. We should prefer to say
that in most cases the mind's aversion from unresolved conflict
acts immediately, like a physical appetite; we do not decide to
decide (or there would be an infinite regress of mental acts), we
just do decide, out of our instinctive interest in—what shall we
say?—in non-frustration. But this is a motive always operative,
and so not usually called a motive; for we commonly reckon as
motives only those reasons for action about which it would be
sensible to ask questions. 'What made him want to push such-and-
such a candidate?'—'Oh, don't you know? He was his pupil for
two years.'—'But what made him hesitate about pushing him?'—
'Why, he found one of his old essays in a drawer.' So far we have a
perfectly sensible piece of conversation. But no one expects it to
continue like this: 'But why ever did he make up his mind between giving a testimonial, and withholding it?'—'Oh, he conceived a strong dislike for the state of indecision.' No motive in
the proper and particular sense is required, to prompt the wish for
decision. And as for the motives on which the decision is taken,
they need be no others than were present in the preceding state of
conflict.

(2) We will now take up the second point of our criticism.
The argument we are refuting disguises the difference in the
function of motive as occasioning initial interest, and as guiding
subsequent decision. Let us take an example of initial interest. A
young man sees a girl in the street, says 'Goodness, what a girl!'
and turns out of his road to keep her in view. It is necessary to

suppose something in the young man which prompts him to act on the spur of the moment in the way he does. And there is no difficulty in specifying what this *something* is; for in this sort of way young men are much alike, and would be even more alike than they are, but for breeding and sophistication. So there is no mystery here about motive, if motive means that without which no one acts.

If motive means something on which an intelligible decision to act might be taken, there may, of course, be a good deal of mystery about motive in such a case. Suppose the young man has no idea of bringing the girl to bay, or of achieving any result which can compensate the loss of time, and the ridicule of friends; we might then fairly complain that his behaviour is absolutely motiveless, and that he ought therefore to be ashamed of himself, and stop it. We complain that he does not know what he is doing; but that does not alter the fact that he does it, and that he has the sort of motive without which no one does anything. In this case we will call it sex; and we may say, by way of epigram, that sex is a motive for doing many motiveless actions.

The universal statement that no one acts without a motive is understood to cover such cases as that of our young man; and to make sense of the statement, we must allow to the term 'motive' the necessary breadth. That no one acts without a motive, means no more than this: (a) some object, or project, must interest the agent and (b) there must be something in the agent which makes him liable to feel such an interest. Now it is obvious that in the initial outbreak of interest choice has no part. Something catches our attention; we find ourselves interested before we can do anything about it. To speak of the motive as a simple determining cause at this stage, is to do no violence either to language or to experience. But if anyone proposes to maintain that motive operates in the same way, when consideration is being exercised and choice made, he is defending an open paradox. Of course the man who considers and judges alternatives remains interested in these alternatives, or why should he trouble to consider them, or to judge between them? But the part played by motivation in his

THE FREEDOM OF THE WILL

action is not now what it was when he first felt an interest. We will proceed to show what the difference is.

Aristotle declared that mere thought had no motive power; only what he called appetite could move us. More recent sages have laid it down that no genuine 'It is so' implies an 'I must', or an 'I wish', or a 'Let me'. The stirrings of action commonly arise in response to what is seen to be the case, but the proper cause of the response lies in that which responds; purpose is born of purpose, not of constatation. How, then, are we to find a beginning of purpose, or a first purpose? If every purpose needs an actual purpose for its antecedent, we shall never come to a beginning at all; and, conversely, a man who awakes from a profound sleep, purposing nothing, can never begin to purpose anything. We escape from the *impasse* by a recourse to the language of potential purpose, or disposition. Our young man going down the street is entertaining no actual interest in attractive girls; on the contrary, he is (let us suppose) doing accounts in his head. But he is dispositionally, or potentially, an amateur of female charm and, on the occasion of a corresponding object presented to the eye, his dispositional or potential interest in the subject springs into actual life.

If the language of disposition may be allowed us, we can proceed to formulate a convenient distinction. Initial interest arises by way of transition from dispositional concern to actual concern. But consideration, and decision, are secondary phases of purposive response, and arise by way of transition from one phase of actual concern to another. For the man who begins to consider, or to pass judgement, was already concerning himself with the alternatives which called for the consideration, or the decision, he now proceeds to bestow. What he had not previously done was to draw the alternatives together into the focus of a single survey; and this he now proceeds to do.

Having laid down our distinction, we will go on to relate it to the distinction between necessity and freedom. A transition from dispositional purpose or concern to actual purpose or concern is a necessary transition, not one we can choose to make; for, in an allowable sense of the words, we are not there to do the choosing. Unless we are already on the job, not potentially but actually concerning ourselves with something, we can steer neither the direction not the expression of our concern. Whereas a transition from one phase of actual concern to another is the typical occasion for voluntary choice; the subject, finding himself already engaged in a line of interest, decides in what way he will prolong it.

In what different senses, then, does the maxim that *no one acts without a motive* apply to a direct expression of initial interest on the one hand, and to a considerative or judicial prolongation of it, on the other! To say that no one acts without a motive in the initial bestowal of his attention, is to say that a determining cause in himself is required, why he should bestow his attention where he bestows it: a cause which for convenience we describe in dispositional terms. Whereas to say that no one acts without a motive in considering or deciding, is to say that he must have been already interested in what he proceeds to consider or decide upon; since otherwise he, as an interested party capable of pursuing consideration or forming decision, would simply not have been there. Now it is manifest sophistry (and this is really our whole contention) so to equate these two applications, or senses, of the formula that no one acts without a motive, as to transfer the deterministic implications of the one, to the account we give of the other. Disposition is rightly conceived of as a sheer cause, excluding the operation of any choice; but actual interest is the basis on which choices are built. An argument for determinism which treats the second as a case of the first, is surely self-condemned.

ii. *Disposition as a cause*

Shall we rest content with the refutation of the motive argument which we have produced? Ought we not, perhaps, to give our attack a more up-to-date and logical air? Let us suppose a logician to be listening to us. In his hearing, then, we repeat our protest: monstrous, we say, to interpret actual interest in its effect on choice, by analogy with disposition in its effect on actual interest. Monstrous indeed, says the logician; and why monstrous?

Because nonsensical, because in violation of logical rules. The proper complaint is not, that a cause determining an effect is equated with a cause enabling a free act; but that two things are equated, which are not causes in the same sense at all; no more causes in the same sense, than the magnitude of an elephant and the magnitude of a calamity are magnitudes in the same sense, or capable of being compared with one another. Actual interest is part of some real and particular mental or personal event; and there is direct evidence for its presence, or absence: a man neither feels nor behaves the same, when he is interested and when he is not. But disposition is neither an event, nor a set of events; nor does it afford direct evidence of its presence in the man who is said to have it. We impute it to him on the ground of his previous conduct. A tutor-who-takes-an-interest-in-his-pupils'-promotion is, up to the moment of awakened concern for a particular case, indistinguishable from a tutor who takes no such interest; only that we have seen him on the job before. Thus, when we say that his present concern springs from his disposition to feel such an interest, we are not tracing the succession of phases in any real process, we are not passing from one link to the next in any chain of events. All we are doing is to cash out, in terms of a man's present conduct, the value of a general expectation justified by his previous history. And what could be more absurd, than to apply to the interpretation of an event-sequence the rules for cashing a general expectation? But this is precisely what people do, who suppose that the sequence of consideration, or decision, upon actual interest preceding it, is like the conformity of actual behaviour, or feeling, to an imputed disposition.

So much for the logician's kind attempt to reformulate our attack on the determinism of motive. It is certainly neat, but does it do the job? Is the deterministic description of initial motive deterministic, for no other reason than that it is a dispositional description? If so, then we have only to bar the comparison between a disposition and an antecedent, and we are rid of the whole determinist case. But it is not clear that this is so. We are inclined rather to suspect, that if we rid ourselves of dispositional language entirely, and spoke of initial interest as consequent upon genuine antecedents, we should still want to call its occurrence necessary or determined. Dispositional language is not, after all, reserved for the human being. As I may say that actual ire arises from irascibility, so I may say that actual explosion arises from explosibility. But I do not agree, nor will you, that our habit of supposing explosions to take place by natural necessity, is a mere consequence of our using disposition-language about quiescent dynamite. When we have got rid of the disposition language, the natural necessity remains. Perhaps the same may be true about disposition-language as applied to mankind. And if it is true, then the determinist can escape the logician's refutation. For he can reformulate his account of initial interest so as to exclude dispositional language, and still make it a determinist account. It will remain, then, that the proper refutation of the determinist is one which distinguishes necessary sequences from free sequences. Granting that initial interest arises from its antecedents by a necessary sequence, we shall argue that consideration and choice follow their antecedents by a free sequence.

The parallel and contrast between explosibility and irascibility is worth developing a little. The unscientific observer does not know the structure of forces in the dynamite, nor can he perceive any signs of the action of those forces when they are, so to speak, marking time within the quiescent mass. And so he does not know what it is which responds to the fuse by flying out so alarmingly. Wishing to say something, he talks about explosibility, putting the effect (explosion) into the potential mood (-ibility) and making it do duty for a cause. In the same way, if we call the man irascible, we are plastering ignorance with verbiage. We believe in, though we cannot indicate, real forces or activities at present playing quietly in the man, very likely in his cerebral cortex: forces of which the balance, or pattern, has been affected by his previous conduct, and will in turn affect his present action. But having nothing but a general supposition about these forces, we are content to plaster them over with the word 'irascibility'.

So far the comparison between the dynamite and the retired

military officer holds good. But no further. For in the case of the dynamite, the area of real events covered by the verbal plaster of 'explosibility' has the same essential character as the area of events directly indicated by the word 'explosion'. If we are talking of dynamite, there is no difference of any philosophical interest between any of the following transitions: the transition from one moment of stable activity to another; the transition from stable activity to expansive activity; the transition from one moment of expansive activity to another. All these steps have the same physical nature; the difference is simply in relation to an observer. To the naked eye, the succession of stable activity on stable activity in the dynamite is imperceptible; the succession of expansive activity upon stable activity affords perceptible signs of what succeeds (the blast) but not of that on which it succeeds (the stable action). The succession of expansive activity upon expansive activity allows perception of both phases (both the first blasting and the spread of the blast). But these differences in perceptibility concern not the action of the dynamite, but only the perceptions of the observer.

The case of the retired military officer is different. For here we have not so much to consider the perceptibility of his successive phases to the eye of his fellow-golfer; we have to consider his own awareness of them. While his irascible old brain is merely ticking over, he is himself unaware of the succession of one tick upon another. But when, upon the ticking-over of his potentially irascible cerebrations, there follows an outburst of wrath over the breaking of his club, he is as unaware as before of the ticking-over, but aware of the succeeding wrath. And when, already tingling with wrath, and knowing the occasion of it, he goes on to employ his wit in the invention of new and curious maledictions, he is aware both of the initial wrath, and of the game of maledictory invention. Now the entry of the colonel's own awareness into the succession of events does not leave them unaffected. He is not the spectator of his conduct, he is the agent in it. When he finds himself angry, he finds himself itching—perhaps actually beginning—to thrash about with his broken club, and to shout. But he chooses to canalise or direct his passion into the ingenious invention of picturesque oaths, hoping that it will pass as a sort of clowning; one of the things permitted, anyhow in the open air, to an officer and a gentleman. For, alongside the itch to shout and to smite, there awakens in him the anxiety not to disgrace his rank; and his game of picturesque swearing is a choice made in view of these conflicting impulses, and by way of a compromise between them.

To return now to the comparison between the colonel and the dynamite. The verbal plaster 'irascibility' covers a set of real events unknown, which we may be content to think roughly similar to those covered by the verbal plaster 'explosibility'. But when irascibility takes effect in actual ire, a train of events is set in motion which develops quite differently from any physical explosion. For anger is a state of consciousness, and out of his anger the conscious being may act as he determines, not as he is determined by any shove from behind. There is all the difference in the world, then, between conscious reaction arising out of a cause in us of which we are unconscious, and conscious activity developed by us, in succession to a phase in which we are already conscious.

iii. *Concomitant motive*

Our whole endeavour, in the present enquiry, is to correct our language about what is called freewill. What we should like to do would be to settle upon a few lapidary formulae, which would fix the proper types of speech about it. But in practice what we need to do is to protect ourselves against confusion by false analogies; and such protection cannot be afforded by a few clear definitions. We cannot bar out all misleading comparisons by an initial prescription. They have to be unmasked as they arise. Each one must be dissolved by the drawing of the appropriate distinction. But often enough, in the very drawing of it, we raise a fresh misleading suggestion, and are obliged to distinguish yet again. Will it go on for ever? We, anyhow, will not; we will go one or two steps further, and then have done.

Here, at least, is an objection which we ought not to leave unanswered, so naturally does it arise in view of the conclusions we have been recording. The objection is that we have distinguished too sharply between the effect of an unconscious antecedent state, and the effect of a conscious antecedent activity. It will not do to say that whereas the former simply determines its successor, the latter does not determine at all; all it does is to put us there, on the job, and in a position to make our next step what we choose to make it. This will not do; for if antecedent actual interest in no way determines the consideration or the decision into which it leads us, we shall have a consideration, or a decision, undirected by interest or motive of any kind; and is not such a consideration or decision a monstrosity in nature? Undirected by interest, how can we ever consider or decide? And not only, how can we get on with it? but why should we even bother to try? Surely the proper way to distinguish between the effect of an unconscious state and the effect of a conscious activity, is to make it a difference of degree. We should attribute a complete determining power to the one, and an incomplete determining power to the other. For surely the already awakened interest out of which we proceed to consider or to decide, delimits an area of concern, within which our consideration or decision proceeds to make a further de-limitation, by picking, as it were, the very ground it chooses to take.

Such a way of talking may seem reasonable enough, but it gives rise to dangerous consequences. The danger becomes apparent when people begin to assign their respective rôles to the two par-tial determinants, motive and choice. For what (it may then be asked) can the operation of choice add to the operation of motive, but an element of intellectual calculation? What can choice choose, but the richest compatible selection from the objects of interest, together with the practical means for encompassing it? For were choice to add an element of direction additional to motive, what could she add but motiveless caprice? It will remain, then, that a man's deliberate action is a function of antecedent motive *plus* practical intelligence. Now, as Socrates said, no one is stupid on purpose in the choice of his own path; or if he is, there will be a motive for his voluntary stupidity. If, then, a man's motives, his practical intelligence and his present intellectual state are all known, it should be possible to predict his behaviour; for the factors determinant of it are all in our hands.

What is the matter with this piece of reasoning? False abstraction is the matter with it. It is like the rhetorical debate between God's mercy and his justice. There can be no such debate, because there are no parties to carry it on; there is only the mercifully just, and justly merciful God. He acts mercifully, indeed, and at the same time justly; but the result is not obtained by a wrangle between a couple of adverbs. So a man who considers or decides acts both motivedly and choosingly; but these are complementary aspects of his action, not interagent forces producing a joint result. We do not have to ask how choice can choose, unless she takes her cue from motive. For choice is an activity to which motivedness belongs.

If we divide motive from choice, and set them side by side, we shall be likely to think of motive as rigid, and choice as flexible. For choice is by definition a capacity for alternatives, whereas motive is a term scarcely used except in asking or answering the question, what is, or was, his motive? We are concerned to name some one definite thing, whether it is a passion, like envy, or a project, such as the promotion of a friend. When, therefore, we bring choice and motive into partnership, we are wedding the vine to the elm, the flexible to the inflexible; and the adjustment between them is obviously to be obtained by the yielding of the flexible to the inflexible. So motive is taken to determine choice.

But the conclusion is the effect of linguistic confusion. If a man freely invents a course of action step by step, as he goes along, it is always possible to ask, what is his motive? and to answer with some sort of generalisation about his aims or his emotions. But the commentator on his neighbour's behaviour, or the ruminator upon his own conduct, takes himself too seriously altogether, if he mistakes a generalisation about purpose for the determinant of choice. If we want to see how choice can really choose, and yet not be motiveless, we must set aside the irrelevant question, 'In what word, or phrase, can the agent's purpose be summarised?' and substitute the question, 'How does choiceful activity work?'

Our best plan will be to take an example, and follow a train of action as it develops. Here is an undergraduate, come up fresh to the University. Like any other normal specimen of his kind, he has an instinctive propensity to make friends and to be liked, a propensity which has received a special development in the life of his family and his school. Here, then, is our dispositional cause. He meets a fellow-undergraduate of the same year, a youth whose desire for social life equals his own; he feels a sudden expansion of the heart, and kindling of delight in this youth's company; and here we observe the birth of initial interest, arising as the mere effect of the dispositional cause. He proceeds to cultivate his new friend's acquaintance: to walk with him, to play tennis with him, to eat and drink with him, and to conduct interminable conversations with him. These things he does with a good deal of that self-consciousness about personal relations, which is not uncommon at his age. We have said that he cultivates the acquaintance, and the phrase fits—he cultivates it as a zealous and scientific farmer may study to cultivate his land; he bestows thought on it, and has policies about it. Here, then, we have the exercise of choice, or self-direction, following upon particular interest initially aroused. And this is the phase of the affair we have to consider, with a view to grasping the part played in it by motive.

We must try to see the whole range of companionable activity through the eyes of the undergraduate himself. Is he interested in it? Of course he is; far too interested, his tutor will say. Would he but attend to his science as he attends to his friendship, he would be less likely to suffer want in his old age. But in what is he interested? Certainly not in the mere formal idea of having friends, and succeeding as a social being—the object, if you remember, of the disposition with which we credited him at the moment of his entry to the University. He has stopped thinking about that, if he ever consciously did think of it—for he is no longer anxious—perhaps he ought to be—about his social ineptitude. What, then, is now the object of his interest? Shall we say, not merely to have a friend or friends, but to have this friend; as a hungry man's general desire to have a meal becomes particularised as the desire to eat a well-grilled steak, when his wife brings it in on a plate, and the aroma assaults his nostrils. All we have to do is to add the particular characteristics of beefsteak on the one hand, or John Robinson on the other, to the sketchy lineaments of the object claimed by undifferentiated appetite; and we shall know what our man is interested in.

Or would this be to press the analogy between a prospective friend and an edible steak too far? The diner has eaten steak before, and has (let us hope) entire confidence in his wife's catering. As soon as he has seen and smelt the steak, he settles his mind about the object of his interest. It is an edible beefsteak. Now no one will wish to deny that for a discerning palate, one steak differs from another steak in glory; but this consideration does not alter the motive of a reasonable man. It merely spices his anticipation with a grain of curiosity. How different is the case of a friend! It may be true that the angels—or perhaps even, the dons—could give an inventory of John Robinson's virtues, faults, capacities, defects, interests, blind-spots, charms, and repellencies. But his young contemporary, when he meets him first, does not take in these characteristics, as the diner at a glance takes in the characteristics of a steak. No: he takes in a smile, an attitude of welcome, a set of features, and a tone of voice; and his bosom conceives a great hope. 'With this youth,' he says, 'I will have a delightful acquaintance; we will—what will we do together? I do not know. We will make it up as we go along.' So they make it up as they go along, John Robinson and Robin Johnson; and we need not ask how long it lasts them. But while it lasts, and while they are making it up, in what is Johnson interested? He is interested in the whole cheerful game: in his fellow-player, and in all the inventions, choices, decisions and cooperations of their relationship. He is interested in what he has discovered, or hopes to discover, about his friend, but also in the discovering. He is interested in what they have invented between them, or hope to invent; but also in the inventing.

Enough of this parable. If anyone asks us how choice can co-exist with interest and not be determined by it, we will answer: 'The chooser is interested in choosing.'

To think straight about this matter, it is vital to distinguish con-comitant interest from antecedent interest. Freely chosen action will not be pursued unless both play their part. Antecedent inter-est, springing out of disposition, must first arise, or, as we have said above, the agent will simply not be there, or on the job. If, when he proceeded to the job, the antecedent interest remained the whole motive of his action, he would be controlled by the dead hand of his own past. The past nothing can alter—not even the gods can do it, says the Greek proverb; a choice determined by antecedent interest would be determined indeed. But a little attention to life as it is lived will suffice to lay the spectre of necessity. Out of antecedent interest is born an interest concomi-tant with the action it motives: an interest inseparable from the action itself, and equally flexible.

iv. Conclusion

Looking back, now, on the argument of this chapter, we can see that what we have done boils down to this: we have drawn two distinctions. We have distinguished between two sorts of transition; and we have distinguished between two sorts of inter-est. The two sorts of transition were involuntary and voluntary: the *involuntary* transition from an unconscious personal state to some conscious interest; the *voluntary* transition from a phase of conscious interest to some further development of our personal response. The two sorts of interest we have distinguished are antecedent, and concomitant: the *antecedent* interest which in-clined us to a line of action, and the *concomitant* interest we take in developing that line of action. It is obvious that these two distinc-tions fit together into a single story. For every voluntary tran-sition we make from one phase of action to another has antecedent interest behind it, and concomitant interest dwelling upon it. These, then, are the two distinctions we have drawn, and this is the relation between them. And our claim about them is this; that if we keep these two distinctions in mind, we can liberate our-selves from the sophistry, which undermines belief in voluntary freedom by the platitude that we cannot act except as we are motived to act.

Even supposing that our argument has been successful, let us remember the very limited scope of it.

Psychological determinism has many faces; and motive is an endlessly ambiguous word. We have talked about motive, but that does not mean that we have discussed every argument built upon it. We have considered life, not as the subject of psycho-logical analysis or of psychiatric manipulation, but as lived by him whose life it is. And we have refuted nothing but the single thesis, that action and motive are so related in our common understanding of them, that action must be determined by motive; and determined in such a sense, that we can do only what we were bound to do.

We have attempted to show that the thesis rests on nothing but linguistic confusion, and can be easily dissolved by logical dis-tinction. If we take the trouble to talk straight, we shall have no difficulty in speaking about a man motived by interest in what he makes up as he goes along. I say, we have no difficulty in speaking so. I do not say that the life we freely live is an improvised fantasy, which we can make whatever the whim takes us to make it. For, quite apart from the question of moral seriousness—the limits which attach to the justifiable use of our time—we have, no doubt, imperious psychological demands to face. Our own nature is a sphinx propounding riddles to us, in a speech which is not even articulate. We must employ our free abilities in both guess-ing how the riddles run, and in devising answers. Unlike the sphinx of legend, our nature does not demand one set answer to each of her riddles; many different answers will satisfy, so there is room enough for invention; but the answer must satisfy the riddle, all the same. If we answer wrong, she does not kill us outright; she fixes her claws in us, and grips us; the grip of the sphinx is called unhappiness, and, since it is progressively tight-ened as we fail to invent the suitable reply, it is a marvellous stimulus to invention. But only up to a point. Beyond that point it produces despair, madness, death.

But, under happier circumstances, we are free to satisfy our nature's demands; and so long as we do, within reason, satisfy them, we have a margin of freedom beyond. Our young man's nature demanded society; many other friends beside the friend he took up with would have satisfied his sociable appetite, and many other ways of developing the friendship beside the way these two invented as they went along, and which was their own creation.

CHAPTER XII

EMPIRICAL PSYCHOLOGY

i. Repressed wishes

OF the several grounds on which an argument for determinism may be built, it remains to consider what is perhaps the most straightforward and empirical of all. We have to examine the claim, that so much of our voluntary behaviour is in fact explained by special sciences in terms of uniformity, as to make it only reasonable to suppose the rest can be.

We may begin by setting aside the philosophical opinions of psychologists and sociologists. They may be doctrinaire determinists, to a man. We are not concerned with their opinions, but with their achievements. Does what they do either require them to presuppose determinism, or oblige them to conclude it? When we speak of their achievements, or of what they do, we adopt the tone of strict empiricism. Can they control, and can they predict? A more or less plausible deterministic theory of thought or conduct is not science within the meaning of the present question, so long as it is a speculation only, and irreducible to the empirical test.

When the layman hears psychology mentioned, he thinks of a body of doctrines: indeed, of several such bodies, for he understands that Freudians and Jungians, for example, hold sharply different views. Evidently, then, the scientific prestige of psychology does not rest upon agreed conclusions. And anyone who knows anything about it will commonly protest that the science is in its infancy, and that it is malicious to require formal perfection of it at the present stage. Indeed, it will be said, it has done all that could fairly be expected of it in the short time it has so far flourished; and already has practical achievements to its credit, which inspire a most reasonable confidence in its continued progress.

What are these achievements? They are of very different kinds. The great and somewhat nebulous body of psychological doctrine hangs in the air like a cloud; but it is not all in the air. It touches practical life at several different points, and it is of the greatest philosophical importance to keep these several touches distinct. It is, in fact, only when they are confused together, that a conclusion of general determinism appears to result.

The first point at which psychology touches earth is in the practice of mental healing. Now healing as such, whether bodily or mental, is an art. Physicians do not claim to control disease, in the sense that they guarantee cures; let alone predict with assurance the exact time and course of the patient's recovery. Conceived as an art of healing alone, medicine would support no more exact or deterministic a claim, than that various remedies are well worth trying; and in the mental realm we know that this is so before we ever hear of psychology. Everybody knows that in broadly classifiable conditions of emotional distress, appropriate remedies are well worth experimenting with. If people are despondent, we flatter them, if they are angry, we concede the justice of their indignation, while distracting their attention from the cause; and so on. No doubt psychiatrists are more discriminating in their diagnoses and more subtle in their remedies, than are the mothers of families; but there is no obvious difference in principle.

Physical medicine as such (we have said) is an art of healing. But we are all very reasonably convinced that the success of the healing art is largely dependent on physiological science. Dissection, microscopy and a dozen other techniques provide a knowledge of how the body functions, which is largely independent of successes in the art of healing. The art, then, is based on a science; and however modest may be the claims of medicine to control and predict the course and cure of disease, the claims of physiology to inhibit, affect, stimulate or predict bodily reactions, are far greater. Turning from medicine to psychiatry, we may too readily assume that the same relationship obtains—that an art of healing, with modest pretensions, rests upon an exact science, with independent access to the matter of its study. But, in the case of mental healing, there is no such exact science. Thought and behaviour are not measurable quantities. The only aspect of the psychologist's patient which can be reduced to anything like physical exactitude, is his body. But though physiological conditions do, of course, have their effect on emotion, thought and behaviour, the effect, so far as observable by us, is highly general, and cannot give the mental healer the detailed basis he requires for the practice of his art. Thus we find him working with speculative and largely mythical theories, of which the verification lies in the success of the healing art, and in nothing else.

If this were all, no one, perhaps, would be inclined to draw very startling philosophical conclusions. Whatever view we take of the freedom of the human will, we know men to be so far alike, that one can have a technique for influencing them, whether in sickness or in health; and the success of the technique is a verification (so far as it goes) of the rules-of-thumb on which it proceeds. We may go further—the believer in freedom will probably wish to say, that mental or emotional sickness of any kind reduces liberty, and tends to place the sufferer under the sway of compulsive patterns. And so it may appear that the psychiatrist works upon compulsive conditions, for the purpose of eliminating them, and restoring freedom. If so, the art of psychiatry may approach closer to verifiable regularity than the art of common persuasion; for common persuasion works upon the normal, and therefore the free; whereas psychiatry works upon the compulsion-ridden, and therefore the bound. If, then, psychiatry had even a hundred per cent. success in restoring mental freedom, this result would have no tendency to show that freedom is not free.

There is one particularly well-known class of phenomena to which the psychologist attends, and which illustrates as well as any his rôle as the restorer of freedom. The patient is afflicted with compulsive thoughts or compulsive acts, which appear to him as irrational as they are uncontrollable. They correspond to no wishes or interests he knows himself to entertain, and so appear to conflict with the great platitude, that we do what we want to do. Not at all, says the psychologist; the conflict is apparent only; you do wish to do these things, or, if not precisely these things, then some other things for which these things are a sort of symbolic substitutes. But your wishes are hidden from yourself; you disown them and manage to be unaware of them. The psychologist sets about to unearth, and to restore to his patient, the missing piece of self-knowledge. What is the use of his doing that? It is, that once acknowledged, our wishes may be dealt with. We cannot, indeed, help feeling them, but we can help acting upon them; or if we do not entirely suppress them, we can choose the form and the degree of expression we will allow to them. Whereas unacknowledged wishes act as blind forces; and how could they do otherwise, since we are blind to them?

This whole province of psychiatric practice may easily have a disquieting effect on the minds of observers. They may lose confidence in themselves, and wonder whether they are not often a prey to unacknowledged desires, when they suppose themselves most rational and free in their decisions. From such a practical disquiet, they may advance to a metaphysical disquiet: instead of asking, reasonably enough, 'May it not be that I am often the victim of unacknowledged blind desires?' they ask 'May it not be that all supposedly free choices are determined by unacknowledged blind desires, and free choice simply an illusion?' The metaphysical doubt can be laid at rest by a logical argument; the practical doubt must be dealt with in detail, and by practical considerations.

That the metaphysical doubt is nonsensical, can be seen by any one who troubles to trace over the steps leading to it. We begin with the assumption that it is normal for our choices to be consciously decided by us, with reference to our acknowledged wishes; an assumption which we should not even understand, unless we knew from experience what it is to have acknowledged wishes, and to make decisions with reference to them. We become troubled by abnormal cases, where this does not seem to happen: cases which would not even appear abnormal, apart from the assumption we have just spoken of. And we explain these cases by the operation of unacknowledged wishes in determining a concealed choice; when, once again, we would not know what we were talking about, unless we were familiar with acknowledged wishes and unconcealed choices. The explanation, even so, remains both unverified and unfruitful, unless the patient is led to acknowledge his previously unacknowledged wishes, and to make an unconcealed choice about them.

It is evident, then, that the whole conception of blind choice and unacknowledged desire presupposes an acquaintance with conscious choice and acknowledged desire. It is an absurd suspicion which insinuates that we have never been acquainted with these things, or that they never occur. Maybe our mind has learnt to deceive itself by counterfeiting choice; but it would not know how to counterfeit what it had never experienced. Indeed, the metaphysical doubt about our choices in general is refuted by the same method as the Cartesian doubt about our perceptions in general. It is enough to bring forward the principle that hallucination presupposes normal perception.

So much for the metaphysical doubt. As to the practical doubt, whether we may not in any given case be swayed by unacknowledged motives, it must be dealt with by particular heart-searchings. We all have some ability to search our bosoms, and psychologists may sharpen our eyes for the enquiry. So, in their various ways, may discreet confessors and candid friends. Even so, there is no invincible guarantee against self-deception, there is only reasonable assurance. But this is not the only field in which we have to make do with moral certainty.

It is easy to prejudice the issue by asking the wrong question. If, for example, in any given situation of choice, we demand even a reasonable assurance that no unacknowledged motive plays a part in the interest we feel one way or the other, then it may well be that no such assurance can be given. It is, indeed, a very plausible opinion, that in all our practical deliberations there is a bias additional to any inclination we manage to particularise. But the bias may be slight, and we may have a moral certainty that we have discounted it; that, in fact, we have decided the issue in accordance with considerations openly entertained. Undisclosed bias may be all-pervasive, and yet be far less considerable in some cases than in others; and that is comfort enough. Our assurance of exercising genuine choice on disclosed grounds lies in the experience of doing it, not in the demonstration of an impossible negative about what is *ex hypothesi* concealed from us—the invisible bias of the mind. Whether our choice is effective through resisting a hidden bias, or through having little of it to resist, is immaterial. Few judges, perhaps, are unbiased by inclination; yet many judges give sentence on the ground of law alone.

ii. Fatal biographies

But that is not the end of the argument; for the deterministic suggestion made by psychoanalytic practice has not been found to lie simply in the psychologists' discovery of the influence exerted on us by repressed wishes. It has lain just as much in the particular origin they have assigned to certain unlucky complexes of desire, which have come to be repressed. It is through no motive of mere theoretical curiosity that the psychologist seeks to explain the origin of a repressed complex; he is intent on his patient's cure, hoping that in accepting an explanation of his condition, the patient may come to accept the condition itself. He will be no longer frightened, guilty or indignant over the interventions in his mental life of a self he does not acknowledge. He will see the place occupied by these unhappy developments in the natural history of himself, and how they have come to be part of the creature that he is. And so he will learn to do his best with them, as he endeavours to do with the faults or eccentricities he has always been aware of.

Now it seems natural to say that what the psychiatrist unearths, is the *cause* of the trouble; and that he is, therefore, working with the quasi-physical category of cause and effect: that by a chain of causes which could not have operated otherwise than they did, he links the patient's present condition to events as remote, perhaps, as the first days of his infancy, or even to what befell him in his mother's womb. Well, if such a chain of causes stood alone, it would not prove general determinism; but it seems irrational to suppose that it can stand alone. Surely it is just a specimen of the connexions to be found in every strand of our psychic life. What is there peculiar about it, except that the psychologist has happened to select it for investigation? To put the argument the other way round: if there were a force of freewill loose in the patient's history, alongside of the deterministic chains the psychologist studies, it would be pretty certain to have cut across the lines of determination a hundred times in the course of all these years, and marred the pattern. If the world is a world in which psychiatric science can operate, it must be a world in which there is no free will. But that psychiatry can function, is evident from its successes; and so determinism is proved.

If the argument we have outlined is set up as a demonstration, it lies open to so many refutations that one wearies of them before one has finished stating them. It is more interesting, perhaps, to consider what, in face of the psychological facts, a sensible man will think, than to hear what a paid advocate for voluntary freedom could urge against it.

The most radical refutation is that which explodes the empirical evidence. It is pointed out that the psychiatrist does not set about, by methods which any historical or biographical discipline would accept, to establish the facts of his patient's previous life. He simply encourages a story to come together out of what is in his patient's mind. If the object is, that the patient should accept the story, and, in accepting it, pull his mind together, no better method could, perhaps, be employed; but as a method of arriving at historically true facts, what can be less reliable than the piecing of a mosaic out of a neurotic's dreams? If the psychiatrist were anxious to establish the truth of his historical reconstruction, he would, like a good historian, put it to the negative test, and see what evidence, or what argument, could be produced in disproof of it. But no psychologist ever does attempt to test his diagnosis in this way. He is content to believe, perhaps, that the success of the cure proves the truth of the diagnostic story. Alas, in certain cases external evidence has in fact exploded the story on which a successful cure has been based; and a few instances of this sort are enough to refute the claim that the cure proves the history. And (the devil's advocate may proceed to ask) why should anyone ever have supposed that it did? For the cure depends not on fact, but on faith. In an age when no myth except the great myth of scientific determinism is easily believed, we heal mental disorder by faith in causal order. The patient is to be convinced that nothing could have happened otherwise than it did; he needn't feel responsible. If he would believe this on the grounds of a bleak metaphysical generalisation, it would suffice; but the causal axiom makes little appeal to the heart; faith must be comforted by a more detailed story, revealing the very threads with which the web of necessity has been woven. The truth of the construction is immaterial, so long as it convinces.

As the refutation of a pretended demonstration, this rejoinder may be unanswerable. It will not satisfy a psychologist, for he will know very well that it presents a travesty of his art. What? Is his aim no more particular, than to persuade his patients that their symptoms have a causal explanation? Is he not trying to put together an individual mind, which has unhappily gone to pieces? That is why he sets out to assemble the pieces, especially those that have shaken loose: the dissociated or repressed wishes and fears, with the systems of thought and habit which cling about them. These he labours to bring back into view, and to set before his patient. The patient, confronting the facts, discovers that he is a stranger to himself; but it is the psychologist's aim to overcome this self-estrangement, by leading him back behind the split from which it resulted. So back into the past they go, by way of the patient's own mind. Very likely the patient sees his past through veil after veil of subjective illusion. Never mind, for these illusions are just what concerns the psychologist; they are powerful psychical facts. There may be no final assurance possible that the analysis has gone behind all illusion, and reached objective history; about what was done, say, to the child by his elders in remote infancy. But need that matter? It may be enough to reach repulsions or resentments, carrying with them a quite fantastic image of what occasioned them; for these resentments, these fantasies, were real facts in the infant mind and, psychologically speaking, the origin of the trouble.

The psychologist will readily admit the elusiveness of his subject-matter, but he will be convinced that to explore the emotional past of his patient, anyhow to a certain depth, is a genuine and hopeful enterprise; and that the recovery of emotional unity is unlikely to be effective, if the most dynamic of the materials buried in memory are not worked into the analysis. The patient must make a genuine effort, with the psychologist's assistance, to recover his past. There may be gross factual errors in the reconstruction, without the main lines of emotional development being materially falsified. The patient recovers his unity by wrestling with his past, a past which exists as an emotional legacy in his own mind. Exactly how much historical accuracy is required for success in such an effort, is a question that must be left for empirical enquiry to determine. But at least the psychologist is clear that the cure is not obtained by an attempt to falsify the past, but by a readiness to be candid about it.

The sketch we have just given of the psychologist's reply is vague, no doubt, and full of metaphors. To reduce it to philosophical exactitude would take a deal of time. We will spare ourselves an effort, which it does not concern us to make. What we have just said, however metaphorical, and what we remember to have heard or read about psychoanalytical case-histories, will serve us as a basis on which to consider the following question. Allowing all the claims the psychologists make for the scope and method of their art, is there any reason to suppose that the chains of antecedents and consequences they link together are of a strictly causal sort? 'Strictly causal' might mean a great many different things in different contexts; but for the present purpose let us accept a simple definition. We will not require that, to be strictly causal, a sequence must be exhibited as the case of a uniformity established on other evidence, and admitting of no exceptions. We will be content to call 'strictly causal' a sequence which we believe to be such that it could not have gone otherwise.

This definition will allow us to rephrase our question in a more illuminating way. If the patient's recovery of his emotional history is to reconcile him with the repressed wishes or fears from which he is alienated, does he need to suppose that the steps of that history were all strictly necessary, and that none of them could have been otherwise? Or will it do, if he can see them as perfectly natural, and, though often alternative to other equally possible steps, still not in any way surprising?

There is an analogy which may both illuminate the meaning of this question, and help us to answer it. The psychologist's patient is to be led to understand his own wishes and attitudes, because part of himself has, so to speak, become strange to himself. We say 'so to speak, strange to himself' because we are conscious that the language is borrowed from a sphere where it more properly belongs. I may become, so to speak, strange to myself; but my neighbour may be, without any qualification, strange to me. It is reasonable, then, to look for light on the process by which I overcome my own strangeness to myself, in the process by which I overcome my neighbour's strangeness to me.

The case we are considering is one in which I am prompted to say, that I cannot understand Mr Smith's going on the way he does. It is outrageous, crazy, inhuman. Mr Smith's old schoolmaster undertakes to remove my bewilderment, or perhaps, my indignation. He tells me the man's history. There have been many things against poor Smith, from his childhood upwards. A heroic mind might have stood up to them, but Smith did not. On the other side, he might have done a good deal worse than he did. None of the steps by which he has made himself what he is was unintelligible, outrageous, crazy, or inhuman; and one led on to another. It may be with tears of pity in my eyes that, after hearing the old schoolmaster's story, I agree that I can understand poor Smith now. But my understanding of him does not require me to make any particularly deterministic assumptions. Fate confronted him, certainly, with inescapable situations; but fate did not dictate his responses. I can see how, so circumstanced, he could do as he did; I cannot, perhaps, flatter myself that I would have done any better.—But we are treading over old ground. We showed in a previous chapter that personal understanding in general is not deterministic.

Let us apply the analogy. If my understanding of my neighbour has nothing specially deterministic about it, why should my understanding of myself have such a character? Surely I do not need to see that I had to do what I did; it is enough that I should be able to see myself doing it, if I am to say: 'Yes, that was I.' Yet the case of my understanding myself, and of my understanding poor Smith, are not in all respects comparable. There is no intrinsic obscurity about Smith's case. It is obscure to me simply through my ignorance of biographical facts, facts easily stated once they are known. If I had been Smith, I should have understood myself. But as it is (let us suppose) I am Robinson; and I do not understand myself. There are phenomena in my mind, and compulsions in my conduct, which are intrinsically puzzling. They cannot be explained as Smith's life has been explained, in terms of unheroic but normal responses to visible circumstances. As we have said, in so far as I repressed some part of my wishes or repulsions, I became alienated from them, and they began to work like blind forces. It is no very startling admission, that compulsions are compulsive, and therefore not free; and in so far as what the psychologist leads me to explore is the history of my compulsions, he turns my eyes upon the least free or self-directed aspect of my development. Yet these unhappy elements of compulsion do not form a causal series insulated from my freer action. Compulsions and choices have interplayed throughout my history. The psychologist, like any biographer, is concerned both with what the subject of his study has done, and with what he has suffered. In what he suffered, he was not free; but that does not stop him from having been free in what he did. The paradox of psychology is that some apparent doings are, like sleep-walking, to be reckoned among sufferings; they are more what happened to the agent, than what he willed to do.

It is, of course, absurd to generalise about so various a matter as psychoanalytic practice. We can only hope that what we have said bears upon a fairly typical case, and that other sorts of cases could be dealt with in a similar manner. Surely it will remain, that the psychoanalytic explanation of a present morbid condition from past events, traces a historical, not a causal sequence; though it concentrates on aspects of the history in which the subject of it has been most liable to causal determination. If this is so, no very interesting metaphysical conclusion results from psychoanalysis.

iii. Social psychology

But, it is very properly urged, practical psychology does not limit itself to the study of particular morbid and compulsive conditions. It establishes generalisations about the way in which various social or other environmental factors affect mankind, and make men what they are; and these generalisations are subject to empirical verification; not merely in the sense, that we can observe more or less perfect instances of their operation, and see whether the formula holds good of them; but in the further sense, that we can experiment in the application of them, by placing mankind under recommended conditions, and seeing whether the promised advantages follow. Ideally, of course, we could supplement the positive experiment with the negative, and see whether by doing all the psychologically wrong things to our human guineapigs, we could make them as bad as they ought to be. But though scientifically desirable, this type of experiment is not socially convenient; and not even chimpanzees provide adequate substitutes, for the purpose of destructive psychological experiment.

In view, then, of these wider psychological claims, shall we not have to revise our opinion, and admit that psychology establishes strict causal uniformities; or at least, that it aims at doing so? If we were to ask our question of the psychologists themselves, they would no doubt answer with the modesty of true scientists, and protest that an ignorant public greatly over-estimates their achievements. So far, they would say, we have been able to establish no more than the loosest generalities; we leave it to our successors to tighten the net of theory, until there is no free play at

all left to the wriggling facts. But meanwhile, the indubitable correctness of certain psychological generalisations surely shows that
we are dealing with a matter about which generalisations can be
framed, and therefore, presumably, a causally-uniform matter. If
human conduct were free from causal rules, then we might expect
to see overthrown at Fagby the generalisations which hold good
for Winton and Harchester; e.g. that a lighter hand on the cane
produces less contrasuggestibility to cultural interests; or that the
absence of a father-figure in early adolescence leads to emotional
instability at university age. But in fact, no one expects to see such
generalisations overthrown. It may be that they are not proved to
the satisfaction of a logical pedant; but when we are talking philosophy we shall be content to take our stand on what, as a matter of
fact, sensible men are going to believe.

It is very right that scientists should entertain almost unlimited
hopes for the progress of their science, so long as they look for it
along a genuinely open path. No one expects the geometers of
even the remotest future to measure square circles or erect four-
sided triangles. Nor can it be expected on the whole, that whenever a net of loose generalisation has been thrown, it will be
practicable to go on tightening it until the facts have no free play
left to them. Against any such overall assumption, the practice and
method of statistics revolt. The first point in statistical method is
to find a numerical basis wide enough to support a given generalisation. The aim of narrowing down your numerical basis until the
rule binds the single instance, is in many fields utterly chimerical.
If psychological generalisations true of Winton and Harchester
hold good at Fagby, it may be because, statistically speaking,
upwards of a thousand boys are enough to flog. Very likely
many fewer would do. But still it may be that Tom Brown,
flogged every morning within an inch of his life, finishes his
school-days pickled in culture to the eyelids, and undulating with
aesthetic sensitivity.

Probably not, one must admit; and this 'probably' is more than
statistical. It is not like the probability against any given throw of
the dice turning up a double six. For nothing has been done to the

247

dice to stop them turning up double sixes—at least, let's hope not. They will not need to show an unusual resistance to countersix influence, if they are to pull it off. Whereas much has been done to young Brown to make of him a young tough. Yet even the toughening of Brown works statistically, though in a different dimension. It is only the general policy of beating Brown which, pursued over a sufficient length of time, makes it even likely that he will be toughened. His reaction to any one given beating is not predictable; it may be anything you like: indignation, nonchalance, penitence, bravado. It is not, in fact, that his freedom of action in meeting this recurrent infliction is limited; but rather that, in whatever way he chooses to meet it, the having to meet it (never mind how) day in and day out, makes him a boy of a certain sort. But then again, by his becoming a boy of this sort, the freedom of his particular action is not necessarily reduced—it may even be enlarged; it all depends on what view you take of the effect of old-fashioned discipline on the human being. No boy can be a boy-in-general; he must be a boy of some sort; and if being a boy of some sort determined him to a single line of action in any given situation, then there would be no freedom anyhow, and it would be unnecessary for us to discuss with solemn faces the new and breath-taking evidence for determinism supplied by psychological science. The common opinion is that some sorts of boys have more freedom than others, in the sense that they are less tied down by one-track attitudes or negative emotions. And those who take the optimistic view that the cane, in beating aestheticism out, beats character in, would presumably say that anyhow in the situations which confront an empire-builder or a big-game-hunter, the well-beaten boy will enjoy a larger scope of effective free choice, than will the product of a namby-pamby education.

It has been pointed out that the general precepts of psychology, as applicable (for instance) to education, are largely concerned with what the ancients called vices and virtues, but we call qualities and faults; the object being to foster qualities, and avoid the formation of faults. We always knew something about the parental policies likely to have the one effect or the other; and if a greater precision can be given to the traditional lore by a careful empirical enquiry, so much the better. We have never doubted that our training, good or bad, has very largely made us what we are; nor have most of us ever questioned the conviction that, being what we are, we are free to make the best we can of ourselves, by conduct freely chosen.

What we feel (if we are at all clear-headed) when social and educational psychology is talked to us, is not that human liberty is being disproved, but that it is being threatened. That psychological generalisations can disprove a freedom of action enjoyed by the human being as such, is a metaphysical absurdity. But if a technique for shaping character and sentiment is perfected and standardised; if it is placed in the hands of an omnipotent state-authority with limited views—and what public authority has not limited views?—then it seems that the infinite artistry of nature is in danger to be botched by a handful of pedants. Suppose they set out to breed, rear and tend a herd of contented materialists. If they succeed, they will not take from their subjects the liberty of choice; but they will determine the range of it. A contented materialist is free—free to be, in his own way, a contented materialist.

A philosophical critic will accuse us here of most unphilosophical rhetoric. 'The artistry of nature is in danger from a handful of pedants.' The artistry of Nature, indeed! And who may the lady be? Well, if you put me back against the wall, and turn out the logical firing-squad, I will confess, and not deny—I will confess that the artist is God. But since this is not the place to define or justify a theology, we will merely ask our reader to put his own construction on an assumption more widely held than any explicit creed. Does it mean anything to him, that the interplay of forces and influences, of materials and circumstances which moulds the individual, and provides a different point of departure for each man's freely-directed pilgrimage, constitutes, as it were, a vocation assigned, or a charter of existence granted to us? Would he distinguish a true education, cooperative with nature, and respectful of God's handiwork, from a false education, forcing an artificially devised pattern on mankind? Is it not a degree of atheism which shocks even unbelievers, when some Kremlin or other asks itself what sort of people it wants for the staffing of a preconceived social machine, and coolly sets about to make them so?

I hope it is plain that nothing which has been said is any sort of attack on psychological or social science. Passive reverence is not enough; we honour the creative handiwork by furthering it, and practical knowledge will make us all the more able to do so. It is merely that here as elsewhere, and perhaps most markedly here, an increase of knowledge increases temptation; the sin of playing Providence may seem a trifling thing, when our control of means is trifling.

We have fallen into a digression. What it concerns us to say, is what we have said already—that psychological and sociological study is not a speculative threat to our belief in free choice. It is not, in itself, a threat to anything; but in the possibility of its misuse, there lies a threat to the human nature which exercises whatever freedom we possess. We have always known that, before we can be free, we have to be; and that something other than our freedom has made us what we are. To some considerable extent, we all owe what we are to the free efforts of others, say of our parents; and a science which directs their instinctive skill does not, of itself, introduce any philosophically significant novelty into the picture.

We have written, perhaps, as though the sciences of which we speak bore upon education only. But psychology can produce generalisations just as well about the way in which formed char- acters react to various policies and influences. The basest branch of the art is salesmanship, together with the other techniques of persuasion and success; a less ignoble department concerns itself with producing public contentment. In thinking about the pre- cepts or generalisations laid down by these disciplines, we can usefully draw a distinction. Either these precepts or generalisations concern the way people will initially react to certain attitudes or approaches on our part; or else they go further, and take in the conduct which will result from their reactions. In the second case, freewill is directly involved, because people's conduct is, or anyhow may be, freely willed. In the first case freewill is not directly involved, because initial reaction is not freely willed. If what you say annoys me, it annoys me; it is only starting from there that I have any freedom, say to nurse my annoyance or to distract my attention. If precepts for producing immediate reactions are useful only on the whole, it is merely because the variety of human character and circumstance is too great to allow of perfect generalisation. But if precepts for producing certain lines of conduct are useful only on the whole, it is for the additional reason that we are generalising about the behaviour of free agents; and here indeed a wide numerical basis will be required if our statistical formula is to apply. 'In 900 cases out of 1000 a man will' . . . does not by any means entail 'In 9 cases out of 10 a man will . . .'.

If there were no rules of thumb for determining our neighbour's immediate reactions, we should be quite at sea, as soon as we passed beyond the family circle. That we know what will please, displease and so forth on the whole, is obvious. An attempt to systematise this knowledge need postulate no new principles, besides what all commonsense concedes.

iv. Conclusion

In the preceding discussion we have dealt with two very different branches of the psychological art. Psychoanalysis detects, derives and attempts to dissolve compulsions; and in so doing shows us that we are morbidly unfree where we should normally be free. Social or educational psychology takes a wider scope, and attempts statistical generalisations about the normal response of free individuals to certain classes of circumstances. It may be that the current belief in the deterministic implications of psychology is based on a confusion between the two branches of the art. We borrow from social or educational psychology the claim to embrace the whole of conduct; while from morbid psychology we borrow the rigorously deterministic account of certain particular thoughts and actions. By rolling into one two completely different disciplines, we get the chimaera of a wonderful science called Psychology, universal in scope, and in its method explosive of freedom. If we dissolve the chimaera we shall rid the mind of an incubus; but we shall discredit none of the real functions which anything called psychology can hope to fulfil.

CHAPTER XIII

RESPONSIBILITY AND FREEDOM

i. *The legal model of responsibility*

THE function of philosophy may lie in the examination of speech; but not all speech offers an equally serious field for philosophical investigation. It is not the triviality of our common talk which distresses the philosopher; it is the contradictoriness, the vagueness of it. The common man may talk about subjects of a high philosophical interest; responsibility, for example. He does not know what he is talking about. He makes emotional, figurative and mutually irreconcilable remarks. And it seems absurd to labour the analysis of what he means, when he means so little, and that little so vaguely. The philosopher who wishes to enquire into responsibility looks for his raw material in utterances which he can take seriously; he looks for the tongue that is taught, for the mind to which the assessing of responsibilities is a profession; for the man forced by his calling to give exactitude and consistency to his speech; the man whose pronouncements have serious consequences, and command a general consent. He finds such a man in the learned judge, and steps with a sigh of relief from the spongy bog of common moralisings to the rock of legal practice. Here is something to philosophise upon; the lawyers know their job.

So they do, and to philosophise about legal responsibility is to philosophise about a solid matter. It is a rash assumption, nevertheless, which makes 'responsibility' in legal contexts typical of 'responsibility' in all contexts. The common man, talking of moral or personal responsibility, certainly talks less well than the lawyer. But it may not be the whole reason, that he lacks a legal training;

it may partly be that he talks of something else, and something more elusive. Legal responsibility, being the original case, is the most straightforward. Moral responsibility bears all the marks of a transferred idea, not to say a metaphor; no wonder, then, if it is ambiguous. Legal responsibility has an undeniable claim to be the defining or standard instance, for it is the literal one. But it would be a tyrannical proceeding to control the extended by the literal meaning, and so conclude that moral responsibility is no more than legal. For the transferred sense of a term is other than the literal sense.

When we think of metaphor, we commonly find our example in a wanton transference. There was no need, certainly, to call a head of criminal conspiracies 'Napoleon of crime'. Holmes could have described him more accurately, if less picturesquely, in proper terms. But there is metaphor more vital than this. There are provinces of thought which are nothing but developments and applications of some metaphor; fields of action which consist in living out a twisted idea. In particular we must believe psychologists and anthropologists, when they tell us that conscience is law interiorised. Conscience begins when social discipline is taken into the mind; when children discover that parental standards are still with them in the absence of the parent. Presently they begin to pass judgement on their playfellows, and become members of the judiciary, as well as of the subject body. Last of all, perhaps, they bring the two rôles into direct relation, and judge themselves. In their earlier attempts, they see their exercise of judgement as the application to cases of a common morality. As time goes on, they feel the duty or the power to improve upon the code; but they do not find it easy to persuade others of their improvements. The sole obedient subject of self-legislation is the legislator. No other is obliged to heed him; but he has little claim to sincerity if he does not heed himself.

'The city that recks not of law, has decreed . . .' is an unmitigated scandal, where the city has but one inhabitant.

We need not dispute the general correctness of this account, or deny the origin of moral responsibility from the interiorisation of rule and custom. The question, however, remains, whether, in becoming interiorised, responsibility undergoes any transformation that is of philosophical concern, and in particular, of concern to the philosophy of will. It would be a mistake, for example, to assume without examination, that if a deterministic account of the legally responsible person will square with legal practice, it will do as well for the person who holds himself responsible in the court of conscience.

How shall we proceed with the question? Is it not plain that we must look at the literal or legal usage first, and then see what modifications take place in the transferred application?

'Responsible' means 'answerable'. Everyone legally responsible is answerable to . . . and answerable for. . . . He is answerable to an authority which can compel him either to do his own duty and respect his neighbour's right, or else to undergo the penalties. This authority is either the judicial power, or a party whose right the judiciary enforces; a cashier is responsible to the bank for the exactitude of his dealings, but only because the bank can call him to legal account. So much for 'answerable to. . . .'.

A man is held, in different senses, answerable *for* his actions, for a province of duty, and for the things or persons his duty concerns. Mr Jones is responsible for the bridge (a thing), that is, he is responsible for keeping it up (a duty); and so he may be held responsible for having used rotten timber to mend it (an action); and his landlord, let us suppose, is the person to whom, in all these relations, he is responsible.

We have taken what may be called a linguistically ideal case; that is, a case in which it would be possible to use 'responsible' in all the four senses. This is not commonly so. A man is not often said to be responsible for an action bearing upon a duty for which he is also called responsible. The law does not consider the responsibility of men for their legal actions; and illegal actions are mostly infringements of rights. Defaults in respect of duties are not actions at all, they are failures to act. The typical default is not patching the bridge with rotten planks, but leaving it unpatched. Even if you patch it with rotten planks, they do not hold you responsible for a rotten action, in the common case; they hold you responsible for repairing the bridge, pronouncing your pretence of having done so to be a rotten pretence. You are only made responsible for using rotten wood if there is evidence of malice; of fraud, for example, in disguising it as sound; of negligence, in callously endangering the passage.

The typically wrongful action infringes a right. If I shot my landlord wilfully, I am responsible; not because I have a responsibility for seeing that he moves about his lands unmurdered, but because he has a right to do so. It is axiomatic that I am responsible for respecting all my neighbour's rights; we may call this duty my responsibility, but no one would call it *a* responsibility of mine. A responsibility is particular and defined, like a right; for example, to keep up the bridge.

Responsibility for duties is laid upon the citizen by the law, or, if the law needs interpretation, by the judge. If the court makes me responsible for the upkeep of the bridge, then I am responsible for it, even though the judgement is a bad one, and though I shall presently succeed in getting it reversed. The reversal of the judgement will not prove that I was not responsible hitherto; it will take off the responsibility henceforth.

So the judge creates responsibility for duties by laying down the law. It is obvious that he cannot create responsibility for actions in so absolute a way. He can lay it down that such-and-such an action, if I committed it, was an action for which the law will hold me responsible; that it was, in fact, an offence. But only if I committed it. If it is disputed whether the offensive thing was in any sense done, or brought about, they do not ask whether I was responsible; they ask whether there was anything I could be thought responsible for. But suppose there was—the thing happened; my landlord got the shotgun wounds in my bushes. Now the question arises, Was I responsible? And the court cannot make me so; it is past history—either I was, or not; the court has to make up its mind on something comparable with a matter of fact. Either my action was such as to square with the standard definition of responsibility, or it was not. If I want to show that it was not, I may plead that I was not to know my landlord would be snooping, and that I thought he was a rabbit. Or I may plead that I did not fire the shot, my companion fired it; which, if granted, will probably clear me, but not certainly. For suppose he alleges that I said to him: 'What's moving over there? Shoot it!' and further, that when we were setting out, I had said to him 'If the old man comes snooping, we'll pepper him'. And suppose that counsel turns the knife in the wound by asking the court to consider whether, without malice aforethought, a man like me would wish to see a gun fired blind into a stirring bush.

To say that I am responsible is to say that I did it, either with my own hands, or through another's. To plead error or accident is to plead that I did not do this very thing, in the direct sense of the verb to 'do'. I did not shoot at a landlord, I shot at a supposed rabbit; that was the form of my personal action: an action of which the peppering of the landlord was but an accidental consequence. Even if the court accepts my plea, it will wish to enlarge my statement; 'Shooting at a supposed rabbit *without making reasonably sure that it was not a man*', will be the legal view of what I did; and it will not acquit me of all blame.

In listening to a case like this, the simple moralist may notice with approval that a lack of intention to do the criminal thing is a sound legal excuse; it must surely be, he concludes, that legal responsibility depends on wilful intention. But if so, how can it be that lack of wilful intention will not clear one from the charge of negligence? The court holds that I ought to have made sure the bush did not contain a man. I enter the sincere plea, that I am not guilty of taking a risk, since I had neither the intention nor the awareness of doing so. I defied no warning; the idea of its being anything but a rabbit never entered my head. I realise that it will be difficult for me to convince the court of the fact; after all, they have no direct access to my inward thoughts; but perhaps they will accept the corroborative evidence offered by my companion, who says that I fired without a trace either of hesitation or of excitement. I am prepared, then, to have my statement challenged; I am amazed to have it swept aside as an inadmissible defence. How can the court hold me guilty of taking an undue risk, if it is not even prepared to discuss whether, to my knowledge and belief at the time, I was taking any risk at all? Is the court indifferent to the guilt or innocence of those it punishes—supposing, that is, that guilt is defined in terms of actual intention?

Only one hypothesis will account for the legal phenomena. Law is utilitarian in its attitude to pleas of error, ignorance and accident. The prime object of the legislator is to discourage certain sorts of actions. His method is, to define a crime, and punish everyone who is caught committing it. The purpose of the punishment is to make an effective deterrent of the threat: 'Whoever does so-and-so will be punished.' But if the threat is to be effective, it must mean 'Whoever *intentionally* does so and so . . .'. To threaten people with penalties for what they accidentally bring about, is perfectly useless; if by accident you understand that which there is no recipe for avoiding. However frightened I am of the law, it won't stop me from having accidents of this sort; and if I am so frightened that my hand shakes all the while, I shall have not fewer accidents, but more. If, on the other hand, accident is defined as what due care could prevent, then it is useful to threaten people with penalties for letting it happen; for there is hope that they will take the care. And so the law should not accept the plea, that at the moment of action I had no thought of risking an accident; for the purpose of punishment is to discourage thoughtlessness. Neither should the court accept the plea, that in the moment of action I was either ignorant of the law, or forgetful of it. For one purpose of punishment is to make the law known; publication, without enforcement, being found ineffective.

Should I have acted otherwise, if, at the time of action, I had had a due respect for the law in its bearing on the situation? If the answer is Yes, then the court will hold me responsible for my infringement of the law. The purpose of punishment is to enliven the legal threat. We enliven it by punishing those who would have felt it, if it had been lively to them. There need have been no historical or psychological possibility for them to have felt it, as things were. It is enough, if they would have felt it, supposing that someone were at that moment being punished before their eyes for the same offence, with an official spokesman standing by to point them the moral. We excuse them if they were mad, for then they might not have felt the threat, whatever demonstration were used to enliven it.

The connexion of legal responsibility with voluntary freedom is indirect. By holding men responsible for breaking the law, we do not express the belief that they could, at the moment of action, have respected it. What we do is to furnish them or their fellows with a motive on which, in the future, they can freely act—fear of the law. Such is the account which a libertarian philosopher will give, because he holds that heedful action in general is freely willed. A determinist will not agree; he will say that the fear of law which punishment creates acts as the determinant, or part-determinant, of men's decisions. Determinists and libertarians agree that the purpose of penal law is to act as a motive. They give different accounts of how motive works: not this motive in particular, but motive in general; that, after all, is the difference between the two parties. Determinists think of motive as a sort of cause, or as a rule for the operation of causes. Libertarians think of it as something to which free action may respond; but that does not stop them from seeing that many motives can be brought to bear with good hope of a high statistical effect; or that the fear of punishment is often such a motive.

The conclusion is, that criminal responsibility has no special bearing on freewill. It offers a motive on which decisions can be freely taken, but so do many other things beside criminal responsibility. We have now to consider whether the situation is significantly altered when we pass from the legal to the moral or personal realm, and take law into the mind. We will begin by examining the hypothesis that there is no radical alteration.

ii. Application to conscience

Legal responsibility, we have said, is fixed upon the citizens by the law, so that social disapproval, backed by penalties, may become an efficacious motive. When the law is transferred from the public court to the tribunal of conscience, need the pattern be seriously disarranged? The disapproval which is to be made effective is now the agent's condemnation of his own faults, and the penalty is self-rebuke. If the fear of self-reproach is to act as an effective deterrent, I must have some conception in general of the actions which my disapproval will strike; the crimes, that is, for which I am to hold myself responsible. In the case of public justice, competent authority has published the statute, and made me responsible for learning it. In conscience I publish it to myself, and I may make myself responsible for memorising it.

The strict application of the political model to the republic of the mind suggests an enforcement of discipline by one level of thinking upon another; the superior level being actuated, like the external judiciary, by utilitarian principles. Every evening, let us suppose, I hold a moral court on the actions of the day, and issue rebukes to myself for my transgressions. The object is not to cry over spilt milk, but to do better next day. I do not worry, if I am a sensible man, to determine how far I was aware of the laws infringed, or how far it was a psychological possibility at the time, for me to have observed them. If I leave it to spontaneous feeling, I may find myself more ashamed of my complacency in doing a bad act under persuasion of its entire innocence, than I am of my villainy in overriding a sensitive conscience. In either case I incur my own rebuke, for I shall be sorry if I do no better tomorrow. So far from my practice of self-discipline implying any acceptance on my part of libertarian theories, it would be easy to argue the opposite case. If my rebukes have a directly causal effect in my mind, leaving traces tonight from which motives will arise to-morrow, then I have every reason to trust the efficacy of self-reproach; the more so, if the resultant motives, when they are called into play, exercise a causal force, in their turn, on the balance of my practical decision.

Shall we let the story pass, then? We will not. It is founded on an artificial evasion of the paradox expressed by the compound word, self-reproach. It keeps me, the judge, and me the criminal at arm's length from one another. It conceives of my mental history as though it were a row of silk in a tapestry: when the green thread is on top, the red is underneath, and vice versa. When action is in, judgement is out; when judgement is in, action is out. Action fills the heat of the day, and reflection the cool of the evening. When judgement has delivered its verdict, it retires into subliminal concealment for another twenty-three hours, content to have impressed upon my active self a fear of the rebukes next evening may deliver.

Obviously, real life is not like this. While it would be an exaggeration to say that self-judgement never sleeps as long as men are awake, it is a safe assertion that nothing but sleep offers a guarantee against its rousing; and that nothing is more likely to rouse it, than a dawning interest in any of the crimes it prohibits. To return to the political analogy; it is as though we were shadowed all day by a discreet policeman in plain clothes, who stands out from the crowd and warns us, as soon as we show any signs of illegal behaviour. Yet even this analogy misleads; for the policeman merely warns us of the penalty which the magistrate may inflict; whereas the warning of conscience is the same in kind as the sentence of judgement. If conscience is a policeman, he is a policeman on the Continental model, authorised to fine you on the spot for spitting on the pavement. All that is needed to turn the warning of conscience into the penalty of self-reproach, is defiance of the warning; and not even that; for the warning itself is already a reproach, occasioned by the inclination to offend.

There are cheerful souls in plenty who make do with the first-instance judgements of their ubiquitous policeman-magistrate, and hold no formal sessions in the court of self-examination. And yet no one will wish to say that they have no discipline, or that their moral life is of a totally different character from one which includes a periodic formal action of the interior judiciary.

Sometimes in civil life the warning of the police, or of some self-appointed mentor, is ineffective; we plunge into crime, but with the nasty feeling in the back of our mind that we cannot hope to get away with it in the end. We may get away easily with the criminal action, but justice will track us down, and haul us into court. Similarly there are occasions in the moral life when the excitement of action, and the heat of passion, make it a comparatively painless thing to stifle immediate self-reproach; but we have the nasty feeling somewhere in the background, that we shall not get away with it in a cool hour; when excitement has died and distractions are few, we must face the process of interior justice. In general the analogy holds good; but if we press the details we obscure the vital difference. Arrest, trial and condemnation for a public crime do not begin until the police have tracked me down. But my moral process begins in the moment of my offence.

The common man, in answer to the question, 'What was the guilty act?' will reply: 'The act in which a moral choice was involved, and in which I chose perversely.' 'Perversely perhaps,' says his determinist friend; 'but you chose as you had to choose. What makes you condemn yourself is not really the hypothetical consideration that you might then have done otherwise, but the practical perception that by blaming yourself now, you may hope to do otherwise.' 'I don't see the advantage of your formula' says the common man—who has, I am afraid we must admit, changed hats meanwhile with a libertarian philosopher, and looks much less common than before. 'I say that I rightly blame myself because, on the blameworthy occasion, I was faced with the question "What shall I do?" and decided wickedly. You say that I rightly blame myself because, faced with the question, "What is it useful to blame?" I decide correctly. You simply choose to think about the decision to blame, instead of thinking about the decision which was blameworthy. You are forced to think of the present decision (What to blame?) as an open question, about which one could go right or wrong—in fact, as a free decision. But you refuse to think of the past decision in this way; you prefer to think of it as a determined event. Why? If you admit that your will is alive now, and deciding what to blame, why pretend it was dead this morning, and necessitated to err?'

By treating my past error as a *corpus vile* for my living moral surgery to dissect, the determinist's story falsifies moral fact. The reflective moral judgement which arraigns previous action is the same in kind, and even, so to speak, identical in person, with the conscience stifled at the time of acting; for both are I. The struggle between moral opinion and immoral action was not settled by the perverse deed. It breaks out afresh in subsequent heart-searchings, and the principle then set aside enforces itself now, as well in remorse for the past as in resolution for the future. This evening's 'Is it right to blame . . . ?' is substantially the same issue as this morning's 'Is it wrong to do . . . ?' The struggle against admitting responsibility now, is the same struggle as that against admitting the rule of law before. Only the circumstances have changed. He who, in however cool an hour, repents his act, does not go on the reasonable persuasion that a dose of blame will do him good; he reopens the still festering wound, and performs the self-cautery he previously shirked. Moral self-judgement is not essentially a habit of blaming past actions, but a habit of imposing on one's conduct the law of one's mind.

What we have been saying may appear trite enough; none the worse, perhaps, for that, in the eyes of those who make it the glory of philosophy to vindicate platitude against sophistry. It needed to be shown how little you have said about moral responsibility, when you have classed it as an interiorisation of the legal kind. What is of philosophical interest is not the external model, but the alteration it undergoes in the process of being interiorised; not that the inward court passes some sort of judgement on responsible actions, but that judge and offender are the same person. When A passes judgement on B, it is a vulgar fact, as when C hits D on the nose. But it is a first-rate philosophical curiosity, when E disciplines his own reluctant self.

iii. The divided will

So far, we have viewed this oddity in the light of our legal responsibility for criminal actions. Perhaps the analogy of our legal responsibility for duties will contribute a supplementary illumination. The court holds Jones responsible for keeping up the bridge. No marvel, if Jones is inclined to default. Very likely he has no personal interest in keeping it up; it is nothing to him but an expense and a bore. The duty is laid on him by an alien will, his landlord's, backed by the authority of the court. But now suppose that Jones is a conscientious man, and holds himself responsible for the state of his landlord's bridge. The will which imposes the responsibility is no longer alien, it is Jones's own. How odd, then, that Jones should be inclined to default, and should need to beat himself, and even then, perhaps, in vain!

The comparison with a legal responsibility for duties does nothing but sharpen the age-old paradox of a divided will. That the will should be divided in a certain sense, is, of course, no paradox; if we had no conflicting interests, we should make no serious decisions. How interests initially conflict, and how we can properly speak of a decision as arbitrating between them, are questions already discussed, and not to be reintroduced here. But there seems to be a quite special puzzle about the reluctance of a man to do his self-imposed duty. For here we appear to have a conflict of intentions when the decision has already been made, and while it continues to stand. Must we not call it an actual conflict between decisions? I am committed, decided on the side of duty; and yet (if I am so wicked) I decide against doing it. In the common case, I am in two minds, my mind is not made up. But in the conscience-case, it is made up. But if it is made up, it is pulled into a unity; and there should be no strand of purpose left loose, no uncommitted voice free to advance a dissident persuasion. Yet the thing happens; I can tell myself that I will not, on the given occasion, do my admitted duty; and following this wicked voice, I may in fact forbear to do it.

The paradox exploits the ambiguity of the phrase, 'to have made up one's mind.' In the absolute sense, the mind is never irrevocably made up, or unified, by anything but action; then indeed openmindedness is out of the question; for I cannot both do, and not do what I am doing, while I am doing it. And for the purposes of this formula, speeches and thoughts must rank as actions; I cannot both say and not say, both think and not think. So, then, I cannot both tell myself to do my duty, and not tell myself to do it, nor can I both do my duty, and not do it. But no

contradiction of this absolute sort is involved, when I tell myself
to do it, and do not do it.

A contradiction of a less preposterous sort does, however, seem
to remain. The canon of self-consistency which we have just laid
down is one which even mania does not violate. We expect more
of sane men; we expect them to avoid flagrant contradictions between their present thoughts; and it is a paradox still, if moral
weakness is to be presented as a defect of sanity. Let us consider
what the nature of the moral contradiction is. There are, no
doubt, several ways of formulating it, or (what is more important)
several ways in which it may formulate itself. We will keep to the
formulation we have been considering, and continue to think
about the man who reminds himself that a certain standard of
behaviour is the rule he has decided to follow, who sees the
standard violated by what he proposes to do, and who tells himself that he will do it, all the same. Is not he intending contraries?
In a sense, yes, he is; but in what sense? Not like a man intending
a project which combines contradictory aims, say those of love
and hate (this is quite common). The morally inconsistent man's
project may be entirely consistent within itself; as when a virtuous
citizen thinks out a watertight scheme for defrauding the Revenue.
The inconsistency is between the plan he adopts, and the rule he
means to keep.

The man is intending to keep the rule, yet in the same moment
intending to do what will break it. The contradiction appears
absolute, only until we recollect that the intention to keep a rule is
but a standing-form intention; and that standing-form intentions,
being general, are necessarily imperfect. Only particular intentions can be perfect; they alone, that is, can be properly intended,
for they alone are fitted to become the forms of actions. General
intentions are no more than resolutions, on which particular intentions ought to be founded. The man we are thinking of refuses to
make the particular intention which would implement the resolution. Very likely he considers making it, as any man choosing
may consider the performance of an alternative ultimately rejected; but he does not make it. His failure may be called a failure

in perseverance; the failure to follow up a first step by taking a second. For a general intention is a first step towards many particular actions, as the opening of a shop is a first step towards many acts of supply. A man may open a shop, and never supply anyone with anything. It would certainly be unusual. But many men open shops, and fail to deal with a proportion of the orders they receive. It is very unshopmanlike of them; and so it is very immoral, when men who have made moral rules fail to act on them. But it is not the logical or psychological monstrosity of intending, and not intending, the same thing in the same sense and at the same time.

The recollection of a resolution on a particular occasion may be reckoned equivalent to the consideration of a demand—the demand that a certain question should be made the question of the moment; for example, 'Is this (that I propose to do) the truthful thing?'—When it is assumed that 'the truthful thing' is part of what I expect from myself. The morally inconsistent man does not disagree with himself over the answer the question requires—he refuses the question; refuses, that is, to make it the question of the hour. He accords that status to some other question, say 'Is this advantageous?' or 'Is it pleasurable?' and answers it by the choice he makes.

Perhaps our readers will recognise what we have just written as a disguised version of Aristotle's teaching about 'incontinence'. They may complain that the Aristotelian account, however glossed, is of no avail to save the formal rationality of the agent; for he is bound to see that the question, 'Is this what I require of myself?' cannot be set aside in favour of any other question. The complaint is, however, unjustified. The acknowledgement that a given action is what I require of myself, cannot be set aside without contradiction. But the question whether this is what I require of myself, or not, can be set aside as a question not so much as needing to be asked. All men who are not moral pedants do, in fact, waive the question of duty with regard to a good half of the projects which occur to them. Is it my duty to keep on writing this argument, or shall I have a drink with Bibulus, who has just rung up? If you like to say so, it is obligatory under my standing rule, to work until lunch-time, and the rule is not without serious sanction. I disapprove of self-employed persons frittering their time away, and if they are in danger of doing so (as I am), I hold that they should make rules of industry, and keep them. Yet in the present case I waive the question of the dutiful thing, and substitute that of the pleasant, or (less discreditably) the friendly thing.

It may be that, on reflection, I could justify my action in the court of duty. Perhaps my rule admits of exceptions, so long as they are not too frequent; or if, perhaps, they are of their nature strongly attractive. Dear old Bibulus! I do not see him every day. I might well make out a case for waiving the rule in his favour; but in fact I do not. I waive the whole question of duty, and attend to another. What is the friendly thing? To go straight round to Bibulus, or to ask him here at six, when he can meet Faustina?

There are whole provinces of conduct in which we habitually throw the onus of proof on morality—we shall not attend to her, unless she makes out a case why we should. If she does not seem to be saying anything very important, we waive the moral question and get on with life. At other times it would clearly be unprincipled, not to hear her out. Yet if we hear her, we may still be unconvinced. We begin to be in bad faith, when we resist conviction. It is the height of iniquity, when we are virtually convinced, and nevertheless make another question the question of the day. 'Yes, that would be the proper thing to do, no doubt; but this will be such fun!'

When we attempt to describe wilful irresponsibility, in what sense are we concerned to save the unity of the agent? It will not do, if we reduce him to a madman, in whose practical thinking there is no continuity. On the other side it will be scarcely less absurd, if we talk his inconsistency away, and bring him out a moral monolith. We must not say that he falsifies the very senses of the words 'right' and 'wrong', but we may fairly accuse him of perverse and partial judgement, a fault not limited to the sphere of a debating conscience. I may refuse to see the superior merit of a man's work, because his rival is a charming companion; and my conduct is not dissimilar, when I refuse to admit the preponderant importance of the moral issue, because it will be such fun to act otherwise. If my prejudice is so complete as to blind me, there is nothing paradoxical in my conduct. But often it is not so—I know that I am indulging prejudice. In the same way I may know that I am going against conscience.

Cases of wilful irresponsibility differ widely in the degree of palliation, or self deception, they exhibit. The mind has no liking for head-on collisions with itself. I may avert my attention from the moral issue, and pretend that it is not effectively present to me. I may grow angry, and cry 'No, I wont!' expelling the decree of my conscience from myself, as though it were an unreasonable foreigner, making excessive demands. In a small matter it may be enough to say 'Be a dog for once', suggesting that the enforcement of the law on every occasion, and especially on this, would be pedantry. The intellectual who decides to get rid of his wife and children, disappoint his kind mistress, and marry a fresh young thing, will require a more complicated formula, a whole morality to fit—happy man, he can buy it off the next bookstall. Now his practice and his precept match, who shall indict his sincerity? He has covered himself from the very eyes of God.

To affirm a rule, and refuse the practical questions it raises, is insincerity, even in the eyes of mankind. Whether the insincerity is aggravated or diminished by the agent's success in blinding himself to the flatness of his moral refusal, we need not here discuss. Our present purpose will be served by a more general conclusion. Insincerity is culpable inconsistency, a wilful violation of volitional integrity. It is not mania, however, nor even intellectual self-contradiction.

Perhaps we have gone further into subsidiary matters than the purpose of our enquiry justifies. The thesis we wish to uphold is, after all, a platitude: that the fundamental work of conscience is a calling on ourselves to fulfil, in active decision, the law of our mind. We will now pass on to consider what bearing such a thesis has on the freedom of the will.

iv. *The choice of questions*

If it were possible to limit the work of conscience to retrospective blame and prospective resolution, conscience-thinking might with some plausibility be insulated from that immediacy of decision, in which the evidence of liberty chiefly lies. But if conscience is concerned with the making of decisions in the moment when they are made, our experience of her must be inseparable from that of self-determination. To feel the force of a moral rule, and to offer a measure of resistance to it, is nothing else but to struggle with a decision between the conscience-question and some other. And no one can approach such a decision in the lively belief that the outcome of it is effectively prefigured in existing facts.

So far we have said nothing much. It is commonly thought that conscientious struggles offer special evidence of freewill; and it is a disappointing conclusion, if all we have to say is that they provide as good evidence as any deliberate decisions, but no better. We shall not, in fact, content ourselves with quite so barren a result; but before we attempt to improve upon it, let us embrace the opportunity to declare that decision as such, any decision, is the foundation of a sound libertarianism. To know that you are free is to understand what deciding is. Any libertarian edifice which narrows its base, and builds on privileged decisions, moral or otherwise, is doomed to fall. For once we admit that most decisions are determined, we cannot resist the contention that all may be. If, then, our readers are dismayed because we do not take our stand on moral ground, we have no comfort to offer them.

We are willing, however, to allow on the other side, that some decisions are more evidently decisions, and so more evidently chosen, than others. After all, decision is a diminishing quantity in the descending scale of action; it vanishes at the debatable boundary between choice and impulse, a line impossible to draw. The higher we stand above that level, the more decisive our decision will be. Conscientious decisions are high in the scale; and they are distinguished by special characteristics, upon which we will venture two remarks.

The first remark is this. The decision for or against conscience is, as we have seen, a decision between questions; I determine that my action shall answer the question, what (in the circumstances) will square with the rule I hold, or the question, what will be fun—to pick one rival question among many. Now a decision between questions presents a special resistance to some sorts of determinist analysis. The claim, it should be noted, is not made on behalf of conscience-decisions only; a choice of questions has no need to be conscientious. Offered a choice of hot mutton or cold beef, I may decide on the issue, 'Which will be palatable?' 'Which will be digestible?' or 'Which will be ingratiating?'—the mutton being, let us suppose, the daughter of the house's first attempt at a roast. In acting on one question, I may be as well aware of setting another aside, as any struggler with conscience could be. 'Bother the child's feelings!', 'Hang my gastric juices!' are examples of such dismissals.

The choice of questions, whether conscientious or otherwise, reveals the inadequacy of a crude psychological determinism; a determinism which asks 'How can I prefer any alternative, save that which I want most?' For if it is to be unambiguous, the determinist's 'What do I want most?' must be put within the limits of a single question. If it is a question of the palate, I want beef. If it is a question of pleasing the family, mutton. 'But which do you most care about, to gratify your palate, or to gratify your hosts?' It will depend on how I think. At the moment, no doubt, one approach to the matter is more to the front of my mind than another; but that accident will not stop me from making a different question paramount. I suppose I might say to myself: 'Do not let me intrude, with my conscious considerations. Let me leave my desires to declare themselves, and show what they—or rather, what I—most want.' But all that would then happen would be, that the question in momentary possession of the field obtained an answer; or if not the question in possession, then some supervening question pressed on my attention by obtrusive circumstance, and requiring no intellectual initiative to bring it forward. It is not obvious that any very profound truth about 'what I really want' is discovered, merely by suppressing reflection, and allowing elementary or immediate mental processes to take their course.

The identity of the thing I want most, alters with the alteration of the question; but so does the very meaning of the verb 'to want'. 'What do you want for your birthday?' 'Do you want to be an engine-driver when you grow up?' 'Do you want the Conservatives to retain power?' The sorts of wanting differ as the sorts of objectives differ. And so, prevented by the incomparability of objects from asking which is the more attractive, we cannot elude the difficulty by subjectivising the enquiry, and asking 'But which promises to satisfy the stronger want?' We shall merely provoke the rejoinder, 'It depends on what you mean by *want*.' I want to understand Wittgenstein's argument before I break off; I want to have my lunch before it is intolerably late. The objectives are incomparable, the wantings no less so.

The objectives are incomparable, in the sense that they have no value-tickets pinned to them, with figures expressed in the same notation; nor have they any identical and desirable quality in different intensities. They are comparable, however, in the sense that both solicit favour, and either can be decided for. As with two candidates for the favour of an electoral committee—they may be incomparable in the sense that their respective qualities or merits can be reduced to no single denominator; yet they are comparable in the sense, that the committee can elect one rather than the other, in the reasonable assurance of making the better appointment. It would be mere verbalism to say that the common measure is eligibility; it would be better to admit that the candidates' rival claims are measured by the particular election. It is much the same with projects, or objects, which answer different sorts of questions. They ask to be adopted on incomparable qualifications; but they enter into competition for the monopoly of some piece of our time, the control of some phase of our action.

The competing questions which claim an answer in our acts are supported, no doubt, by different growths of instinct or interest, each more or less firmly rooted in our mind. The psychology of mania and mental health is much concerned with them, and with the balance between them; a balance we may crudely represent by arithmetical ratios or geometrical diagrams. By fixing an appropriate sense on the word 'want', we could make it axiomatic that the standing balance between various instincts and interests determines what we most want at a given time; but it would be quite unplausible to maintain that it determines which question we shall make the question of the moment. Thought often forces the balance of psychological need; all that the balance can then do, is to revenge itself presently, by throwing up disproportionate desires on the other side, or by some such trick. And that in turn will constitute a situation which thought and choice may variously handle.

We have said enough to show that the choice between questions is a specially awkward subject for a certain sort of determinist; the choice between questions in general, not the decision for or against the conscience-question in particular. The conscientious struggle is not, indeed, a typical case of the choice between questions, nor even, in all respects, the best case to quote in support of freewill. Perfect freedom may seem to lie in the exercise of an untrammelled preference; whereas the conscience-issue is always in a manner prejudged. If I do my duty, I merely persevere in a line of choice initiated already; if I default, I produce a mental conflict, and it becomes possible to say, in a fair sense, that I do not want to do the thing I do. All this is true; but the conscience-issue has compensatory features which endear it to the apologist of liberty, and the mention of them brings us to the second of the two remarks we proposed to make.

Though the prejudgement of the issue by conscientious conviction impairs in a manner the freedom of choice, it enhances the awareness of it. The grating of our decision against an established rule makes us acutely observant of the fact that we are deciding; it produces that painful consciousness of what we are about, which first gave 'conscience' a name. We may be most invincibly certain that we do decide, when decision is a moral agony; as we are most conscious that we breathe, when we need to struggle for breath.

We breathe all the time, nevertheless, and never so freely as when we are least aware of it. To treat agonies of choice as our only genuine choosings is a philosophical blunder of the grossest kind, whoever may have committed it. We have written about it on an earlier page, and will not repeat what we said.

v. Conscience de-legalised

In conclusion to this chapter, we will raise a consideration affecting the whole basis of discussion which we have adopted, or accepted, in the course of it. For the purpose we had in mind, we found it convenient to seat law on the interior, no less firmly than on the public, bench; for we wished to compare the responsibility imposed by civil rule, with the responsibility imposed by moral self-discipline. But to keep the parallel up so rigidly as we have done, is to take a very partial view of conscience. Moral responsibility may derive from legal, but it may proceed to de-legalise itself by a whole series of steps. We will be content to indicate a few of them.

Legal responsibility, as we have seen, attaches to us in respect of our actions, only if there is a law, or a custom with the force of law, prohibiting what we do. The case of moral responsibility which comes nearest to this, is that of the worthy citizen who respects public law, enforcing it upon himself without any thought of danger from the police. The next nearest case is where the law concerned is not enforcible by the courts, but required by public opinion, and avenged by social disapproval. Here again the good citizen does not care whether he is detected or not, whether he incurs odium or not; he keeps the custom, as he expects others to keep it, out of honesty, not out of fear. At a third remove is the man who holds himself to the keeping of formal or tacit agreements with individuals, where fidelity to the general requirements of the social body is no longer in question. Fourth, we come to the man who keeps rules or resolutions he has himself laid down for the guidance of his life, no party being involved except himself— no human party, that is.

We seem now to have come a long way from our starting-point, but even at this stage two important features of the original model survive. There is a fixed, interpretable formula with a limited range of application; and there is the promulgation of it to the person responsible for keeping it, even though the promulgator is no other than himself. But at the next step, the fifth, both these features virtually disappear. This is where the rule a man holds himself responsible for keeping, and guilty for breaking, is not a rule which is legally interpretable, even by the man himself. If I resolve not to smoke or eat sweets in the season of Lent, I have made a legally interpretable rule. If, in the course of the forty days, I swallow either sweetmeats or tobacco-smoke, I break the rule; if not, I observe it. But if I acknowledge the duty to be sympathetic, or not to judge harshly, then my resolution (if you call it that) is not patient of legal interpretation. There are, no doubt, extreme cases of culpable harshness which are evident breaches of the rule; but to have avoided such transgressions is not to have kept the rule well, nor (hardly) to have begun to keep it at all. For this so-called rule is not so much a rule prohibiting definable actions or, even, definable thoughts, as it is a rule of keeping one's eyes open for certain sorts of demands in certain types of situation. What we must do in response to them is not laid down by the rule, it has to be extemporised on the occasion. I am not to judge harshly; yet it is often necessary that I should sum up my neighbours, and never desirable that I should lie to myself about their characters. What severe assessments are or are not culpable, cannot be determined by the rule prohibiting harsh judgement. All the rule does is to set me on my guard, whenever I think I have adverse judgements to make.

Because the rule here is no longer an interpretable law, it is absurd to say that my responsibilities for keeping it are the simple consequences of its having been promulgated, even by myself. For what the rule tells me to do, is to look out in situations of a certain sort, and to act as the circumstances require. If I have looked out, I have done all that the rule simply and directly prescribes; yet if that is all I have done—if I have failed lamentably to do what the circumstances required—I hold myself guilty in

RESPONSIBILITY AND FREEDOM

respect of the rule; and my having 'looked out', so far from diminishing my guilt, may only increase it. For now I have sinned against the light.

It seems clear that, in such cases, my responsibility (if we are still to keep the word) is a compound one. It is only partly defined by the rule; in part it is defined by the circumstances of the case: let us say by the persons involved, and by their several situations. My crime is, that though the rule directed my eyes towards these persons, and towards their claim on my humanity, I failed to respond to their claim, or even, perhaps, to respect themselves.

Now let us take another case, the sixth and last. Let the rule drop right out of the story. I am a moral Hottentot. No one ever edified me by lecturing me about the crime of harsh judgement; nor did I ever make a resolution against it. But now suddenly, in the darkness of my native jungle, Dr Livingstone accuses me of harshly judging my village catechist. A flood of moral light bursts upon me. How badly I have acted! Still, says Mr Stanley, don't let that worry you. You weren't responsible. You didn't know it was wrong.—Shall I accept the shallow consolation of the facile journalist? I doubt it. The catechist is a man. I should have seen that I was being a beast about him. Dr Livingstone has not manu-factured the evil by propounding the definition. The evil was there; and but for my general selfishness, and hardness of heart, I should have owned it. If not specially in that single case, yet in my whole way of living, I am responsible for being closed to a human claim.

I am responsible. But what sort of responsibility is this? Surely the original metaphor of law has become so stretched, that it has lost the substance of meaning. To whom, or what, am I now said to be responsible? Not, surely, to my own mind, as to an author-ity which has fulminated the law I have neglected; for that is just what my mind has failed to do. I may still be called upon to be my own executioner; but I have not been my own legislator. No; if any comparison with the citizen under law remains, it will prob-ably be this: that just as the statutes have been fulminated by authority, and it is the responsibility of John Doe or Richard Roe to acknowledge them; so moral claims are shouted at me by the very existence of my neighbours, and it is my responsibility to acknowledge such claims. But facts do not shout, not even personal facts; they have no voices. All they can do, or need do, is to be important for practical decision. What has the word 'responsibility' to do here? All it does is to call attention to a characteristic of certain ranges of importance, or of value; that their claim to be recognised is not optional, but obligatory. If you say to me, that there is an important play at the theatre, and that I must not miss it, you exaggerate. I can miss it if I like; and by giving it a miss, I discredit neither its dramatic merit, nor my own sincerity in accepting your estimate of it. I agree that the play is interesting, significant, what you will; but I am in no mood for plays. Whereas if Lazarus is dying on the doorstep, Dives is free neither to deny the importance of the fact, nor, if he concedes it, to keep his hands in his pockets. That the values of human life, virtue, and happiness lie upon us with a unique incumbency is evident; and what else is meant, by saying that we are *responsible* for doing something about them?

It may be that we can restore a fuller sense to legal analogy, and make its application more natural at this level, if we throw over responsibility for actions, and take up with responsibility for persons or things. Let us put it like this. Some responsibilities for things and persons are defined and enforced by law. But the good man accepts many of them on their merits, and is his own judge with regard to them. Parents, for example, seldom need the magistrate to teach them their responsibility for their children. The next step is to extend the notion beyond the extremest range of law. The legislator, we will say, is a rough schoolmaster to train us in a few typical responsibilities, and to enforce a few vital ones. But the good-hearted man comes to acknowledge responsibility for everything human which falls in his path. He is his brother's keeper; his neighbour is whoever meets him; the responsibilities that may arise for him are defined neither by law nor by custom, but by the pull of facts.

Such a way of putting the legal parable may seem more

natural; but the advantage is no more than rhetorical. It is hard to attach any meaning to unlimited responsibilities for all and sundry. I can be charged with a defined responsibility for a single party, because it can be reasonably hoped that I shall be able to give the obligation priority over other claims; or that the occasions of my being unable to do so will be so few, and themselves so definable, that they can be made the subject of exceptive clauses. But how will you hold Dives responsible for Lazarus on his doorstep, when the doorstep is the world, and Lazarus is every ascertainable distress? We cannot be held responsible for mankind, nor for all the men who come our way; but only for seeing them, and for praying to be given discretion, whom we should help, and whom let be. It does not matter what formulation we employ; it will always remain that the uncovenanted well-doing by which good men are good, is not a performance of duties.

We began by asserting that legal metaphor was the form and substance of moral conscience; conscience being but the interiorisation of the law. We have seen that in working out the metaphor, conscience works herself right out of it; and in her most developed, most sensitive activity, leaves law clean behind. Any deterministic flavour which may seem to haunt legality is left behind too. Philosophers have sometimes reasoned as follows: 'There is no freedom in the moral will except to do right or wrong. But even the option of right or wrong is a choice between determinations: to be determined by desire, or to be determined by the rule of right. This is our only freedom, to step into the up-train or to step into the down-train; in either case we shall run on the rails.' Nothing, in our view, could be more mistaken than this thesis. It is false in both its parts. When we are untouched by moral considerations, we need not be determined by desire. But neither, if we choose the right, need we become fixed in the track of law. To do what is right often means to make a succession of serious or virtuous decisions in face of the morally relevant facts. And such decision can be as inventive as any. We have to make it up as we go along—we have to; the moral facts put us on our mettle, and forbid our invention to flag.

CHAPTER XIV

VALUATION AND INVENTION

i. Libertarian implications of Moore's anti-naturalism

WE set out to discuss responsibility, but in the upshot we found ourselves discussing valuation. For it seemed that the ultimate responsibility acknowledged or enforced by conscience, was of acting in accordance with our serious valuations. Let us make a fresh beginning, and consider the bearing of valuation on freewill.

English philosophers, when they take up the subject of valuation, are still inclined to make *Principia Ethica* their starting-point; and we will follow common example. No one, indeed, accepts the form and conclusion of Moore's anti-naturalist argument, exactly as they run; and we make no apology for putting our own complexion on the doctrine.

It is convenient to see Moore's argument as a gloss on Aristotelism, the one 'metaphysical' position which, oddly enough, in a criticism offered as systematic, he fails to criticise. The good, said Aristotle, is what everything is after; that is the definition of it. He did not mean, 'What any particular being happens to pursue', for that would make the bad aims of bad men good, because they aim at them. He meant, 'What any *kind* is after', say, the human kind. He took it as axiomatic that there are proper objects of human aspiration, and so, determinate goods for man. But (anyhow in his wiser moments) he rejected Plato's belief, that these goods or objects could be determined *a priori*, by a theoretical consideration of the human essence, or of any other 'idea'. He agreed that aspiration claimed to pursue what was good for man, and not merely what she happened to like. He denied that she could in the long run show any evidence that her pretended good was good, except her being moved by it. So, then, the good is good, in virtue of a relation between it, and the requirements of the human essence. But the bearing of this relation can be perceived only from the human end, and in the individual case, and by the awakening of aspiration. It is only when the observer's own aspiration is aroused, either directly or sympathetically, that any object or project possesses in his eyes the relational property of 'goodness'; and he will always be insincere in calling 'good' what his serious aspiration fails so to designate.

At this point we may append Moore's gloss to Aristotle's position. The empirical Englishman turns his gaze in a direction from which the Greek formalist was inclined to avert his own, when he points out that it is always theoretically open to enquiry, whether anything, or any type of thing, will attract, or continue to attract, aspiration. You might say that life, anyhow, is a good. Yet Cleombrotus was seriously persuaded of the contrary; and the poet who wrote 'Die, if thou wouldst be with that which thou dost seek,' had almost to be restrained from plunging after the suicidal Platonist. No set of distinguishing marks, attaching to an object, an aim, or a state of being, can settle the question of its goodness. It must seem good in the eyes of aspiration (or of approval, which for present purposes it will be sufficient to regard as an exploratory, imaginative, or sympathetic aspiration). An object will very likely be seen as good, in virtue of characteristics which can perfectly well be listed. But this is only to say that it is in the listed characteristics that the goodness of the object is found; or, to put the same thing in other words, that it is they which move our aspiration. Our aspiration has, nevertheless, to be moved, if the good is to be identified. The presence of good can never be defined by any set of nameable characteristics, but only by the claim they exert on aspiration.

It is not objectively describable characteristics alone, which are incapable of guaranteeing that anything will be accepted as good. Relational properties are just as incapable of guaranteeing it, so long as they accrue to the object in virtue of its relation to any fixed appetite or aptitude. Examples of such relational properties are edibility, pleasantness, amusingness. The only appetite (if it can be called such) by relation to which anything becomes good, is our total aspiration, or serious approval; a limitation unaffected by the possibility, that it may be in the pleasingness, amusingness and so forth of things, that their goodness is seen to lie. For it is not seen to lie is such properties otherwise than by moving approval or aspiration.

It is obvious that aspiration and approval are practical in their intention and effect. We approve, indeed, many types of conduct which we are not at the moment called upon to imitate, just as we appreciate the worth of many beings, who make no present claim on our help or cooperation. But it is scarcely to be supposed that such responses would have any place in the life of the human mind, if they did not, on occasion, run out into action. Aspiration and approval are, in fact, a sort of inchoate, exploratory, and imaginative decisions; a doctrine of valuation is a doctrine of decision, at least by implication. When Moore denounced as heresy the supposition that any 'natural' characteristics in the object automatically made it good, he was saying, by implication, that our decision in favour of anything is not necessarily determined by a nameable set of features in it, nor even by its felt appeal to any one among our appetites, or to any complex of them.

It would certainly be a false simplification, to make a doctrine of value coextensive with a doctrine of decision. Not all decisions settle values; not, for example, those decisions which go, alas, against our valuations. But the converse is true—all values are settled by a sort of decisions, and our doctrine of value means nothing, unless we agree that such decisions as these can be made.

Moore established his doctrine by appeal to a sort of logical experiment. If a man holds that any describable set of characteristics in a thing or in its environment simply define its goodness, there is a short way to refute him. 'Tell us,' we say to him, 'is it meaningful to ask whether a thing having these characteristics, and thus situated, is good or not?' And he will be bound to agree that the question can be meaningfully put; that a man might conceivably be found so perverse, as to judge evil what we take for a typical embodiment of good; like those who condemn aesthetic beauty as sensuous temptation. Such a man is wrong, in our judgement; he is wrong, in placing his value-tickets outrageously; as wrong as a judge at a flower-show, who gives the first prize to the worst exhibit. Yet he, the eccentric judge, and we, the sound judges, both mean the same thing by 'first prize' and by 'deserving of the first prize'. And in like manner the perverse valuer is in no disagreement with us about the meaning of the label 'good'; his error is not like that of a man who should stick the ticket 'chrysanthemum' on an aster, and vice versa, and who should stand by his identifications, when challenged. It follows that the absolute meaning of 'good' cannot be identified with the presence of any characteristics; for they are all open to valuation, or disvaluation, in terms of it.

We will proceed to translate Moore's experiment from the language of valuation into the language of decision, and see what result we get. A man's decision (we shall find ourselves saying) is not in such cases logically bound by his recognition of any characteristics in the object or project, nor yet of any relations borne by object or project to his felt responses. He can acknowledge all or any such factors, and still decide, without contradiction, against what they might be taken to recommend; as is done by the ascetic who, feeling pleasure, turns against it because it is pleasant.

Can we claim Moore's thesis, so translated, as an argument for freewill? It might seem, on the face of it, that we can. If nothing can settle the value-question but a man's personal decision; if no one can settle it for him by looking, as it were, over his shoulder, indicating the relevant factors, and showing him how to work the sum; then it seems that his decision is free from determination by the complex of factors present in the situation; it is simply the attitude he chooses to take up in view of them.

A pleasing conclusion, this, for the libertarian, but one which a moment's reflection will show to be quite unjustifiable. All that Moore's argument can be stretched to prove, is that our value-judgement is no deduction from any set of facts which can be arrayed before the deciding mind. And why? Because the good is that which appeals to a certain sort of (subjective) response. Nothing set before the mind can be taken as good, unless the heart replies; and the reply which the heart is to make cannot be set among the facts or considerations which call for it. The heart's reply is hidden from the eyes which make the scrutiny designed to evoke it; a limitation of vision which, however, has no tendency to prove what the libertarian desires—that the heart's reply is unaccountable-for in terms of any causal or quasi-causal analysis. Why, libertarians themselves must admit that something can sometimes be said about dispositions and so forth in a man, affecting his value-decisions, dispositions necessarily excluded from his view when he decides. They cannot therefore claim the invisibility of a certain range of subjective factors to the valuer, as providing evidence of their inefficacity in his decision.

We have, as the reader will perceive, fallen back into the lines of an old argument (see pp. 127–139 above). We had there to meet the more general determinist contention, that the apparent openness of choice was due merely to the impossibility of placing among the facts deliberated on, those subjective responses which it was their function to evoke. To vindicate the real openness of choice, we found it necessary to shift our ground, and appeal to the subjective form of sheer decision-making. We might follow the same course in the present connexion, and it would, perhaps, be our strongest argument. But it would be an argument from decision as such, not specially from value-decision; whereas what we are at present considering is the particular bearing of value-decision on liberty of choice. And some sort of argument can, indeed, be erected on the narrower ground, even though the weight it carries may be less logical than moral.

The contention will be, that the determinist account involves a moral paradox, since it makes the appeal to value-judgement a submission to the arbitrament of blind psychological force; and surely that is not what we can believe it to be. To make good this contention, we begin by observing that in a certain area of action, determinism allows a man to deliver himself from mere actuation by psychological forces; in the area, that is, over which reasoning extends. For though reasoning, according to this philosophy, necessitates, it does so by a principle which is eminently respectable, being, indeed, that of reason itself. Unless a blinding passion or the like interferes, I am bound to see that a thirty-foot bridge will not span a forty-foot river. And so, if I am a military officer in a hurry, I shall nevertheless not advance on the supposition that the prefabricated bridge I carry will deal with the liquid obstacle before me. Consideration in general will reveal the viability or the reverse of projects which passion recommends; and then the passion, as an effectual motive force, will be suitably modified. My enthusiasm for jumping a fence will be cooled by the observation that there is a wide and dirty ditch on the other side of it. Such examples are trivial. More interesting and more relevant are those surveys which establish the expediency of proposed policies, or their inexpediency, for a harmonious realisation of our desires upon the whole. By efforts of reasonable thinking along these lines we may deliver ourselves, and our neighbours too, from much conflict and frustration.

Reason, then, is a luminous cause which delivers us from the sway of blind causes. But the implication of Moore's doctrine is not, that the magic halo of value invests our projects, or our objects either, in proportion to their thought-out-ness or perceptible rationality. When we have done all the thinking-out we like, it remains to see whether the heart will move; whether the policy we have subjected to every reasonable and practical test will be embraced, in preference to any alternative policy—including among alternatives the policy of inaction. And, quite independently of Moore's theories or observations, we are convinced that the rationalisation of purposes, the harmonisation of aims is only one half of moral concern. The other half is a just assignment of priorities between the goods which any harmonising policies are to harmonise for us. Not any harmonisation will do, but only one in which certain priorities are respected. And how are the priorities established? How, but by the movement of the heart, as when we respond to our fellow-creature, and put his happiness above our own convenience?

It is at this point that the paradox of the determinist position strikes us. Must not the movement of the heart appear in determinist eyes to be mere subjective brute-fact, the working out of a balance of power between psychological forces of some kind, in a part of the mind sealed off from immediate inspection or control? And however theoretically tenable such a view may be, it does not seem that the morally serious man can entertain it as a practical belief. He must put love and knowledge, reason and will on the same personal level; must hold that as one can see truth, so one can embrace worth; that to do so is an act of the man, directed towards the object, because it is the proper object.

To such objections as these, we have heard a determinist retort, that our own eyes are obfuscated with moral pessimism. Could we but rid ourselves of an atavistic belief in original sin, and think cheerfully of the human heart, we should see no difficulty in his position. On any showing, indeed, many men make and hold what we think degraded valuations. But, of the nobler valuations that are made, why should a naturalist hold our nature incapable? Why not take a favourable view of her determined workings—as favourable, anyhow, as the facts demand?

Well, but surely this 'nature' of ours, as naturalists know it, is the product of culture. Cut the child off from his cultural inheritance, give him to the wolves to rear, and where is his humanity? Take an adult at a given cultural level, and you have a being with a certain system of organised and graded purposes, to which (though not without strains and frictions) the instinctive forces of animal desire have somehow been geared. Take him as he is, and you may call his human nature no bad thing, nor incapable, perhaps, by its determinate process, of throwing up the valuations he makes. But you have surely no right to take him as he is. For valuation cannot without moral paradox be made the mere *de facto* expression of an existing culture. Cultures themselves are valued and disvalued, and not only cultures themselves, but culture itself. In answer to the question, what makes us think it better to be cultured than not, to be Socrates than to be Silenus, is it enough to say, 'Because we are conditioned by our culture to do so'? Must not we say, 'Because we are by our culture enabled or set free to do so'?

Any number of depressing and cynical arguments can be advanced, with abundant empirical support, to show how painfully our valuations are controlled by breeding and interest, by superstition and prejudice. But if there is no margin of sheer aspiration anywhere, going out to the objects of a creative choice, can we either explain the history of our race, or find a basis for our moral convictions?

Once the least particle of such aspiration is admitted, our case is made; for it does not seem that the proposal to give a deterministic account of it can mean anything. A deterministic account would have to explain the result (in this case, the new value-decision) by a combination of already given principles or forces, according to already given modes of combination. Such an account can perhaps cover the value-decisions of a merely conventional citizen, if such a being anywhere exists. For are they not in some fashion the joint product of changing circumstance, and of the breeding he has received? But how can it account for advances (as we deem them) in valuation, for a stretching of inculcated principles until they are virtually transformed? Every moral pioneer must start from base, that is, from upbringing; but he must also advance, or he is no pioneer; and if his advance is merely by learning from those who have advanced before him, his pioneering neither deserves the name, nor illustrates the process by which fresh advances are achieved.

It is said of our electronic engineers, that they can construct machines capable of learning from experience, and of surprising their inventors; and yet (it is pointed out) no one supposes machines to work otherwise than mechanically; and is not the mechanical the stock instance of the determined? No doubt; but the variations of action which the clever machine develops, remain within the limit its construction sets. If we make a fabulously ingenious self-directing missile, we may, perhaps, give it an undefined and self-developing capacity for dodging obstacles or countering hostile radiations, and even, perhaps, for attacking any of several among a given range of targets, as circumstances allow or recommend. But it is not going to change its basis of action, repent its destructive mission, and immolate itself by plunging into the bowels of a volcano. There is an obvious sense in which no machine exceeds the principle of its construction, or rises above a function assigned. A deterministic account of innovation can only be a virtual denial of the *novum*; the new pack must come out as a reshuffle of the old cards.

ii. *Freedom of valuation, and of practical decision*

It may be that a critical reader, wading through the arguments we have been developing, will feel that they are misdirected, even if they are sound. What is the use of labouring the case for freeing value-decision from causal necessitation and the dead hand of the past? It will still be no true example of free choice. On the contrary, a genuine value-decision is one which we find in ourselves no liberty to make otherwise than we make it. There come before us

> *Proposals which, like Luther at the Diet*
> *Of Worms, we can't do otherwise than shy at,*

or which, alternatively, we cannot do otherwise than embrace. This is not to deny that in the very moment of valuation we can begin to falsify and obscure the act we are making, by misdescribing our own decision to ourselves; or that in the next moment we may begin acting contrary to it. But as for the valuation itself, if we really do make the effort of valuing—if we experiment, as it were, in relating ourselves to the object or project to be valued—then either we are for it, or we are against it; unless, of course, we make no clear reaction either positive or negative. But we have no power to aspire after what we disvalue, or to disvalue that after which we aspire.

We have not described with any subtlety the experience to which we have referred, but neither is it of any importance we should do so; for the point which is troubling us here is not psychological so much as verbal. If we complain that a value-decision is not a free choice, what sense are we putting on the word 'free'? Or, a question which may come to the same thing, what standard example of freedom are we holding before our minds? A value-decision is not free—not as free as what? If I have indulgent friends to amuse, I can follow the whim of invention in the choice of conversation; and so exercise a freedom, which in serious value-decision I do not possess. But what is that to say, but that the choice is trivial; that it does not matter what I do, within certain wide bounds? It is foolish to complain that value-decisions are not like this. How could they be? In deciding a value, I must pull myself together and make a serious choice. But in making it, I simply choose; choose honesty, or kindness, or whatever it may be, either in general, or in the particular instance. Nothing enslaves me, I choose what I choose; even though in such a case I cannot choose one moment and unchoose the next, as, in my conversational whimsy, I may tease one moment and flatter the next. I am bound by my value-choices as I am bound by my beliefs; but such binding is no bondage.

The special character of decisions about the good is determined by their subject-matter. The things decided on are universal objects, about which it is proper to hope that human preferences will be stable, and will agree. We recognise that neither individual stability nor general agreement will be achieved without effort, or prove entire. All we hope is, that as understanding and mutual sympathy proceed, there will be more, not less, both of stability and of agreement. The proper answer to those who say that the assigning of the epithet 'good' goes by personal taste, is that, on the contrary, the serious use of 'good' begins when we reach a sort or level of objects, which are not the objects of personal taste. Our preferences about such things claim in some sense to speak for the human heart, and it is this claim which distinguishes the serious use of 'good'.

Everyone making a serious value-decision passes an implicit judgement on the discrepant decisions or attitudes of others; they, we cannot but feel, are failing to fall in with the rule of a true aspiration. And the conscientious man, anxious about his own valuations, may wonder whether they conform to the true standard. Thus it may come to look as though the decision or choice involved is not free; that it is not a matter of choosing what one wants to choose, but of toeing the line. But to view things so, is only to fall victim to a false comparison. We are thinking of the true good as proposed to us by an invisible authority, say, of Nature, which we cannot but obey. But—to accept for the moment the mythology of the parable—that is not how Nature works in the case. She works, not by prescribing the object of our choice, but by inspiring our choice of the object. If we are in error, our way out of it is simply to discover more deeply what we want, or to aspire more genuinely; and this we may hope to do, by concentrating more singlemindedly on the object to be valued, or by appreciating more open-heartedly the aspirations of others.

In substance, the attack on the freedom of valuation, which we have just considered, is the complaint that it is not the freedom of whimsy, or of invention; much as though we were to commiserate the constrained condition of a flying eagle, because he is not a swimming porpoise. There are no limits to the range of such an assault; a sophistical determinist might go the whole round, attacking each form of voluntary action in turn, for not being some other. By the time he had come full circle, and was found to be using as his type of freedom the activity he first pilloried as an example of constraint, the most gullible of us would have seen through the device; there might even be a hope he would see through it himself.

But there is an allied sophism less naive than this; one more likely, therefore, to deceive its proponents and to puzzle their public. To appreciate the bearing of it, we require a less elementary diagram of voluntary conduct, than that which our last few paragraphs have presupposed. We have been thinking of the human person as capable of expressing his voluntary freedom adequately, in any one of a number of different ways; as a man can exercise the power of vocal noise, by the utterance of any one among a whole range of sounds. But an ability to utter distinct and unrelated notes, though it is the ability to do just that, is not the ability to sing; and a freedom to perform distinct and, as it were, staccato acts of various types would not be freedom to live, in the human sense of the word. Human life is a living-out of complex purposes, which lose all meaning and character if they are pulverised into atoms of action. It is a free decision on my part, if I leave off writing to go out and catch the post. But taken by itself, the action is meaningless; I must have written the letter, say in acceptance of my correspondent's invitation; and I must mean to visit his house at six o'clock on Wednesday week.

On such a level of generality, the point is really too commonplace to deserve illustration. What is more to our present purpose is a more special point: that actions of a given type may be, in their whole function, complementary to actions of another type. There may be more complex cases than this; perhaps it takes a combination between three or four different types of act, if certain sorts of human purpose are to find expression. The precise degree of complexity is irrelevant to the sophistical determinist. All he has to do is to isolate the actions belonging to one among two or more complementary types, and he can point out that the freedom to perform them is not the freedom to fulfil human purpose. Or rather, employing a better disguised and therefore more effective formulation, he will ask us to observe that ability to perform such actions falls short of anything we should accept as the enjoyment of human liberty.

We need not look beyond our present subject for an example of the sophism. We have been talking about value-decision as a case of free choice. Well, but when we have done our best for it, is it not still a disappointing instance? A value-decision is one which, ideally, should last us a lifetime, and one which should chime with the decisions of all our fellow-men. Is human freedom to find its expression in standard decisions on stock subjects? If that is the libertarian's contention, is it even worth arguing about? Very likely not; the libertarian would certainly be foolish to accept such a field of debate, when he can move on to superior ground so easily. He has only to remind his antagonist that value-decisions, as such, are incomplete actions, actions which find their complements in acts of invention, alternative choice, and so forth.

The sophism will work just as well, or just as ill, the other way round. It may take acts of practical decision, and point out that those of them which are uncontrolled by value-decisions or by value-attitudes are trivial, not at all the sort of actions about which libertarians made much to-do. Whereas those controlled by prior or standing value-decisions are, *ipso facto*, not free; or if free, only in a marginal way, and in so far as our application of generalised valuations to the case in question may demand the exercise of casuistical extemporisation. The refutation of the sophistry is the same as before, the appeal to unity of action. The man who embraces the values is the man who makes the day-to-day decisions, and in the whole complex activity he expresses or enjoys a human freedom.

It is, in truth, proper to say that a man is free, not that his acts are so. And yet the man, the free agent, is expressed in nothing but his activity; and we cannot comprehend the whole of that in a single view, even if it is right to speak of it as composing a whole; and, what is more material, neither can the man. He must live his life, and actualise his freedom, in single successive actions. Yet there is continuity of purpose, his life is not a series of flashes. What is neither the focus of attention nor the subject of action is somehow present in the penumbra of the mind. While I frame this sentence that I write, only a single clause is formulated at a time; and yet the formulation takes shape in view of what I have just said, but no longer distinctly remember, and of what I mean to say, but do not yet distinctly conceive. The unity of consciousness through time is a function of its inexactitude. It is only by losing, or by not yet achieving, the distinct outlines of present imagination and present discourse, that the vast matter of memory and purpose can lend support or direction to what occupies us here and now.

The inexactitude, the elusiveness of the mental penumbra plays its beneficent part in our life, but what justice can it hope from our philosophy; a philosophy which has never unlearnt the Cartesian lesson, that it should banish all but the clear and distinct from its consideration, and break down baffling complexes into simple constituents? Certainly a man would have no grip on his activity, he would not be self-directive, if he could not focus his attention in a limited area of concern, and make the contents of it clear and distinct to his intelligence. But again, if that were all he could do, if his decision could not feel, and feed upon, the half-remembered and the scarce-conceived, he could not exercise the wholeness or continuity of purpose which are proper to a human being.

iii. Invention

We have spoken of a sophistical method for reducing freedom to an absurdity, by driving a wedge between types of act which, split off from one another, fail to express it sufficiently. But the wedge may alternatively be driven not between one type of act and another, but between the constituents of a single active process. An example of what we mean may be provided by a type of free act to which we have many times alluded, invention. What seems more characteristic of freedom than to invent, or, as it is almost blasphemously said now-a-days, to create? The very word compares our action with the sovereign freedom of God, and provokes the philosophical critic of metaphysical inflation. Come now, he says, what is there in it, after all? You say that 'Hamlet' is Shakespeare's creation, and that such an achievement of the mind is a hard nut for determinist explanation to crack. Let us take the creative process to pieces. What do you suppose to have happened? Shakespeare came to the task equipped with several well-practised skills, and he had the ready-made outline of a plot to work upon. He could apply his skills to his undertaking direct, and study the best way to knock his play into shape. But then, of course, he has to invent. Not in a vacuum, however; at any given point the story is going in a certain direction, the characters are in a certain posture. Now what shall Hamlet say? Through processes of mental association, quite ungoverned by conscious direction or by any exercise of voluntary control, a number of suggestions rise in the poet's mind, out of the deep caves of his memory. It is the part of conscious skill and good sense to make decisions, admitting or rejecting notions which have welled up of their own accord, and working into shape what is adopted for use. Last of all the poet tries it on his ear, and decides whether or no he is satisfied with the result.

Let us list the voluntary actions, and the mental events, which belong to what is presumably the most 'creative' moment: that at which Shakespeare finds something for Hamlet to say, when that something is no mere matter of course.

1. Shakespeare turns his mind over the situation of his character, or broods upon it. There is nothing in this more than in any process of thought, specially calling for a non-deterministic account.

2. Phrases or images rise in the poet's consciousness, never mind from where; for whatever their source, they come, they are not picked or chosen; so there is nothing in the occurrence to concern the freewill argument.

3. The poet passes judgement on his hunches, arranges them, mends a word here or there, and so forth. Once more, if any thinking can be deterministically explained, this can be. The poet's practised abilities, his arts of rhetoric and verse, offer principles to govern his decisions; principles which require heed and thoroughness, rather than liberty of option, for their application to the matter in hand; while the plot and the characters, already conceived, provide a standing form to which reference can be constantly made.

4. Finally, the poet tries what he has written on his ear, or rolls it round his mouth. But then either he finds he likes it, or that he does not; either sees that it will do, or that it will not. He does not *decide* to like or to dislike it. So, unless we have already conceded the libertarian account of value-appreciations in general, we see nothing here to shake us.

We have set out the skeleton of a whole determinist account, even though several of the topics it employs have been discussed

already. We have, for example, no more to say about valuation
(4), or about decision as such (3). We will concentrate on (2). It
is here that we observe the operation of the sophistic wedge,
driven in this case between the supposedly passive and the admittedly active phases of the inventive process. The author is
supposed to run over, or brood upon, what he has already constructed or imagined; this is action. In response to it, ideas shoot
up out of the subconscious, while the poet, as a voluntary agent,
remains passive in regard to them. He is like Aaron when,
according to his own account, he stood by the fatal cauldron and,
to his vast surprise, 'there came out this calf.' Still, like a bear
rather than a calf, it needs licking into shape, and he gets to work
on it with a graving-tool—here, once more, there is activity on
the poet's part.

Surely no one who has invented a poem or story or any such
thing, will accept an account like this. We have been told that
whole stanzas floated into Housman's mind, and that Coleridge
dreamt 'Kubla Khan'. We have nothing to say to these singular
examples, except that they are not typical. It is plain anyhow that
'Hamlet' did not occur to Shakespeare, nor did he dream it up.
We have no desire to discuss whether 'Kubla Khan' is or is not the
product of voluntary thought. 'Hamlet' is, and so are the little
pieces of verse we have all ourselves attempted—not to mention
these interminable lectures.

The deterministic falsification lies essentially in the separation
between active and passive. There is a passive element in invention; something takes the beating, when we are said to cudgel our
brains. But equally something does the cudgelling. To use a less
crude metaphor, we do not wait for something to come, we
fumble for it. In an earlier discussion, we compared the constructive mind to a mason who can lay his hands on his materials, since
he knows his way blindfold about the builder's yard. The parable,
like all parables, is imperfect; the resources of comparison are
defeated by the procedure we are trying to illustrate. Before we
go to look for what we want, must not we know what it is we
seek? Whereas in the case before us, to know what we seek is to

have found already; if we know what phrase or image to seek, it is already ours. Even this is not the end of the trouble. In the case of truly inventive composition, we may not even know the function which the missing phrases are to perform, or the general shape which they are to fill out; for, as we say, we simply do not know how to go on. We make up the pattern by the same act, by which we hit on the material. The two things suggest, or call for, one another; who can say which comes first, if either does?

Invention is a voluntary activity right enough, a supremely self-directive endeavour. It lacks, of course, the mastery and the clarity which belong to decision between formulated alternatives, or to manipulation of finished materials; as when we decide which way round to place a couple of virtually self-contained stanzas, or paragraphs, already composed. Invention makes up, however, in sheer innovation what it lacks in control; and since both control and innovation belong to our idea of human freedom, decision and invention are equally required, to give it substance.

There is, as we have seen, a special paradox for the imagination, in the effort to diagrammatise invention; and logic cannot help us out, since logic deals with what is formulated or formulable, and is therefore *ex hypothesi* invented already. But it is bad philosophy to make these difficulties an excuse for denying that there is such an activity as invention, or for driving a wedge between passive 'inspiration' and conscious manipulation.

iv. *Reasonable conduct free as such: conclusion*

We will mention one more example of the wedge. We need not develop it in any fulness, having in principle discussed it already. A libertarian philosopher cries 'Heureka!' and runs into the street, to gladden a philosophical public with his news—the long-sought proof of freewill at length is found, and (like most epoch-making discoveries) turns out to be of a convincing simplicity. All we need to show, he says, is that reasonable behaviour takes place; not, that is, behaviour to be judged reasonable by some external observer, but behaviour animated or directed by reason. For once it is made clear that we do things for sensible and objective reasons thought out by us, it must be conceded that we are not simply actuated by cerebral mechanism, animal passion, psychological habit, or any other compelling cause.

In our view, as we have, let us hope, sufficiently indicated, this moral Archimedes is unquestionably right. But if he is to make his case wedgeproof, he will need to say more than he has, in the first excitement of discovery, managed to say. For all he has so far asserted, his critics are free to reply: Men act from reasons. Well and good. But what does this mean? Children are taught to think, as they are taught to talk; the two lessons are one and the same. Now no one, I trust, will be so uncharitable as to suppose determinists committed to the denial that talking plays any part in the causation of behaviour. Of course it does. What, then, is 'reasonable behaviour'? Not motiveless behaviour, anyhow; no one would call that reasonable. Now motives are initially supplied by appetite or disposition; no free choice there. But then the project in which motive interests us, brings some reasoning-habit into play; and the habit acts according to its own technique, whether to analyse the aim or to calculate the means. No step of the reasoning is arbitrary (or so much the worse for it); every one is in accordance with principle and art; no free choice here, either. And when the project is thought out, and begins, perhaps, to wear a somewhat different appearance from anything originally proposed, appetite, disposition, feeling, or whatever we are to call the sources of motive, act once more; the man either does, or does not want to carry out the project. And where is the free choice in that?

The wedge has been driven in, we observe, between reasonable thought on the one side, and motive or interest on the other. What needs to be done, if the discovery of our Archimedes is to obtain the credit it deserves, is to reunite the two sides of the split. It must be shown that the constructions of reason do not simply evoke formed appetites or dispositions; they provide novel objects in which we freshly interest ourselves. But we have had enough of that argument on earlier pages; and here we are turning the last page that we mean to devote to the direct discussion of freewill.

How shall we fill it, then? What single topic, hitherto neglected, calls loudest for a mention? What but the last spectre of the mind, the final and most metaphysical of doubts? We have all through debated on the supposition that freedom is vindicated, if our action proves irreducible to any combination of determinate factors, of which the joint effect could ideally be calculated. But now it may be asked: 'Granted that no such analysis is even ideally possible, and that there is nothing to be said about the course taken by my action, but that I do what I do; may it not still be suggested, that my doing what I do is as it has to be, and cannot be otherwise?'

There are two exorcisms available for laying this spectre. The first of them is strictly philosophical. We persuade the haunted man that his misgiving is meaningless. He allows, after all, that we simply act, unhampered by any constraint which can be in any way particularised, or which comes to bear on us at any specifiable point; that there is, moreover, no way of establishing the supposed destiny we fulfil, except the evidence of what we do. To all appearances our free action writes our history. The horrid misgiving amounts to nothing but the suggestion, that the narrative has been written already, and that our pen is always tracing over invisible letters. The supposition is not only wanton, but senseless; for there is no hand that could have written the first draft ahead of us.

'Is not there, though?' says the fate-haunted man; 'what is the absurdity in a prescient Omnipotence?' Ah, now (we say to him) you are talking theology, and you will need a theological exorcism to conjure your devil. That will mean a lengthier and less glib incantation. We must lead you to see what sort of theology makes sense, under what charter God can be believed to have placed the exercise of human liberties, or how the action of a creaturely and finite will can be thought to be limited by a will in a different plane, the will of its creator. If you are for theology, there are no short cuts; you must think your theology out.

CHAPTER XV

LIBERTY AND THEOLOGY

i. Existential and 'We think' philosophies

THE time has come to survey the question of voluntary freedom with a wider sweep. We have done what we could do in the hand-to-hand fight with deterministic misconception. Let us stop arguing about the freedom of the will, and ask ourselves why, after all, it matters. Let us beg the question of liberty, and say: Supposing that we have a voluntary freedom, what is the use of making the fact clear, or stripping away the sophistries which obscure it? For, as even determinists admit, men must be allowed to think as though they were freely inventing, and to make choices as though they were freely deciding. Will not the libertarian and the determinist, therefore, live and act in an identical way? If there is a difference between them, it is that the determinist hopes to perform a feat of which the libertarian despairs. For the determinist thinks that, reflecting after the event on his neighbour's conduct or his own, he should be able to descry in it the structure of reason, the lineaments of necessity; whereas the libertarian renounces any such hope. And so it may seem that the practical value of libertarianism is nil; it makes a metaphysical fuss about deciding and inventing, things which the sensible man does as he goes along, with no fuss at all. Whereas the practical value of determinism is tangible; it holds before us the hope of causal explanation; it gives us a programme to work upon.

The determinist claim which we have just stated contains an implicit admission, which the counter-argument will seize. What is determinism? It is not a hypothesis, it is a hope. Whatever patterns or regularities are to be found in human behaviour, a libertarian is just as free to recognise, study and profit by them, as a determinist can be. The determinist is in no position actually to plot out the most part of human conduct, as the simple exemplification of established uniformities, whether before or after the conduct occurs. He is singular merely in holding the hope, the pious hope, that under ideal conditions it could be done. Now where we have a general and pious hope entertained about what can be done, we may postulate, as the counterpart to it, a pious faith about the way things are. If some form of action or achievement is held to be in general an ideal possibility, it is surely held to be so in consequence of the general nature of things. If we hope that we will reduce conduct to causal explanation, we believe conduct is such as to be causally explicable. The hope and the belief belong together, and they share the same pious character. If the hope is a pious hope, the belief is a pious belief; not the sort of belief I have when I believe Viet-Minh to be a republic, but the sort I have when I believe the Yellow Race to be a messianic people.

Once it has been seen that determinism is a faith, the way is open to consider libertarianism as a faith also. Now the determinist attack which we were just now considering, amounted to saying that bare libertarianism is an empty faith; it makes a fuss over assuring people of their freedom to do what they will do in any case—contrive, invent, decide. The point ought to be conceded. Bare libertarianism is an empty faith; and if we cast fate out of liberty-hall only to keep the rooms empty, swept and garnished, the demon will return with reinforcements. For the patterns of necessity play so large a part in our thinking, they will always encroach on empty ground. Bare libertarianism is an empty faith; but then libertarianism need not be, and commonly is not, held as an isolated conviction. It is supported by other beliefs, beliefs which both give it signficance, and themselves borrow significance from it. We will recall two of them: about creativity, and about responsibility, the believer in freewill has his own way of thinking. We will take the two terms in order.

It may be true that, for practical purposes, the doctrine of necessity concedes the felt freedom of our acts; but it teaches us, when we reflect on them, to view them as the expressions of a natural inevitability. And (the libertarian complains) such a teaching cannot but undermine in us the seeming importance of what we do. For it tells us that there is some nature of things, or of ourselves, in accordance with which we are bound to act; whose tendencies our decision merely applies to the case, and, as it were, precipitates. To employ again the gross metaphor we have used—the statute-laws of our universe, or of our kind, are fixed; our decisions are, at the best, those of judges; our discretion is limited to an application of law to instance. By contrast, the libertarian may see himself as making law. Within the limits which physical and psychological facts prescribe, man may have the sheer liberty to make himself the sort of creature he chooses to be, by adopting a certain sort of life, and building up the customs and aptitudes required for it. No doubt our power to make ourselves is much restricted; by the time we take the task in hand, our elders have done so much to us already. But they have done it, and we shall do the like to our children, pupils or charges. The fact that man-making by men is exercised on others, not on one's self, does not diminish the portentousness of the undertaking. Any one of us, it is true, will over-estimate his importance, if he supposes that he alone, in independence of other individuals or of the social mould, can shape any single soul, his child's or his own. Nevertheless, according to the libertarian belief, the total moulding force will be a function of the number (whatever it be) of free agencies; whether aware, or unaware of their freedom; whether employing it to carve a destiny, or asleep on it, in a nest of convention.

Certain existentialist thinkers on the Continent have carried self-creation to the limit, and have boldly proclaimed (without, in their own eyes, discrediting their doctrine) that liberty is so absolute, it topples over into an absurdity. It may amuse us to compare Sartre's estimate of our condition with Pope's mockery of man. 'Go, wondrous creature' says the poet to the featherless biped, 'teach Providence to rule; then drop into thyself, and be a fool.' Yet, according to Pope, we need not resign ourselves to cosmic folly, for we need not undertake to play providence. We can play the fool in a corner, and it will not be calamitous; *dulce est desipere in loco*. Whereas according to the existentialist philosopher, the sceptre of Providence is forced into our fingers; if we do not play providence to ourselves, no one will; there is no other God. The ordeal of Phaeton is ours; the reins are in our hands, the doors of dawn are open, and we must guide the chariot of the Sun. We must—but it's absurd; our ignorance, our liability to passion, the mutual frustration of our aims, present the spectacle of forty Phaëtons drunk, driving wild on the Place de la Concorde.

'Now, my child,' they used to say to me, marking the end of a penal silence, 'Now you can say what you like.' My young lips were struck dumb by so portentous an option; and so it is, when existentialism throws my life into my lap, and says 'Be yourself, my boy, and make it up as you go along'. The effect is like a paralytic stroke. I come to again, however, at last, and begin to remember—with what consolation to remember—my responsibilities. There will, no doubt, be occasions for sheer personal option, but thank heaven I have not to meditate *in vacuo* on what to make of myself, as the God of Leibniz meditates on what to make of the world. Thank heaven I have this lecture to write, and beyond that, my pupils to see to; and ah, beyond that, if I dare to look, there is Lazarus on the doorstep, covered with sores.

What is it, then? I must, by my effort, and invention, and fidelity, make my life; but always responsibly. Now we talked of responsibility in a previous chapter. We saw that the notion derived from the law-court, and might, even in morals, have a very limited application. The flattest determinism could allow that we are, through the operation of fairly obvious motives, swayed by a social code, for the keeping of which we feel responsibility. But we suggested in our discussion that the most interesting extension of the notion is that which stretches it furthest, and makes us responsible for acting or not acting on our basic valuations; and it is this extended sense of responsibility that we shall consider in the present chapter.

Here, then, is our trinity of notions, our libertarian battlecry,

Liberty, Creativity, Responsibility—or death! We are free, and free to make our lives, but always in response to claims; claims which we may be psychologically free, but are not morally free, to ignore. What is it, then, that ultimately exerts these claims upon us? The philosophy of 'How we think' may point out with complacency that we do not commonly trace our responsibilities to a higher source than the custom of our kind, or cite an authority superior to the American way of life. And doubtless a Gallup poll, say of the Civil Service and other black-coated workers, would do much to support the contention; especially if the questionnaire were suitably framed. *Vox Gallupi vox Dei*; still, we must be careful not to misinterpret so august an oracle. It may be that people are content to find their authority in custom; but authority for what? Not, ultimately, for what they should do, but for what they should prize. The man who follows the American way of life does not see in the customs of the tribe obligatory performances, which are their own justification; he takes them both to express, and to be inspired by, a respect for humanity.

The citizen is found, then, to have two objects of respect; and he can easily be reduced to that bewilderment produced by Socratic queries in the common breast, if we ask him which is supreme, humanity, or the American way of life? Let Socrates clear up the confusion Socrates has caused. It is plain to the philosopher that humanity, and the American way of life, are not objects of respect on the same level, or so as to be possible rivals to one another. We may respect the American way of life as a sound indicator, pointing out to us what there is in humanity most deserving of respect, as well as how that respect may in practice be paid. Humanity we respect absolutely, if once we can see it straight; and this respect obliges us; we hold ourselves responsible for acting, or failing to act, in accordance with it.

We say that our respect is payable to humanity. The word is almost too convenient; indeed, to the modern ear it is an actual equivocation. It means mankind, and it means the characteristic excellence of human nature. Both are objects of respect, or of regard. But so far from coinciding in practice, they are inclined to tug us in different directions, and, on occasion, to tear us apart. To regard mankind is to accept men as they are, to spare them frustration, to give them their will and pleasure. To regard humanity, in the other sense, is to look for what a believer calls the divine image in us, and the unbeliever the human ideal. It is to censure vice or folly, and push against the tide of appetite, as well in other men, as in ourselves.

To all working moral systems, or ways of life deserving the name, some respect for humanity in both senses is common ground. All direct us to accept mankind as it is, and all uphold a standard of what it should be. And all, no doubt, have their practical ways of dealing with the tension which results; of squaring (if we are to take the Christian example) the law Christ delivers on the Mount, with the indulgence he manifests to sinners. The perplexity is a practical perplexity; it cannot be exorcised by logical analysis. It is no use telling us that there is no rivalry between our two aims; that the human ideal, or divine similitude in us is no concrete entity, let alone person, capable of competing for our attention against John Robinson or Robert Jones; that it is merely a way of conceiving what either of these characters has it in him to aspire after. Such philosophical solutions offer no practical consolation, because the perplexity concerns our action. We have either to accept our children as they are, or (however tactfully) edge them towards what they should be.

The modern world has not even yet got over the antique method of reconciling our two aims; a method reflected in that equivocation in the word 'humanity', on which we have just remarked. To the Greek philosopher it was no equivocation at all. Just as, to the old-fashioned botanist, a spotted orchid was simply a specimen of the kind, more or less perfect, the teleology of nature being single-mindedly bent on making it as typical as circumstance allowed; so equally, to the Greek thinker, human individuals were simply specimens of mankind, in each of whom the form of the species was, as it were, doing its best to realise itself. To the great scandal of the modern student, everything distinctive of a person, all that makes the individuality of a character, was written off by the Greek as accidental to the essential man, and irrelevant to the teleology of existence. 'Be human, my son' was the supreme moral injunction; 'Be a Man with a large M.' What we call the pull of the ideal was simply the self-realisation of the natural species *man*, on all the levels of being or action; and especially, of course, on the highest. A bad man was a bad specimen, limited, frustrated, warped, unhappy. The art of felicity and the art of virtue were one, and to respect men as they are was the same thing as to respect what they should be. For what are they, it was asked, what have they in them capable of moving respect, beside their human nature, struggling to be itself? Who could seriously respect in a man what was accidental to his being?

Ideal humanity was to the Aristotelian a timeless form of natural substance, a typical object of natural science, engraved in the order of the world, and unalterable as long as heaven revolves. It was conceivable—though God forbid!—that a concentration of disastrous accident might exterminate us, like the dodo; but nothing could change our essence. Had dodos survived, they would have remained incurably (or, I suppose we should say, triumphantly) dodonian. While men survive, they will be as human as ever.

How hopelessly the Greek position has been shot to pieces is a thrice-told tale: shot to pieces by individualism in ethics, historicism in sociology, and evolutionism in biology. It is not this that we wish to dwell upon, but upon the fact that the Greek did at least know what he was regarding, and towards what he held himself responsible, when he set up the common human essence against the trivial claims of individual deviation. He was respecting a form of nature, timeless and virtually divine. He and his metaphysical faith are gone into limbo, never to return. But what do we, we Anglo-Saxon intellectuals, respect, when we balance regard for the human ideal against our regard for mankind?

The answer of 'We think' philosophy to this question is not always mere academic mumbling. There are the forthright prophets who declare: 'We learn to have confidence in our volitions', our aspirations for the future of mankind. It is too hasty a dismissal which rejoins: 'And did not Stalin have confidence in *his* volitions, when he collectivised the farms, and several million farmers died?' For Stalin's trouble was practical miscalculation. The Socialist utopia was only just round the corner, when the Germans began engaging him in an arms-race—was not it a pity? Otherwise the tears of the peasants would soon have dried, in the dawn of a glorious day. Anyhow, we are not marxist doctrinaires—we have not got ideas into our heads; we keep them at arm's length, and scrutinise them. So we may have confidence in our volitions, our directives for the moulding of mankind; as, according to an ancient myth, God had confidence in his volitions, when he made us this being that we are, and surveying it, called it very good.

Let us pause for a moment, and see what has happened to us. Alarmed by the existentialist predicament, unattracted by the task of being Phaeton and running amok with the horses of the Sun, we took refuge in responsibility. We would create our lives, perhaps, but responsibly, in answer to the claims of mankind, and the truth of our nature. But has not responsibility proved a broken reed? If we are responsible, after all, to our own volitions, are we not back in the car with Phaeton, making up our minds which way to drive? What advantage have we over the most self-intoxicated existentialist, except a sort of cautious collectivism? We are not Stalin, we are the Civil Service; *we* are to have confidence in *our* volitions; not *I* in *mine*. And the volitions in which we have confidence are not the dramatic decisions which existential novel-writing, and historical disaster, throw into relief, they are policies somehow settled, and acquiesced in, by a communal complacency. It is this that does duty for 'the truth of human nature', when the philosophy of 'we think' expands into the field of 'we approve' and 'we decide'.

ii. *Positivism and natural faith*

We have been moving too rapidly and shouting too loud. Let us sit down and consider carefully what is at stake. Our philosophers will point out to us that whether we believe in Aristotle's truth of human nature, or whether we put our confidence in their and our volitions, there is no getting round the sheer fact of approval and disapproval, in either case. It is on this indicator that we must rely, for determining what belongs to the human good, and what does not. We have seen that Aristotle himself, however confident in nature as providing the rule of right, defined 'good' as 'whatever any sort of being is after'. The definition is general, covering the good for animals and plants, and even, to our amused delight, the good for stones; they find it in cuddling down as near as they can to the earth's centre. If we are speaking of man, and his moral good, we may wish to specialise the verb, and say that 'being after' on our level has the name of 'aspiration'. So what human nature aspires after is determined, according to Aristotle, by the lineaments of nature herself; but that is only a metaphysical belief. In practice there is no way to discover what humanity aspires after, but experiencing or observing the aspiration. If our good is that towards which aspiration naturally jumps, there is no way of knowing what it is, save by dropping the cat on the floor, and seeing in what direction it does jump.

Even then, merely to observe in what direction our neighbours' aspiration jumps, will not convince us of the good. After learning all we can from others, and sympathising with them as much as we are able, we may still wonder whether they are not the victims of a common perversity, so long as our aspiration fails to jump with theirs. No good can convince us, that does not win us; the good being defined as what attracts, it cannot be seen as good unless it is felt as attractive; always bearing in mind that we are not now talking of any and every attraction, but of that serious attraction only which can draw our total aspiration.

Well then (say our philosophers) since in practice the human good is known as that which we aspire after, why not leave it at that, and cut away the dead wood, the metaphysical part of Aristotle's doctrine? What use does it serve, to allege that the direction of a healthy aspiration is laid down in the unalterable nature of things, if all we can in practice do is follow our aspiration whither it leads? Why regret the collapse of Aristotelian dogmatism, as though some other dogmatism were needed in its place, which we cannot supply? No substitute is needed, when a chimera has been exploded.

Those who are familiar with this type of debate will see immediately to what issue we have brought the question down: the issue between positivism and natural faith. Not in this question only, but over a whole range of questions, positivists have wished to restrict belief to what a practical test can verify. As with morals, so (for example) with physics. We have no way of discovering physical being outside us, except through its interferences with our bodies, or our instruments; and a strict positivism would reduce physical doctrine to a systematisation of such interferences, actual or potential. But natural faith, including the natural faith of physicists, rebels. It may be (we protest) that we do not know the physical world, except as that which we sound by our interferences with it. But we believe that what we are sounding is a mass of energies carrying on business out there in space, on their own account and, as it were, under their own names, whether any soundings of them are taken or not. There is no circumventing or bypassing the soundings, to reach a direct acquaintance with the physical-in-itself; yet we believe it is something in itself, and if we are theological as well as physical believers, we attribute to God a simple knowledge of it.

It is much the same with natural faith and positivist reduction, in the matter of the good. We cannot bypass aspiration, so as to grasp the good after which it aspires; we can only grasp it through aspiring after it. Yet we cannot cease to believe that there is a true or proper good after which aspiration 'feels, if perchance she may find it'. For aspiration is always endeavouring to be right aspiration, and to respond to objects, or pursue aims, intrinsically meriting it. Divorced from this endeavour, aspiration is no longer aspiration. If we have confidence in our aspirations, or, in the phrase we previously took up, confidence in our volitions, it is that they are sound, healthy or right; that is to say, that they are after the proper objectives. There is, of course, a striking difference between our natural faith in physical realities, and our natural faith in genuine goods. Physical things would be ideally definable without reference to any soundings of them; goods would not, even ideally, be definable without reference to any aspirations after them; the good being nothing but the proper object of aspiration.

Let us be clear, anyhow, of this: that what Aristotelianism offered, and what positivists have rejected, was a metaphysical, not a directly practical, conviction. Aristotle did not tell us, even if he sometimes thought he did, any other means of descrying the good than approval, aspiration, love. He claimed to tell us what, in its general bearings, that good was, to which these sentiments or attitudes were the natural pointers. It was all that served or expressed the due expansion of an eternal essence, human nature. 'Well,' it may be asked, 'and what was the use of the metaphysical belief, even while men could still believe it? It did not direct their aim.' No; but it grounded their faith. To reverence, to worship our own volitions, though backed by those of the Civil Service, is flat idolatry. Whereas nature was divine perfection to the Greeks; and even to Christian Hellenists she was a divine ordinance.

Well, but (we shall be told) this is scarcely news. Who does not know that metaphysical belief, the world over, supplies men with something to adore? But our philosophers will tell us that the wish has everywhere been father to the thought; the pathetic, the essentially childish or recessive desire for an object of un-qualified reverence, disappointed by every empirical reality, creates a metaphysical one. The Greeks virtually deified an immanent perfection, supposed to be working itself out in the transience of event. Christians have set their divine perfection further back, a creative will behind, rather than within, the cosmic process. If you want something to worship, this is the sort of thing. We deny ourselves the childish luxury.

'We deny ourselves. . . .' Such language is damaging, if it is not ironical. We cannot take seriously men who talk as though they were free to entertain metaphysical beliefs, or not to entertain them; to say (in the extreme case) 'No, I don't think we will have God, thank you' or to say 'Yes, let's have him'. For either we believe or we do not. What pattern of conviction about the basis of action can we in fact entertain? If we have wrestled with the sophistries of determinism, it was only to clear or to liberate an actual conviction of our power, in some measure, to make ourselves. But if we indeed have the conviction, have we a conviction complementary to it—the conviction of our responsibility for the exercise of this power? The questionnaire proceeds: Responsibility to what? And desiring to voice a common agreement, and to steer clear of metaphysics, we answer, Responsibility to mankind, in others and in myself. What I do with my life, what I do to my neighbours, comes under the claim of something I cannot but hold sacred, their humanity, my integrity. But leave me out of the picture; even if I am free to damn myself, I am not free to betray or outrage them.

So far, surely, we have been drawing out practical convictions which we actually entertain. Do we, then, desert the path of moral realism and begin to chase wild metaphysical geese, when we take a step further and ask, what it is in any man, that demands this practical reverence? It is not just what he happens to think or to desire, that is sacred to me. I am not to respect the villainy of villains, nor to forward the self-dehumanisation of the perverse. I may say that I respect what they have it in them to be, their proper destiny. But this may not be anything that they want, even in the depth of their hearts; and simply to say that it is what I want for them, that my volition about them commands my limitless regard, does not satisfy me; by which I mean, that I cannot believe it. Can you?

Well, what am I to do about it? What alternative is there? It is too late, surely, to hanker after Aristotelism, or hope to reinstate the timeless essence of man, the identical shaping everywhere at work in different qualities of clay, the one way of growing right, as against twenty thousand ways of growing wrong. It is too late to reinstate the changeless rule of essence, for reasons we have named already: individualism in ethics, in sociology historicism, and in biology evolution. No, if we are to believe an objective rule of human good, it must be a flexible rule; and they are surely right who say, there is nothing for us to put our confidence in, which has not the inventiveness of volition. Only, whose? Whose will do I respect, as a will expressed in the facts and possibilities, the hopes and the claims represented by my neighbours' existence —or, indeed, by my own?

So, then, when it is said that theological belief is morally irrelevant, because after all, God or no God, we have to explore the facts to decide a policy of action, and in deciding, trust our aspiration, we make answer that moral policies are at the service of reverence and love, and that as soon as we consider what we reverence, what we love, the practical bearing of theology appears. For it is no trifling difference, whether we value our neighbour simply for what he is, or for the relation in which he stands to the will of God; a will establishing his creation, and intending his perfection. Those that are so minded reverence not a single, but a double object, God in their neighbour, and their neighbour in God. The divine is not far removed from them, but touches them as nearly as physical things touch them. For the physical is known to us by the way it conditions our physical motion; and the divine will, which is God himself, is known to us in limiting or evoking our dutiful action, through all the persons with whom we have to do.

iii. *Paradox of creative and creaturely wills*

A Gifford Lecturer exercises his office in a country against which it has been made a reproach by her neighbours, that she has too much tormented herself with nice reflection on the mystery of predestination. It may be indeed that the formulations of this problem by old Calvinist divinity do not greatly commend themselves to us. But the mystery itself, so far from being a needless mental agony, or subject of extreme curiosity, lies, surely, at the centre of practical religious thought; and if the Scottish people have retained a keener sense of divine power than their fellow-islanders, it may not be unconnected with a habitual dwelling on this mystery by the ministers of the word. It is true that the Calvinist paradoxes belong to revealed theology, and concern the last end of man. But this sublime issue merely draws out and emphasises a paradox already implicit in the natural theology of common moral belief. For we have seen that what commands the theist's moral response is the divine will expressed in his neighbour's being. Our neighbour is a piece of the divine handiwork, still in the making; it is the process of creation still continuing, which demands our instrumental cooperation. God (it is the theist's belief) is making our neighbour. And yet our neighbour is, in some measure at least, making himself. The same thing is true, we suppose, of ourselves; a providence shapes us, and it is this very work of God upon us, which commands our obedience in the ordering of our lives. But how, in the creating of a single life, can we accommodate two wills, one all-knowing and divine, the other fallible and human? Not, perhaps we should say, two wills side by side, for that would be a blasphemous equalisation; but rather, as it were, ranged in depth, the one behind the other, the one acting through and in the other.

To consider how best to handle such a paradox, and how philosophers or theologians have tried to handle it, would involve us in an entire theodicy, and require another book at least as long as this. All we have in mind to say here is that the mystery of the two wills is not the peculiar property of revealed theology, but arises as soon as we acknowledge in the objects of moral reverence not human volitions simply, but divine. How it arises, we may see by recurring to the comparison between Aristotle's world, and ours. The Philosopher needed to distinguish, just as we must, between the proper direction of human endeavour, and the uncertain self-direction of actual men. He managed the distinction by enlarging and extending the analogy offered by organic growth, as seen in any single generation of a species. If puppies grow to be dogs, not chimaeras, it is because the formative principles of the canine species control their growth. But not all puppies come to be perfect dogs. We attribute such deviations as we find to the awkwardness of circumstance, and the intractability of material. The whole world of creatures, anyhow beneath the moon, is to Aristotelian eyes a multitude of vital forms, renewing themselves by propagation, and going right, but only in the main. What the form is, as it were, trying to do in moulding its matter constitutes the good; what comes to pass is the actual approximation. In the business of his physical growth, man is like any animal; he undergoes, and cannot directly influence, the struggle between form and matter, which makes him what he is. But in the shaping of his conduct he plays a conscious part; his thought and choice become as it were the living voice, the sensitive hand of Nature, imposing human order on what would else be the chaos of his acts. Thus the principle of our lives is perfection (for it is the human form, and form is perfect); but the performance is no more perfect than it is; the humanity in us being sidetracked and frustrated by a thousand complications of adverse circumstance.

We observe that, for Aristotle, the distinction between the standard good and the varying approximations is not a distinction between two wills, or two creative activities, both bearing upon the same material. It is the distinction between principle or form on the one side, and activity or will on the other. Form is of its nature perfect, and functioning all more or less defective, anyhow beneath the moon; for nature is a principle which achieves its end (says Aristotle) only in the main.

Now we have found the Aristotelian picture false to science, and false to sentiment; our empirical discoveries have destroyed the doctrine of timeless, inviolable species, our moral perception sees more in the person than an accidental embodiment of the kind. The shape of that perfection after which individuals aspire is, for us, only less variable than their several aspirings after it. It is a flexible rule which, if it is to be accorded any objective being, must find it in the unsleeping creativity of a faultless mind. And so the paradox of two wills in one existence, the perfect and the imperfect, is forced upon us. And not merely as an intellectual puzzle; it is experienced by the theist as the way in which the personal world environs him.

311

Let us be clear what we are doing. We are presenting the relation between theism and morals; and we are bringing out its distinctive character by touching on the contrasting shape of rival systems, atheistic existentialism, philosophic humanism, or antique naturalism. We are not claiming an easy triumph, in absence, over opponents whose counter-arguments we have not so much as heard. To show that nothing but a doctrine of divine volitions will do justice to the moral sense, would be a task indeed. Should we not have to examine every philosophic alternative that has ever been propounded? If we believe our theology, it is probably because we accept a divine voice as having actually spoken; and that is not a claim which a Gifford Lecturer has any business to investigate.

What we will do here, rather than attempt any argument or justification, is to spread the trouble over a wider field. The paradox of two agents to a single activity, one finite, the other infinite, cannot be confined within the limits of personal and moral existence. For if we recognise a creative will within and behind our own, we acknowledge it as that by which we are what we are, as though it were the wellspring out of which we draw our being. And if we are insufficient to exist without the operation of such a cause, how much more insufficient are slighter and less enriched existences, such as we reckon to be the physical elements or forces of the world. There will scarcely be a theist who recognises a divine will in his neighbour and in himself, who does not believe it to be manifested in the existence of whatever is. But what is essentially the same metaphysical paradox confronts us in inanimate nature. The physical world, as well as the vital world on all its levels, operates through an activity inherent in itself, or rather, an activity which is itself; since activity is, to our present mind, the very stuff of things, and it is of this activity that we suppose our science to study the patterns. Yet, in virtue of our theism, we must take the activity to express the prior action of its creator.

We do not, indeed, attribute to the action of physical energy the special character of will; so that we do not meet, in our con-

.templation of the physical scene, that duality of wills which confronts us, when we consider our own dependence upon God. In the physical scene we have duality of activities, one finite, the other infinite, of which only one, the infinite, is a will. Yet the duality of activities in nature is scarcely less mysterious than the duality of wills in personal existence. We have two stories about what works the world, and each on its own level and in its own idiom appears to be complete. Omnipotence not only can dispense with, but even seems to exclude, additional or subsidiary agencies. But then on the other side the pattern of physical forces fills all the time and all the space there is, and allows of no irruption from the divine.

Men live and act under God, natural forces energise under God. Which of these two relations is the more mysterious? Here is a question which it will be illuminating to discuss, even though we shall scarcely be so simple-minded as to hope for a decisive answer this way or that. It will turn, we may suspect, on the sense we put upon the word 'mysterious'.

On the one hand, the case of physical nature seems the less mysterious. Natural forces, having no will of their own, do not give rise to the supreme paradox of our own case, the opposition of a finite, and often a perverse, will to the creative omnipotence. When we think of nature acting under God, we easily satisfy ourselves with familiar analogies. We can ourselves manipulate natural forces, and make them serve our will, and notably by the construction of machines. How much more readily, then, we say, can God both make and employ the mechanism of the universe. Or again, we think of the even greater immediacy and facility with which we impress the direction of our will on the forces composing our bodies. In some such manner, we may think, the whole universe answers to the control of the divine thought in every part; and following this line of analogy, Leibniz, we recall, came to see God as the transcendent Soul of his physical creation. Neither the analogy of our mind in the direction of bodily movement, nor of our person in the employment of instruments, can supply a physical theology which bears thinking out to the last point. But we need not be so rigorous. Entertained lazily on the surface of the mind, either analogy looks well enough; what a contrast to any image we may form of the relation between created will and creative! For that looks outrageous from the moment we begin to frame it. When will is set over either instruments or organs, hierarchical order is at least respected; when will is set over will, it is ignored, even if it is not flouted. If will operates physical forces, their essential character is not violated; but if will operates will, how can the subject will retain the character of being will? Is not will, by definition, self-operative? It appears, therefore, that the dependence of physical nature on divine activity is less paradoxical, or mysterious, than is the dependence of human life on divine activity.

That is as far as we will take the statement of the first case. We will now pass over to a statement of the contrary; and our initial move will be to attack the analogies on which the first thesis relied. The dependence of nature upon God is certainly not that of machines or an engineer, or of bodily motions on an embodied will. Such figures are pitiful props to a halting imagination. They give no insight whatever into the nature of the mystery on which they pretend to comment. What is it, after all, for any created act or being to draw its existence out of the Creator's act? We can have no real notion of such a relation, save by generalisation from the case where we can (however imperfectly) experience it; and what case can this be, but our own? We say of ourselves, at least, that we embrace, cooperate with, or draw upon the divine will, in doing what is right. It may be hard indeed to set out our creaturely response as an experiencing of God-dependence; and yet such phrases as we have cited mean something to theists, whose belief has become incorporated with the stuff of their lives. The insight we have into our dependence upon God is dark, when compared with God's vision of what that dependence is. But it is brightness itself, compared with the fog we are in, over the dependence on God of any physical substance.

So much for the opposing pleas. What are we to say of them? Each is, perhaps, justified in what it advances, but that is not to say that what the two advance is of equal importance; and we have, no doubt, allowed it to appear which thesis, in our judgement, has the greater weight. All that the first can honestly claim for itself is that it shows us a relation of creature to Creator which is more easily imaginable; and the second thesis may even go so far as to deny that this is any advantage. As God himself is unimaginable, so also must be the dependence of his creatures on his power. And if the relation appears imaginable, we have reason to fear that we are viewing it unrealistically, and, as it were, from a great distance. The nearer we come to it, and the more we are involved in it, the less imaginable, the more paradoxical we shall find it to be. But what we lose in imaginative clarity is made up to us in actuality; just where we cease to conceive our dependence on God, we begin to live it.

Will, action, the creative moment in man, is the only object of consideration which opens a dimension of metaphysical depth, or promises to let through a single ray of uncreated light. Here alone we find a power of making anything to be or not to be, and it is this that raises all the questions of theistic philosophy; leading us to ask, whether there is not such a power underlying all things, not merely the things we make to be; leading us to ask, whether our own creative power is underivative, or whether it does not spring continually out of a deeper source of will, the wellspring of the world; leading us to ask, how nearly analogous that prime creative will would be, to the secondary form of volition we ourselves possess and exercise. Here are questions which to formulate shortly, as we have just formulated them, is but to clothe them in stale metaphor; questions which we have not opened in this book, and will not open now. But to evoke them is to see what an importance attaches to the preliminary work which, however inadequately, we have undertaken; the work of clearing obstacles from the serious contemplation of any will whatsoever, whether human or divine; and even, perhaps, of casting some positive light on that human will, from which alone the divine can be conjectured.

SUMMARY OF THE ARGUMENT

I. BODY AND MIND

By clarifying the Freedom of the Will we prepare the ground for theology, since the Divine Person can only be understood through the free human person. But the treatment we employ is purely philosophical and, as we hope, contemporary. (pp. 1-2)

Before we examine the problem on a mental level, we must make sure that the ground is not cut away under our feet by the evidence for physical determinism. Recent brain-research has revealed the physical correlate of thinking to be a system of electric circulations, which it is difficult to describe otherwise than mechanically. Nor can this evidence be offset by the evidence for indeterminacy in nuclear physics. The brain-system is a high-level system, and to be credited with having discounted the indeterminacy of its lowest constituents. (pp. 2-6)

We open the question with an account of contributions to *the Physical Basis of Mind* by Lord Samuel, A. J. Ayer and Gilbert Ryle. We take from them in turn the following points: (*a*) The working of our brains and nerves is uniform with the mechanism of external things; the distinct character of consciousness nevertheless remaining its own evidence. (*b*) In the nature of the case, physiology and psychology stand in a mere *de facto* parallel, however far research may go in clearing it up. (*c*) What we commonly mean by the unity of body and mind is not the concurrence of physiological and psychological data, but the experienced exercise of thoughtful bodily action. (pp. 6-13)

We develop the last point (*c*) by an examination of the Cartesian dualism attacked in Ryle's *Concept of Mind*. We show how largely Descartes was the victim of historical accident, and the slave of the Aristotelism he rejected. His error was to start from

316

pure thought, instead of starting from that heedful bodily action, which it presupposes. (pp. 13–21)

II. THE SEAT OF CONSCIOUSNESS

In heedful bodily action, the movement we intend corresponds with part of the general sweep of a line traced by minute nerve-events in series, from the brain to the executive organ—with a part only of it; for consciousness 'dwells' on that part of the movement which needs direction. She never *dwells* on the roots of it, which are in the brain. She nevertheless *depends* on the occurrence of the brain-events, as can be proved by physical interference. (pp. 22–28)

To understand the correlation of neurological events with pure thoughts can only mean, to bring it into intelligible relation with the model instance already discussed. The way to do this is to arrange intentional acts in series, from conscious bodily doing, through conscious use of the vocal organs, to thinking aloud with disattention from our production of sounds; and so on to silent thought, in which we merely flick the organs, and are unaware of doing so. (pp. 28–31)

Such a series omits imagination, in which we do not 'ghost' executive action (e.g. talking), but sensuous response (e.g. hearing). It would appear that the responsive nerves are set into 'ghostly' action by the anticipatory disposition of the organs; a 'ghostly' listening and looking produces a 'ghostly' hearing and seeing. But neither in imagining nor in verbal thinking is the brain the organ of our act; it is rather our instrument of organ-control. (pp. 31–39)

III. THE INSTRUMENT OF PERSONAL ACTION

Intentional action is not concerned with the brain, but with acts carried by action-patterns rooted in the brain. In the simplest cases of practical decision, cerebral mechanism may be credited with raising alternative projects in consciousness. Two or more action-patterns tingle in a ghostly way; decision is simply the full-blooded enactment of one among them. In more complex cases,

THE FREEDOM OF THE WILL

invention enters; and she does not choose among alternative projects which 'arise', she fumbles and finds them. Physiologically, she turns energy through the paths of a cortical maze; consciously, she steps from one action-pattern to another and never sets foot in the brain. (pp. 40–46)

'Intention' is ambiguous. Our intention (what we intend) has its physical counterpart in the discharge of an action-pattern. Our intention (act of intending) has its physical counterpart in the brain. It is because intention (2) is about intention (1) and never about itself, that we have no consciousness of the brain. Whether we can be said to 'use' the brain, is a linguistic question. The brain is rather the physical aspect of the user, than anything used. Consciousness identifies herself with the use to which the 'used' is put. The action of the 'used', i.e. of the limb, is itself mechanical, once it has been set going thus. But 'mechanical' is here employed in an extended sense, which does not imply 'lifeless' or 'no suitable vehicle for consciousness'. (pp. 46–52)

IV. THE ACTION-PATTERN, AND ALTERNATIVE THEORIES

If anything is to happen because it is intended, it must be something on which intention can bear. Intention cannot, and does not, bear on minute nerve-events of which she is unaware; but on a large-scale sweep of movement. Minute neural events must be really organised in an action-pattern working towards such a movement, or intention cannot bear on them. This action-pattern is, then, a real principle in the causal order. And it is required not only in the interpretation of intentional consciousness, but equally in that of animal behaviour, whether intentional or not.

An analogy for the relation of action-patterns to their minute constituent movements is offered by the control of higher over lower systems of organisation in the hierarchy of physical nature. It is true that natural scientists often wish to deny the independent efficacy of higher organising principles; but there are several reasons why a philosopher may be pardoned for not taking such denials at their face-value. (pp. 53–60)

Two objections: (a) 'Interaction of mind and body' is non-sensical. Granted; but not so an active relation in one bodily system between several patterns of movement, one of which is linked with consciousness in a way in which another is not. (b) Philosophy should not make her own hypotheses in the realm of natural fact. Answer—Not if she can help it; but she must sometimes fill gaps in a physical story, before she can interpret it. And perhaps the 'action-pattern' does have a place in science somewhere. (pp. 60–63)

We cannot be satisfied with parallel descriptions (here, of human action in physical and personal terms) unless we can see how they fit together; that is why we speak of the action-pattern. Alternatively, we might attempt to probabilify the naked parallel by the analogy of other acceptably-fitting parallels—'physical-object statements and sense-experience statements', or 'secondary-quality statements and physical-force statements'. The former analogy proves useless, the latter lands us in epiphenomenalism. (pp. 63–72)

Epiphenomenalism is scandalous for three reasons. (a) It misrepresents the balance of mental life, making perception the whole business of the mind and rendering action illusory. (b) It takes mind clean out of the system of nature, by denying it any physical effect or animal utility. (c) It counters the assumption of logical study, that meaning governs the formation of discourse. (pp. 72–80)

An appended note explains the fallacy of a rival doctrine, psycho-physical parallelism. (pp. 80–81)

V. MECHANISM OVERRULED BY MENTALITY

We know best those parts of the neural system which we should expect to be the most mechanical, and so most intelligible—the receptive machinery of sensation, and the executive machinery of action. The machinery of transition between the two is scarcely known; and this is where decision must take place. Ignorance at this point does not, however, help the libertarian case; what would help it, would be the exact knowledge of a system building up to a

THE FREEDOM OF THE WILL

delicate balance with many alternatives, such that the inclination of the scale in favour of any of them was fortuitous, relatively to the system. (pp. 82–86)

J. C. Eccles has put forward some evidence that such is indeed the case. But he combines his perhaps sound physical speculations with a discredited metaphysic, making a separate spiritual substance, the soul, exercise the influence to which the delicate physical balance reacts. We should wish to say that one embodied action of the soul responds to another such; as one signaller responds to another, by signalling on. (pp. 86–92)

To talk like this, is to apply to parts of a man's personal action that sort of mixed description, half physical and half intentional or mental, which is naturally and properly applied to the whole man. Otherwise put, we personify his several acts. The purpose of doing so, is to break personal action small enough, to stand in parallel with distinct physical actions succeeding one another in the brain. The language is artificial, but the parallel is real. (pp. 92–95)

To reject physical determinism is not to deny that some physical causes have inescapable mental effects. Commonsense recognises this over a wide field, but is disturbed when a sensational new example comes to light, e.g. the psychological effects of lobotomy. There is nothing new in principle here; yet the shock makes the unphilosophical talk determinism. (pp. 95–98)

The essential refutation of *physical* determinism is the proof, that our acts can respond to our previous acts, or to our previous perceptual reactions, not in virtue of their physical efficacy, but in virtue of what they mean. (pp. 98–100)

An appended note shows how the position adopted might be squared with belief in the immortality of the soul. (pp. 100–105)

VI. FREEWILL DEFINED

The qualification 'free' does not distinguish one sort of will from another (unfree). Free will is simply full, or proper, will; 'free' negates privations of the power or exercise of willing. The use of the adjective expresses a positive valuation of the ability to deliberate, resolve, execute, persevere; but the valuation is not, in fact, contested by anyone. (pp. 106–109)

Freewill is just (perfect) will. But 'will' in turn is just 'action' in the personal sense of 'to act'. 'Act' calls attention more to the performance, 'will' to the intention, in our doing. We ask, for example, *what* was a man's will (intention), or *how much* will (intention) was present; if there was none, there was no action either, but only a bodily event. When will is present, it is the soul of the event, not another event external or previous. To err on this point is to incur a notorious logical absurdity. Similarly, 'I would have acted otherwise, had I wished' does not mean that a different prior condition (a wish) would have had a different consequence (act); but that I could have acted otherwise, in merely willing otherwise. (pp. 109–115)

The most unfree act has some freedom, or it would not be an act; as the most unhealthy man has some health, or he would not be a (living) man. Freedom is most enjoyed when least constrained, but most heroically asserted against constraints. (pp. 116–117)

The hero vindicates freedom against real constraints; the libertarian philosopher vindicates the notion of freedom from notional constraints, theoretical descriptions which do not allow it to be what it is. We revolt against the misdescription of our free being almost as we revolt against actual constraint on our liberty; so upset are we by what conflicts with our practical attitude towards the life of day-to-day decision. Nor can our attachment to the conviction of our liberty be plausibly regarded as morbid vanity. So says the libertarian. The determinist replies, that his doctrine does not misdescribe choice so as virtually to deny that we choose. He merely claims that our choice will be found to have been predictably prefigured in its antecedents. The libertarian rejoins, that no man can believe so about a choice, when he is making it. The determinist may admit this, but plead that the incompatibility is one of attitudes only. We cannot be in the mental posture of deciding, and in that of explaining, the same act at the same time. But this is not to say that the nature of choice precludes prefiguration. (pp. 117–125)

VII. A DETERMINIST ACCOUNT OF PHENOMENAL LIBERTY

Should not a determinist be able to give a 'causal' reason why we cannot, in deciding, regard our decision as 'causally' pre-determined? He might argue thus: The causal efficacy of decision-thinking lies in its evocation of subjective responses which would otherwise be unevoked. It works by developing objective considerations, and letting the responses come. To think about the responses as determinate factors is merely obstructive to the evocation of them. (pp. 126–132)

True, says the libertarian, but irrelevant. Consideration may show a man how he feels about alternative projects, and merely sharpen the issue of a hard choice. It is the choice itself, about which we want a causal explanation, why it cannot be made in the lively belief that it is causally prefigured.—Not a *causal* explanation, says the determinist. The explanation here is *logical*. The form of a decision is, of making it; the form of causal explanation is recognising an inevitability. We cannot recognize as an inevitability what we are making as a decision. Causal explanation and decision have each their own idiom; this is merely tautological, and nothing follows.—On the contrary, my whole case follows, says the libertarian. We have not here a common subject-matter (decision) and two alternative idioms in which to talk about it. One of these idioms is the only recipe for doing it—without decision-thinking, there are no decisions. The idiom is the form of the act, and must be taken seriously as revealing the nature of the act. (pp. 132–139)

Why so? says the determinist. A recipe for doing something is not a recipe for understanding it. Decision-thinking is merely practical; the subsequent act by which we explain our decision causally, is truly theoretical; and explanation has the last word.— Never, says the libertarian. Explanation is itself a chosen human activity, and itself in need of explaining; and so *ad infinitum*. Only freedom can do any explaining; and when freedom turns to explaining herself, she must not explain herself away. (pp. 139–142)

VIII. CONDUCT AS UNDERSTOOD AND PREDICTED

The libertarian does not accept the contention, that the personal idiom of choiceful action is merely practical, and no instrument of understanding. On the contrary, we understand men's behaviour not by causes, but by seeing what they are up to. This is, indeed, the basic form of understanding and prior to all other. It is thus that we understand speech; and speech is nothing but a formalised and symbolising piece of behaviour. (pp. 143–148)

We may consider the objection: Nevertheless, there is no great difference between causal explanation and personal understanding; to explain an explosion is to appreciate it as what, under given circumstances, dynamite does; and to understand our neighbour's behaviour is to appreciate it as what, under given circumstances, a man does.—Answer: 'What dynamite does' means 'what dynamite always does'. 'What a man does' means 'What we can conceive a man's doing, and what a certain man (Henry) is here understood to do.' Both sorts of interpretation rest on analogy, but in different ways. In physical explanation we analogize between one observation and another. In personal understanding we do not analogize at all. We make a direct use of powers which are *de facto* analogous with our neighbour's powers, and therefore understand him. (pp. 148–157)

Another objection: But personal understanding can predict, and therefore views behaviour as predetermined.—Answer: It is not prediction which implies necessity, but prediction from causes. Could we genuinely and directly foresee free decisions, it would cast no shadow on their freedom. Personal understanding neither foresees, nor predicts from causes; it predicts from standing decisions, or policies of choice, which we do not expect the agent concerned to revoke. But on occasion, he may. Nor are occasions causes; they are occasions. (pp. 157–165)

The belief that our friends' dependability involves determinism, is due to a confusion between the many different grounds of our confident expectations, and the many different degrees of exactitude in what we expect. (pp. 165–168)

IX. THE ANALOGY OF NATURE

What is the philosophical importance of the fact, that freewill plays so minute a part in a law-ridden universe? If it is true, that it is only by a freely-pursued investigation that the determined order of the world is discovered, the fact of universal order can never be more certain, than the liberty of the mind which discovers it. (pp. 169–173)

Nevertheless, we have an interest in unifying the objective picture of nature. Hence the temptation to give a paraphysical account of the personal or mental. The unreality of the resultant story leads to a reaction, pan-psychism, which falsifies no less on the other side. What we need to see is that freedom and necessity belong together; for only in a world of causal order can freedom be hopefully exercised. (pp. 173–178)

The study of natural uniformities is the abstract study of the patterns in which natural force acts; and personal freedom appears a stranger in a world of causal diagrams. But besides the patterns, there is what throws them—natural force; and freedom is not a stranger among natural forces, since she has her being in exercising force reciprocally with them. (pp. 178–184)

We know natural force as what interacts with our action and is somehow *in pari materia* with it. We are bound to speak of it somewhat anthropomorphically, but we need not be taken in by our own language, or drawn into absurd inferences. (pp. 184–191)

X. CAUSAL LAW AND MENTAL CASUISTRY

Can we find an agreed compromise between determination and liberty? It will not do to say, that liberty lies in the exercise of action and determinedness in the patterns enacted; for the claim of liberty is, to choose or make the pattern. Nor yet to say, that for logical reasons uniformity-rules can never exhaustively specify the particular event, so freedom has room to act; for this need not be to make human conduct any freer than clockwork. A more hopeful approach points out that a complexity of uniformity-rules will only yield a determinate result by the aid of arithmetic, and that arithmetic is inapplicable to psychology. But so far from producing an amicable compromise between liberty and determination, this consideration seems to preclude any meaningful statement of determinism whatever. (pp. 192–197)

Since scientific determinism is the child of the mathematical method, it is relevant to ask, how men thought before that method prevailed. Aristotelian physics imposed on nature an operation of formal principles, which perhaps had and has its valid application in psychology. It is arguable that our minds really work by a sort of *ad hoc* casuistry, finding secondary rules by which to adjust the conflict of primary rules in various types of situation. If we regard decision as a mere working out on the conscious level of a casuistry of appetite which was already at work on a preconscious level, we shall have a doctrine which we may call 'Aristotelian naturalism'. (pp. 197–204)

Aristotelian naturalism may be defended against the charge, that it is too elastic to pass as any sort of determinism. It cannot, however, provide a compromise formula which will be acceptable to libertarians. It attributes all the motive-principles of action to the necessity of nature, leaving freedom no scope, but that of applying the motive-principles to cases, or to classes of cases. But the libertarian will claim for freedom the choice or invention of many motive-principles on which she acts. (pp. 204–213)

Can the libertarian support his claim? Not so easily from single cases—it will always be possible to allege that the really motive principles of a man's choice were already given. More easily, however, from a wide survey of history. If man has not invented the principles of human culture, human culture was somehow virtually contained in the appetites of our animal ancestors. And this seems absurd. (pp. 213–215)

XI. MOTIVE AND CHOICE

Objection: Nevertheless, no one acts without a motive, in the full sense of 'act'; and the motive determines the act. If there is a conflict of motives, either the stronger prevails, or a decision is imposed. The decision, being itself an act, must have a determining motive. If there is still an unresolved conflict, there will be need of another decision, and so *ad infinitum*, unless some motive takes effect. It follows that all action is determined by motive.— Answer: The argument equivocates on 'motive'. We cannot deliberate or decide without interest in the business, but such interest does not determine our choice, in the way in which an initial outbreak of interest determines our attention, apart from any initiative of ours. (pp. 216–223)

The point is not merely logical—that initial interest is thought of as arising from the touching-off of a disposition, whereas the prolongation of it into a phase of decision arises out of an actual event. The point is psychological—in the former case we are not there on the job, in the latter case we are: the initial reaction overtakes us; in view of it, we take a further step. (pp. 223–227)

We cannot act, or decide, without motive or interest. But the interest which sees us through the decision is not simply identical with the (involuntarily aroused) interest which prompted it. The interest antecedent to decision is determinate; the interest accompanying decision is flexible. (pp. 227–232)

We must, then, hold fast, and correctly relate to one another, two distinctions: (*a*) between a voluntary, and an involuntary, mental transition, (*b*) between antecedent and concomitant motive. Then we shall see that decision is a free creation. But we must not exaggerate our freedom. Oedipus is free to decide on his replies, but he is not free to evade the answering of the Sphinx. (pp. 232–234)

XII. EMPIRICAL PSYCHOLOGY

Whatever psychologists or sociologists may hold by way of philosophical opinion, do their scientific methods or results imply determinism? We will take a few test-questions. Psychiatry shows that we are often impelled to act by suppressed wishes which we do not acknowledge. But the whole meaning and utility of the diagnosis depends on the contrast between such wishes and avowed, conscious intentions; it cannot, therefore discredit our whole claim ever to act freely. (pp. 235–240)

The psychologist, however, goes further and traces a fatal history almost as long, may be, as life itself, through which misunderstood desires have festered and proliferated; and he proposes to heal us by getting us to accept his story about us. For the cure to succeed, it is not, however, necessary for the patient to take a deterministic view of his whole past, nor would it be logical for him to do so. He will merely be required to admit certain strands of unfreedom in it. (pp. 240–246)

Social psychology, and any general prescription for conditioning men (let us hope) to their advantage, is bound to rest on statistics. Statistical rules are true *for a sufficient number of instances,* i.e. for the number of which they prove true; and do not bind the single instance. Statistics about human *reactions* may be like physical statistics simply; statistics about human choices have to reckon with the special factor of variability, freewill. (pp. 246–251)

The belief that 'Psychology disproves freewill' is commonly based on a confusion between the methods of several quite distinct disciplines. (pp. 251–252)

XIII. RESPONSIBILITY AND FREEDOM

Responsibility is a public and legal idea which has become delegalised and interiorised. In its original, legal form it has nothing directly to do with freewill. The law holds us responsible, not when we could (in the psychological sense) have done otherwise, but when our punishment will provide a wholesome motive for future obedience. (pp. 253–259)

Private conscience begins, when we hold ourselves responsible for keeping the public law. What is significant here is not the legal model, but its drastic modification when judge, policeman, executioner and offender are the same person. Our offence is against our ever-present self, and involves the conscious treason of an insincerely divided mind. (pp. 259–263)

The self-betrayal of unconscientious decision appears to contain the paradox, that I go against what I myself decide. But this 'What I myself decide' has the form of a standing decision, and a standing decision is not a decision proper. It is a demand upon oneself seriously to consider the claim of a principle, where it seems to apply. The claim can be set aside either justifiably, or unjustifiably; and if unjustifiably, with either more or less attempt at self-justification. (pp. 263–268)

The demand of a standing principle is, that we should consider a question, e.g. What is the kind, veracious, honest thing to do in the case? But we can, often justifiably, refuse to make this the question of the hour, and let our action answer another question, e.g. What is the agreeable thing to do? In moral temptation we have a supremely anxious, but neither unique nor altogether characteristic example of the choice between questions. Any such choice is difficult to explain for a crude determinism of the 'Every-one does what he most wants' variety, because it is only within a single question that 'What one most wants' has an unambiguous sense. (pp. 268–273)

Though conscience begins by merely interiorising law, she may go on through several steps to discard it entirely. We may hold ourselves responsible for acting not by rules but by valua-tions, and even for evaluating sensitively: for making a total and due response to facts. There may be no rule to follow; we are obliged to invent the right course. (pp. 273–277)

XIV. VALUATION AND INVENTION

Moore's antinaturalism carries the conclusion, that no charac-teristics in an object or project to be valued, allow its value to be simply inferred; it is valued by a 'motion of the heart' towards it. If this motion is passive, or 'pathological', valuation becomes a brute fact, and it becomes a paradox that we should be expected to risk our lives in implementation of it. Must we not believe, that valuation is a free self-orientation towards the object, and so a sort of decision? (pp. 278–286)

It will be objected that valuation is not free choice; like Luther, we can't choose but value as we do. But that is not to say that we do not choose; only that the choice is serious, and made on behalf of humanity. It is not the choice of whimsy, nor yet of invention.

We rightly feel that such a choice as that of valuation fails to embody certain aspects of human freedom; but that is not a reason for denying it to be free, only for remembering that freedom attaches most properly to men, not acts, and that it takes many different types of act to make up the freedom of a man. (pp. 286–291)

A given exercise of freedom may spread over two or more complementary acts of different types. A determinist can trick us by taking them one by one, and challenging us to find the freedom in them. He may even take severally the complementary aspects of a single act. Invention, for example, can be split into its passive and active aspects—something occurring to the mind, and the mind's response to it; and so Shakespeare's creativity can be made to disappear. (pp. 291–294)

The forthright statement of the libertarian position—that people do act out their reasonable thought—has to be guarded against this determinist trick, if it is to convince. And here we conclude our straight discussions of the determinist issue, merely adding a remark on the metaphysical doubt: 'However free my act is in its operation, how do I know that I am not merely tracing what has been invisibly written for me by destiny?' (pp. 294–296)

XV. LIBERTY AND THEOLOGY

Has the proof of freewill any human importance? Determinism is at least a practical faith. It tells us never to despair of causal explanation. Whereas we shall decide, invent, etc. just the same, whether we are libertarians or not.—Yes, but bare theoretical libertarianism is commonly coupled with the conviction that we have our lives to make, a conviction which profoundly affects our attitude. The extreme form of this conviction is seen in a dramatic existentialism, which puts us in the predicament of Phaeton. The corrective is found in responsibility towards an object of supreme respect, our neighbour's being, and our own. Yet it is not so clear to us, as it was to Aristotle, just what the object of respect is. If not what we find men to be, is it what we will them to be? (pp. 297–304)

329

If we cannot believe that our own will requires our measureless respect, we shall find ourselves believing a divine will. In so doing, natural theology does not substitute a different object of moral respect, or lead us to value anything but what moves the heart. It will therefore be brushed aside by positivism as superfluous or meaningless. The answer to the positivist dismissal will follow the lines of the vindication of natural faith, familiar to us from other fields. (pp. 304–309)

If we believe a divine will, we are confronted with the supreme theological paradox—two wills on different levels, the creative and the creaturely, shaping our human existence. The mystery of predestination and freewill, so far from being an extreme conclusion of revealed theology, is the immediate form of moral theism. It is the crucial case of the creature-creator relationship; most difficult, only because most present to us; and for the same reason, best known and most experienced. It is through our freewill that we know the divine will, which is the divine being. (pp. 309–315)

3002